Program Evaluation

Pragmatic Methods for Social Work and Human Service Agencies

Be prepared for your future role in a service-oriented agency. This textbook provides practical guidance on program evaluation while avoiding replicating other course material. Drawing on over forty years of subject knowledge, Allen Rubin describes evaluation methods and designs that are feasible for service-oriented agencies and that match the degree of certainty needed by key users of outcome evaluations. The utility and easy calculation of within-group effect sizes are outlined, which enhance the value of outcome evaluations that lack control groups.

Instructions are also given on how to write and disseminate an evaluation report in a way that maximizes its chances of being used. Conducting focus group interviews and capitalizing on the value of non-probability samples will become second nature after following the effective and pragmatic advice mapped out chapter-by-chapter.

Allen Rubin has been teaching courses on program evaluation for over forty years. He is the Kantambu Latting College Professor of Leadership and Change at the University of Houston's Graduate College of Social Work, past president of the Society for Social Work and Research, and a fellow in the American Academy of Social Work and Social Welfare.

Program Evaluation

Pragmatic Methods for Social Work and Human Service Agencies

ALLEN RUBIN
University of Houston

CAMBRIDGE
UNIVERSITY PRESS

CAMBRIDGE
UNIVERSITY PRESS

University Printing House, Cambridge CB2 8BS, United Kingdom

One Liberty Plaza, 20th Floor, New York, NY 10006, USA

477 Williamstown Road, Port Melbourne, VIC 3207, Australia

314–321, 3rd Floor, Plot 3, Splendor Forum, Jasola District Centre, New Delhi – 110025, India

79 Anson Road, #06–04/06, Singapore 079906

Cambridge University Press is part of the University of Cambridge.

It furthers the University's mission by disseminating knowledge in the pursuit of education, learning, and research at the highest international levels of excellence.

www.cambridge.org
Information on this title: www.cambridge.org/rubin
DOI: 10.1017/9781108870016

First published 2020

A catalogue record for this publication is available from the British Library.

Library of Congress Cataloging-in-Publication Data
Names: Rubin, Allen, author.
Title: Pragmatic program evaluation for social work : an introduction / Allen Rubin, University of Houston.
Description: Cambridge, United Kingdom ; New York, NY : Cambridge University Press, 2020. | Includes bibliographical references and index.
Identifiers: LCCN 2019059898 (print) | LCCN 2019059899 (ebook) | ISBN 9781108835992 (hardback) | ISBN 9781108870016 (ebook)
Subjects: LCSH: Social service — Evaluation. | Evaluation research (Social action programs)
Classification: LCC HV11 .R824 2020 (print) | LCC HV11 (ebook) | DDC 361.3—dc23
LC record available at https://lccn.loc.gov/2019059898
LC ebook record available at https://lccn.loc.gov/2019059899

ISBN 978-1-108-83599-2 Hardback
ISBN 978-1-108-79909-6 Paperback

Additional resources for this publication at www.cambridge.org/rubin

Contents in Brief

Contents in Detail

Figures

Tables

Preface

During the nearly half a century that I have been teaching courses on program evaluation I have not found a textbook that fit my course as well as I preferred. The main problem has been that some books cover too much research methods content that duplicates what students learn in their research methods courses, while other books don't have enough of that content. The problem is understandable, because program evaluation is carried out using research methods. Another reason why I have been dissatisfied with the books with heavy doses of research content is that so much of that content is pitched to well-funded evaluations of national and international projects for which program evaluation is a key component of the program from its outset. Very sophisticated research designs are not only feasible in such projects, they are expected. Program evaluation in local social and human service agencies – where most of my students begin their careers – is unlike program evaluation in those projects in several important ways.

First, the need for program evaluation activities tends to emerge later, after the agencies have matured. Instead of being a key program component with the charge of evaluating all aspects of program activities beginning with the birth of the program, the program evaluation activities tend to be less ambitious and more circumscribed around a particular agency need that arises. Consequently, the evaluation – and its evaluator – are more likely to be viewed as alien outsiders to agency personnel who feel that they have been doing just fine without a strange new evaluation annoyance that they probably don't understand. In turn, the evaluator is likely to encounter significant constraints that limit the kinds of evaluation designs and data collection methods that are feasible in a service-oriented agency setting. Thus, a book that implies that they should strive to implement gold- or platinum-standard-type research methods and randomized control trials risks setting them up for disappointment and perhaps failure. Moreover, if they have already learned about rigorous research methods and designs in a previous research methods course, they can resent the redundancy if the coverage of those methods is excessive.

Students about to start their careers in social and human service agencies should not be led to expect that the program evaluation assignments awaiting them in their careers – especially early in their careers – will require heavy adherence to many of the attributes and criteria that make research studies rigorous but that also can be less feasible in agencies that are committed to service provision. For example, the agency's routine and long-standing measurement and record keeping procedures might not meet standards of measurement reliability and validity and might not fit the variables a program evaluator hopes to assess. Moreover, agency practitioners might resent and resist a program evaluation plan that requires additional measurement instruments, data collection, or record keeping. Not to mention the notion that some "unlucky" clients will be assigned to a control group that does not receive the same interventions that are provided to other, "luckier," experimental group clients.

Although methodological rigor is desirable in program evaluation, students should learn how to design feasible evaluations that have value despite lacking ideal levels of rigor.

Therefore, this book attempts to balance the need for methodological rigor with the need to have realistic expectations consistent with becoming a successful evaluator in service-oriented settings. That's why the word *pragmatic* appears in this book's title. Being pragmatic can be compatible with being idealistic. In that connection, the following phrase appears in Chapter 6 of this book: "Don't let the perfect become the enemy of the good." Similarly, that chapter points out that the degree of internal validity in outcome evaluations should match the degree of certainty needed by primary users of the evaluation. Insisting on conducting ideally rigorous but infeasible evaluations and refusing to make pragmatic compromises can result in accomplishing nothing of value beyond gratifying the evaluator's own egocentric quest for purity. Conversely, it can be more idealistic to put aside the need to feel pure so as to accomplish something good by not insisting on perfection but instead making the pragmatic compromises required to accomplish the best evaluation that is realistically possible and that fits the degree of certainty needed by stakeholders.

Guided by the foregoing conception of idealistic pragmatism, this book will focus on the practical aspects of what students need to learn to be successful in performing evaluation tasks in social and human service agencies. Some content typically covered in research methods courses will be included, but with an effort to minimize the degree of overlap and redundancy with research methods courses that typically are prerequisites for program evaluation courses. Likewise, the length and complexity of this book will not exceed what instructors and students in social work and the human services prefer for their courses on evaluation. Instead of attempting to prepare students to work as evaluators as part of major new national or international program or policy initiatives, the book will be pitched to agency-level evaluation activities and maximizing the value of feasible evaluations that may lack ideal levels of rigor or internal validity. For example, one new and unique feature of the book will be the attention it gives to the easy calculation and utility of within-group effect sizes in outcome evaluation designs lacking control or comparison groups.

Key Challenges for Program Evaluation Instructors and Students with Which This Book Aims to Help

- Minimizing redundancy between research methods course content and program evaluation content
- Matching the focus and level of the book's content with the needs, capabilities, and interests of students whose aptitudes and needs call for an approach that emphasizes practical utility and application regarding their eventual practice roles in local service-oriented agencies.
- Gearing the content to more feasible types of program evaluation that commonly can be conducted in service-oriented practice settings and that fit the degree of certainty needed by key intended users of the evaluation.
- When covering data analysis, not exceeding student aptitude levels and the basics of what social work and human services students *must* know.

Organization

This book's chapters are organized into four parts. Part I contains two chapters that provide an overview of program evaluation and relevant ethical and cultural issues. Part II offers two chapters that discuss quantitative and qualitative methods for formative and process evaluations.

Part III contains five chapters that cover outcome evaluations in service-oriented agencies. Chapter 5 looks at how to select and measure outcome objectives. Chapters 6 and 7 discuss feasible outcome designs that may not meet all the traditional criteria for ruling out threats to internal validity but that meet the degree of certainty needed by intended users. Chapters 6 and 7 also will discuss how to strengthen the logic and value of the various designs. Chapter 8 is devoted to the use of single-case designs. Although those designs are geared primarily for practitioners to use in evaluating their own practice, they can be aggregated for evaluating programs. Because the latter use of these designs is infrequent, some instructors might want to skip Chapter 8. However, some other instructors feel very strongly about including this chapter, and some prefer even more coverage of the topic. The latter instructors might want to use the chapter on single-case designs that appears in my research methods textbook (Rubin & Babbie, 2017). Part III concludes with Chapter 9, which discusses practical and political pitfalls that can hinder outcome evaluations.

Part IV provides three chapters. Chapter 10 addresses how to analyze and present quantitative and qualitative data produced by formative and process evaluations. Chapter 11 covers analyzing data from outcome evaluations. Chapter 12 discusses how to write and disseminate an evaluation report in ways that maximize its chances for utilization.

Finally, an Epilogue provides tips for becoming a successful evaluator – tips pertaining not only to steps to take throughout the evaluation process, but also to people skills that can foster the success of an evaluation as well as help evaluators throughout their careers. I particularly enjoyed writing that part of the book.

Pedagogical Features

Each chapter of the book will include shaded boxes with examples and brief case studies. Many of the boxes will ask questions that can be used by instructors in class discussions. A list of the chapter's main points will appear at the end of each chapter, as will exercises and a list of additional reading.

Supplemental Resources

- Chapter-by-chapter **PowerPoint** slides will be available to instructors who adopt the book. The slides will include experiential learning exercises that reflect the major content areas of the book.
- An **Instructor's Guide** that provides in-class exercises and exam or quiz questions and answers.

I hope you find this book useful. I'd like to hear from you regarding what you like about this book as well as about any suggestions you have for improving it. My email address is arubin2@central.uh.edu.

Allen Rubin

Acknowledgments

This book would not have been written without the support and encouragement of Stephen Acerra, my editor at Cambridge. The helpful support of Emily Watton, Senior Editorial Assistant at Cambridge, is also greatly appreciated. Thanks also go to the anonymous reviewers who made valuable suggestions for improving an earlier draft of this book.

Special thanks go to my delightful daughter-in-law, Heske van Doornen, for her help in constructing infographics. Finally, I want to thank my wife of more than forty-six years, Christina Rubin, to whom this book is dedicated. I owe all of my career successes to her love, support, and sage guidance.

PART I

INTRODUCTION

Chapter 1

Introduction and Overview

> **WHAT YOU'LL LEARN IN THIS CHAPTER**
>
> In this first chapter you'll get an overview of program evaluation and a foundation for reading the rest of the book. You'll learn about the history of program evaluation and the various reasons to evaluate, including the field's finding out that some programs that seemed like good ideas at the time turned out to be ineffective or harmful. Program evaluation is largely about obtaining evidence to inform program activities and decisions, and therefore it is particularly germane to the current era of evidence-informed practice. Consequently, you'll learn about the process of evidence-informed practice. You'll also learn about philosophical issues that bear on the quality of evidence. The chapter provides definitions of some key terms in the field of program evaluation – terms that appear throughout this book. The chapter will conclude by discussing different purposes and types of evaluation.

1.1   Introduction

If you are like most of the students taking a course on program evaluation, you are not planning to be seeking a position as a program evaluator. You might even doubt that you will ever help to plan or conduct an evaluation. In fact, you might be reading this book only because it is a required text in a course you had to take, but did not want to. You probably are looking forward to a career in an agency that prioritizes service delivery and that views program evaluation as one of its lowest priorities. Well, you are likely to be surprised. Even in service-oriented agencies that do not prioritize program evaluation, the need to evaluate often emerges. For example, questions might arise as to whether the agency's target population has unmet needs that the agency should address. Answering questions like those might indicate the need to conduct a needs assessment evaluation. (Needs assessment evaluations will be discussed in Chapter 3.) Perhaps some new services or treatment modalities should be developed to meet those needs. Perhaps the ways some existing services are provided need to be modified to make them more accessible to current or prospective clients. If the agency's caseload has recently experienced a large influx of clients from a minority culture, for example, there may be a need to evaluate the cultural sensitivity of agency practitioners as well as support staff (i.e., receptionists, intake interviewers, etc.).

1.2   Why Evaluate?

The most common impetus to evaluate often involves funding – either persuading an existing funding source to continue or to increase its funding or convincing a new funding source to fund a new service initiative. For example, early in her career one of my former students – let's call her Beverly – was co-leading a community-based support group for women who were being verbally abused by their partners. The group was sponsored by a battered women's program that was not well funded. Beverly strongly believed in the effectiveness of her support group and wanted to conduct an evaluation of its effectiveness in order to seek external funding for it so that it would not draw from the limited resources of the larger program. Another former student – we'll call her Jennifer – was a clinical supervisor in a child welfare agency. Her administrator asked her to write a proposal for funding from a new federal family preservation initiative. One requirement for funding was including a design to evaluate the impact of the proposed program. With my help Jennifer was able to design the evaluation and secure funding. However, I hope in your career your motivation for evaluating the impact of your agency's services is not based exclusively on funding considerations. Your motivation should also stem from your compassion for clients and your professional ethics, both of which should impel you to want to find out if your services are really helping – and not harming people.

1.3   Some Programs are Ineffective or Harmful

It might seem far-fetched to you to suppose that the services you believe in and are devoting your work to every day are not helping people and much more far-fetched to imagine that they possibly could be harming people. But you might be surprised to learn that some programs that seemed to be well grounded in theory and that were widely embraced by leading theorists and practitioners in the helping professions were found to be ineffective. Some were even found to be harmful. Let's take a look at two of them now.

Critical Incident Stress Debriefing. Critical incident stress debriefing (CISD) has been one of the most popular group modalities of crisis intervention for survivors of mass traumatic events such as natural disasters. In it, the group participants discuss the experiences they had during the traumatic event in small details such as where they were when the disaster occurred, what they saw, what they heard, how they felt, and so on. Current emotions and physical symptoms are also discussed. The group leaders normalize those reactions to reassure the participants that such reactions are commonly experienced by survivors and do not mean that there is something abnormal about them per se. The leaders also provide advice regarding what things survivors should or should not do to help alleviate their (normal) distress (Housley & Beutler, 2007). That all sounds pretty reasonable, doesn't it? It sure does to me! Indeed, the CISD approach incorporates various generic principles of trauma treatment (Rubin, 2009). Well, here's a surprise. Multiple evaluations have concluded that CISD is not helpful and can actually be harmful in that it slows down the normal recovery process over time for many trauma survivors. Speculations regarding why CISD is harmful note that people who are not particularly vulnerable to longer-term posttraumatic stress disorder (PTSD) (which includes approximately 70 percent of natural disaster survivors – those who will not develop PTSD) would benefit sooner from the healing effects of time if the CISD did not engage them in imagining a reliving of the traumatic experience (Bisson *et al.*, 1993; Carlier *et al.*, 1998; Mayou *et al.*, 2000; Rose *et al.*, 2002). But until the evaluations were completed such harmful effects were not anticipated, and as recently as 2018 it was portrayed as helpful on the *Web*MD Internet website.

Scared Straight Programs. During the 1970s a program was introduced that aimed to prevent criminal behavior by juveniles. It brought youths who already had been adjudicated as criminal offenders as well as other youths thought to be at risk of becoming offenders into prisons where convicts would describe the sordid nature of life in prisons and thus attempt to scare the youths so much that they would be turned away from criminal behavior. The program, called *Scared Straight*, seemed to make sense. It became very popular and was portrayed in an Oscar-winning film in 1979. The film's narrator claimed that the program was successful in scaring juveniles "straight." The narrator was wrong. In fact, an evaluation at that time found that the offenders who participated in the program ended up committing more crimes than did similar offenders who did not participate. Despite its reasonable-sounding premise, therefore, the program was not only ineffective – it was harmful. In trying to explain why it was harmful, the author of the evaluation speculated that rather than scare the "tough" youths it motivated them to commit more crimes to prove that they were not afraid (Finckenauer, 1979).

Thus, among the various reasons to conduct program evaluations, perhaps the most compelling one is our desire to help people coupled with our awareness that some programs that sound great in theory – even some that have been widely embraced by experts – can be ineffective and even harmful. Our desire to help people can motivate us to conduct evaluations for other reasons, as well – reasons that can bear on program effectiveness but do not examine effectiveness per se. These reasons – or evaluation foci – pertain to obtaining answers to questions that can help us improve the way our program is being implemented. One such question is "What unmet needs of our clients or prospective clients should we be addressing?" Another pertains to whether the agency's staff members are implementing the program appropriately and whether there are any problems in how they are performing their roles. Box 1.1 lists some of the most common reasons for evaluating programs.

Box 1.1   Reasons to Evaluate

Required for funding	To answer these questions

• To seek new or continued funding for agency
• To seek new or continued funding for a new unit or intervention
	1 Are we really helping (harming?) people? (Are we effective?)
	2 How can we improve the program?
	  • What needs of our clients or prospective clients should we be addressing?
	  • Are staff members implementing the program as intended?
	  • Are clients satisfied with our program, and if not, why not?

1.4   Historical Overview of Program Evaluation

Although some have traced program evaluation as far back to 2200 BC in China (Shadish *et al.*, 2001), it emerged in the United States early in the twentieth century with evaluations of the effectiveness of alternative educational approaches that compared outcomes on student standardized test scores. During the ensuing early decades of the century, as concerns emerged regarding the impact of industrialization, evaluations examined worker morale and the impact of public health education on personal hygiene practices. The growth of evaluation accelerated with the emergence of New Deal social welfare programs during the 1930s, and included evaluations of the effectiveness of financial relief policies, public housing, and programs to combat juvenile delinquency. After World War II that growth accelerated even more as public expenditures increased to alleviate problems in public health, housing, family planning, community development, and juvenile delinquency. Rubin & Babbie (2017) note that "by the late 1960s, textbooks, professional journals, national conferences, and a professional association on evaluation research emerged" (p. 322). Interest in program evaluation continued to accelerate during the 1970s, but less so in response to the development of new programs and more in response to increasing skepticism being expressed by conservative pundits and politicians, and consequently the public overall, regarding whether the (dubious) effects of existing public programs were worth the amount of public expenditures being invested in them.

Growing public skepticism about the value of social welfare and human service programs, coupled with a trend toward a more conservative electorate in the 1980s and 1990s, resulted in substantial funding cuts to those programs and put more pressure on programs to complete evaluations in the hope of obtaining results that would justify their proposals for renewed funding. That pressure intensified the political context of program evaluation, as program personnel wanted their programs to be evaluated in ways that maximized the likelihood of obtaining findings that would portray their programs as effective and therefore worthy of more funding. (Chapter 9 will discuss the political context of program evaluation.)

Another major historical development affecting demands for program evaluation during the late twentieth century was the emergence and popularity of the concept of managed care. This concept emphasized various ways to control the rising costs of health and human services. One way to control those costs is to fund only those programs or treatments that have had their effectiveness supported by the findings of very rigorous experimental outcome evaluations that randomly assign participants to treatment and control groups – evaluation designs known as randomized control trials (RCTs).

A similar influence on evaluation during the first decades of the twenty-first century was the growth of the evidence-based practice (EBP) movement, as leading thinkers in the helping professions promoted the idea that practice decisions about programs, policies, and interventions should take into account the best research and evaluation evidence regarding which policies, programs, and interventions are most effective and how best to implement them. The EBP concept, however, was not without controversy, as some opposed it on the grounds that it was nothing more than a way for managed care efforts to reduce costs by reducing the range of efforts to help people that would be funded. While recognizing that implementing the most effective policies, programs, and interventions offers the opportunity to do more with less, proponents of EBP countered that its priority was not cost saving and pointed out its consistency with the professional ethic of seeking to ensure that clients received what is known to be effective and not harmful. This book is being written during the evidence-informed practice era when program evaluation – despite historical fluctuations influencing its prevalence and nature – continues to be an important concern among human service programs and agencies, both for utilitarian reasons and for humanitarian reasons.

1.5   Evidence-Informed Practice

The current era also is a time when evidence-informed practice is being emphasized in the educational preparation of social workers and other human service professionals (CSWE, 2015). The term evidence-*informed* practice has replaced the term evidence-*based* practice in response to critics who misconstrued the use of the word *based* to mean that evidence should be the *only* thing that informs practice decisions. The original term, *evidence-based practice*, was never meant to imply that practice decisions should be determined only by research evidence. Those who coined the term, as well as its early pioneers (Sackett *et al.*, 1997; Gambrill, 1999; Gibbs & Gambrill, 2002), emphasized that the evidence-based practice model recognized that practice decisions should take into account *all* of the following considerations:

- Client characteristics, needs, values, and treatment preferences
- Practitioner expertise and treatment resources
- The environmental and organizational context
- The best available research evidence

Five steps were proposed for the model, as follows.

1. Formulate a question concerning practice needs.
2. Search for evidence to inform the answer to that question.
3. Critically appraise the methodological quality of the research supplying the evidence.
4. Answer the posed question in light of the best available evidence as well as client characteristics, needs, values, and treatment preferences; practitioner expertise and resources; and the organizational context.
5. Implement the action (intervention) implied in step 4.
6. Evaluate the action taken in step 5 and provide feedback based on the results of the evaluation.

1.6 Philosophical Issues: What Makes Some Types of Evidence Better Than Other Types?

Not all evaluators or leading thinkers agree about what makes some types of evidence better than other types. Leading thinkers representing different schools of thought – or *paradigms* – have argued about this question for decades. Three main paradigms are currently prominent regarding evidence in social work and the human services: contemporary positivism, interpretivism, and the empowerment paradigm.

Contemporary Positivism. Contemporary positivists emphasize objectivity and precision in measurement and the logic of causality in designing evaluations and appraising the quality of evidence. They recognize the difficulty of being purely objective and of conducting flawless evaluations whose findings and methods are immune from warranted criticism. They tend to notice the imperfections in any individual evaluation and see all forms of research (evaluation included) as an eternal and self-correcting quest for better evidence that involves a replication process in which any particular evaluation is followed by subsequent evaluations to see if the conclusions of the previous evaluation(s) are upheld or merit modification or rejection.

Interpretivism. Interpretivists do not focus on maximizing objectivity in measurement or on logically isolating the causes of social phenomena. Instead, they emphasize probing for a deeper, subjective understanding of people's experiences, the meanings and feelings connected to those experiences, and the idiosyncratic stated reasons for their behaviors. They believe that the best way to evaluate what people need and how well services meet their needs is to take a flexible and subjective approach to evaluation that seeks to discover how people experience things on an internal and subjective basis.

Empowerment. The empowerment paradigm puts less emphasis on the priorities of contemporary positivists and interpretivists and more emphasis on using evaluation to empower oppressed people. Thus, for adherents of this paradigm, the best evidence is that which best empowers people and advances social justice. Evaluators influenced primarily by the empowerment paradigm might use evaluation methods favored by contemporary positivists or methods favored by interpretivists, and the choice of which to use will depend largely on which are most likely to produce findings that are consistent with their empowerment and advocacy aims. One type of evaluation design geared specifically to the empowerment paradigm is *participatory action evaluation*. In this design the evaluation participants are members of disadvantaged or oppressed populations. Those participants make decisions about the goals and design of the evaluation. The evaluation's priority is not only to produce its ultimate findings, but also as a means of educating the participants, raising their consciousness about social injustice, and mobilizing them for action. Box 1.2 summarizes a participatory action evaluation that involved university students who were welfare recipients. The box also illustrates how an evaluation can focus on social policy.

Constructivism. Another paradigm, one that shares commonalities with the interpretivist and empowerment paradigms, is called *constructivism*. This paradigm has different versions, or types. Its most extreme version rejects the notion of absolute truths, or of an objective social reality, and argues that people only

---

Box 1.2   A Case Example of Participatory Action Policy Evaluation

Quoss *et al.* (2000) reported an evaluation involving welfare policy in Wyoming. Using participatory action methods, economically disadvantaged university students – many of whom were welfare recipients – participated in the evaluation with the aim of persuading state legislators to allow postsecondary education to be deemed "work" within the regulations of the state's new welfare reform policy. The evaluation began with the students creating an organization called *Empower*, which involved making on-campus presentations to mobilize support from faculty members and students. The students next gathered and summarized existing research studies related to their aims and developed relationships with state legislators. Next, they distributed fact sheets and their research summaries to the legislators – both on a one-to-one basis and in legislative committee meetings that they attended. When opponents of their policy aims argued with erroneous or misleading information, the students pointed out the errors and offered corrections. Their evaluation succeeded. The Wyoming regulations were modified to allow the pursuit of postsecondary education to be considered work, which thereby represented a way for the students to escape poverty and no longer need to rely on welfare.

---

have their own subjective views of reality. Some support this version of constructivism by citing Plato's cave allegory. People in a cave might believe that shadows, and not real people, are reality if they sit in the cave facing a wall with the cave entrance behind them and see only the shadows on the wall cast by people walking outside the cave entrance. Other constructivists are less extreme and believe that, although we all distort reality through our own subjective filters, it is possible to try to gain a more objective understanding of an objective social reality. Constructivism can overlap with interpretivism in its emphasis on the notion of multiple social realities and thus the need to probe into subjective understandings of people's experiences and deeper meanings. Constructivism can overlap with empowerment in that a political version of constructivism maintains that our views of history and the social order are merely social constructs dictated by people in power. If objectivity is elusive and dictated by those in power, then guiding evaluation with a contemporary positivist philosophy using objective methods in search of objective truth takes a back seat to using whatever methods seem most likely to produce evaluation findings that can be used to advocate for the empowerment of the powerless.

Each of the above paradigms is evident in different parts of this book. The contemporary positivist paradigm is apparent in chapters that emphasize minimizing – or at least recognizing – bias in survey questionnaires and survey samples, selecting outcome measures that are reliable and valid, and inferring causality in outcome evaluations. The interpretivism paradigm can be seen in this book's content on using focus groups to assess client needs or using probing interviews of staff members and clients to better understand program processes. Although the empowerment and constructivist paradigms are not noticeable in this book's discussion of various evaluation methods, they are implicit throughout this book in that the services and programs provided by social work and human service practitioners commonly address the needs of oppressed people and the rights of marginalized groups. Thus, evaluating how to improve those programs and services ultimately is aimed at better empowering them.

1.7   Qualitative versus Quantitative Evaluations: A False Dichotomy

If you have completed a research methods course, you probably learned about the differences between quantitative and qualitative research methods. You should also have learned that these two categories of methods are not mutually exclusive; they are complementary and can be combined to improve the quality of a study. When they are combined, the study is called a *mixed-methods* study. Simply put, quantitative methods aim to produce findings that are precise and generalizable, whereas qualitative methods emphasize subjectively understanding deeper meanings. Quantitative methods emphasize using data collection procedures that are highly structured and specified in advance; measurement procedures that are reliable and valid, unbiased, and that mainly use closed-ended questions; and deductive data analyses focusing on statistics. In contrast, qualitative methods aim to generate tentative discoveries and understandings rather than statistics that test hypotheses or can be generalized to a population. Likewise, they emphasize using flexible procedures that can change during the course of an investigation and less structured and more open-ended measurement procedures with more probing.

The evaluation methods covered in this book traverse both quantitative and qualitative evaluation approaches. For example, a mixed-methods evaluation might use a quantitative approach to evaluate whether a program is achieving its objectives (as discussed in Chapters 6 and 7) and combine it with a qualitative approach involving client and staff open-ended interviews (as discussed in Chapters 3 and 4) to better understand the reasons for the program's successful or more disappointing outcomes and how to improve the program.

1.8   Definitions

At this point we need to take a moment to make sure that we have a common understanding of the meaning of some of the prominent terms that have been mentioned so far and that will continue to be mentioned throughout this book. For example, what is meant by the term *evaluation*? Evaluation is ubiquitous in the decisions we make every day – both professionally and personally. Evaluation in personal decisions can involve what consumer products to buy, what health care providers to see, what movies to watch, and so on. Sometimes we make those decisions on the basis of how people we respect evaluate things and what they tell us. Sometimes we rely on what experts say. Sometimes we are influenced by Yelp ratings on the Internet, ratings by *Consumer Reports*, or movie reviews that we read. Everyday evaluation in professional decisions can be influenced by what respected colleagues or supervisors tell us, what professional experts (such as accreditation visitors) say, or the results of evaluation research.

From the broad standpoint of a dictionary definition, evaluation can include all of the above things. In this book, however, the term *evaluation* will be limited to an empirical context involving *the use of research methods to develop evidence about the operations and results of social welfare and human service policies, programs, or interventions*.

The terms *program* and *policy* refer to *a set of rules, resources, or activities that aim to improve the well-being of a target population in need*. Although the terms *policies* and *programs* are closely related, they are not synonymous. To illustrate the distinction, a state government might establish a new policy requiring all school districts to offer sex education classes. *How* they offer the education would be the *programs*. Some districts might offer it in the form of electives; others might make the classes required. Some programs might emphasize abstinence. Others might emphasize safe-sex practices. Thus, policies are like big tents under which various program components reside.

The terms *program* and *intervention* also are closely related. Both refer to *a service delivery or treatment approach that aims to improve the well-being of service recipients*. To illustrate the difference, a *program* might be funded with the aim of preventing suicide among military combat veterans. Within the program might be different interventions, such as referral services, a suicide prevention hotline, cognitive behavioral therapy for PTSD or depression, and so on. Thus, programs also can be viewed as big tents within which various interventions can be applied.

An additional term that will appear throughout this book is the term *stakeholders*. Stakeholders are people who have an interest (i.e., a stake) in a program. As

---

Box 1.3   Stakeholders in a Formative Evaluation of a Homeless Shelter

Suppose your homelessness program is planning to establish a shelter in a particular neighborhood, and you need to conduct a planning evaluation regarding the likely need for and potential success of the shelter. Who would be the potential stakeholder groups? To begin, there are the funders, who would want evidence of the need for the shelter and, if funded, its eventual impact. Community residents would be stakeholders because they might object to having the shelter in their neighborhood, and their potential resistance would need to be assessed. The same applies to nearby businesses. Your board would have to approve the initiative and therefore will be keenly interested in the results of a planning evaluation. As to prospective service recipients, to what extent do they feel they need the shelter or intend to use it? Are there other agencies whose personnel can refer people to the shelter, and how do their staff members feel about the shelter? How do your program staff feel about working at the shelter? They are all stakeholders.

---

illustrated in Box 1.3, stakeholders can be funders, public officials, community residents, program administrators or managers, board members, program practitioners who provide services, other program personnel (receptionists, intake workers, etc.), businesses affected by the program, referral sources or recipients of referrals from the program, and service recipients and their families (including current, former, and prospective clients). In Chapter 10, when we examine political issues in program evaluation, you will see the importance of involving stakeholders in the planning of evaluations so as to foster compliance with the evaluation's methods and the utilization of its results and recommendations.

1.9   Different Evaluation Purposes

Most evaluations have one or more of the following three purposes:

- To assess the ultimate success of interventions, programs, or policies
- To assess how well interventions, programs or policies are being implemented
- To obtain information needed in planning or developing interventions, programs, or policies

You understandably might be wondering "What is the difference between *evaluation purposes* and the *reasons to evaluate* that were listed earlier?" To answer that question, let's begin with the first purpose in the bulleted list above. An evaluation of the ultimate success of an intervention, program, or policy might be done because it is required for funding reasons or because we altruistically care about whether we are really helping people (and not harming them). As to the second purpose above, an evaluation of how well interventions, programs, or policies are being implemented might be conducted to illuminate results regarding the success of a program. For example, if the results are disappointing, is that because the program, policy, or intervention was a bad idea or because it was not implemented properly? Our reasons for wanting to know that could be funding-related (such as to support the rationale for the program despite the disappointing results or because the funding body required an evaluation of the program's implementation). Or the reasons can be related to our desire to help people by making sure that we are doing things to help them in the correct manner. Similarly, an evaluation for the purpose of program planning – such as assessing the needs of our target population – might be conducted because it is a required component of a proposal for funding, because we want to maximize service utilization for administrative or budgetary reasons, or because we altruistically want to maximize the extent to which we are addressing the most important unmet needs of the people we care about.

1.10 Types of Evaluation

Three main types of program evaluation that are connected to different evaluation purposes are *summative evaluation*, *formative evaluation*, and *process evaluation*.

Summative Evaluation. Summative evaluations aim to assess the success of interventions, programs, or policies. They typically employ the kinds of designs to be discussed in Chapter 7, based on the inferential and logical considerations to be discussed in Chapter 6. These designs and logic pertain to developing implications regarding whether a program, policy, or intervention is achieving its intended impact. For example, a summative evaluation might look at trends in crime rates during years before and after a state legalizes marijuana or implements a new crime prevention initiative. It might compare a group of parents at risk of child neglect who receive a new child welfare intervention with a similar group of parents who do not receive the intervention to see if the intervention recipients have fewer reported neglect incidents than do the non-recipients. Those are just a couple of the myriad types of summative evaluation. The key point here is that summative evaluations are most likely to use quantitative designs that are highly structured in advance in ways that attempt to maximize the consistency and validity of measurement and logical arrangements that enhance our ability to infer whether a program, policy, or intervention is having a causal impact on its target population.

Formative Evaluation. Formative evaluations aim to help programs that are still in their *formative* phases. As such, they are more likely to draw upon a variety of more flexible, qualitative methods while seeking to identify or understand potential problems in the way a program, policy, or intervention is being implemented in its early stages. For example, staff members and clients might be interviewed to detect any problems in staff–client interactions (perhaps regarding cultural sensitivity). Are clients prematurely terminating treatment or having difficulty accessing services? Unlike the highly structured quantitative measurement approaches in summative evaluations, formative evaluations might use unstructured or semi-structured qualitative interviews to search for new insights about program processes and ask non-directive, open-ended probing questions to obtain a deeper understanding of what clients or staff members are reporting. One illustration of a formative evaluation can be seen in Box 1.3.

One way to think about the distinction between formative and process evaluations is to imagine that you are a chef at an Italian restaurant and are creating your own brand of spaghetti sauce. You are not sure if you have included the correct amounts of herbs and spices in the sauce, so you taste a spoonful and ask your assistant to do the same. That's a formative evaluation. You both agree that it needs more garlic. You add it. "Yummy!" Next, you serve it to some customers and ask them if they like it. You get thumbs up from every customer. Those are the results of your summative evaluation. At some point, perhaps on a subsequent evening, the restaurant manager notices delays in getting your prepared dishes to the waiters and in turn to the patrons – delays that might cause the meals to lose their warmth. On the basis of her observations she recommends ways to improve the process from chef to waiter to patron. That would be a process evaluation, which we'll examine next.

Process Evaluation. Process evaluations resemble formative evaluations and use similar methods. They can be used to *describe* a program or to *monitor* its implementation. Describing a program can provide important details for others who want to implement the program in another setting – especially if the program had favorable summative outcome results. Monitoring a program can help in detecting and understanding problems in how a program is implemented. Process evaluations are hard to distinguish from formative evaluations, the main distinction being whether the evaluation is conducted early during a program's formative phase or later on.

To illustrate how a process evaluation conducted in a later phase can have value, suppose a community-based program serving older adults with early-stage dementia who live at home initiates a new intervention to alleviate depression symptoms among those older adults. Further suppose that well after the program is under way, perhaps near its end, a summative evaluation finds that the depressive symptoms are not improving very much from pre-intervention (pretest) scores on a depression measurement instrument to post-intervention (posttest) scores. Or the evaluation might encounter difficulties in obtaining the posttest measurements. Process evaluation interviews might discover that the disappointing level of improvement is connected to an unanticipated degree of decline in the cognitive functioning of the intervention recipients. That decline could have various implications for the disappointing posttest phenomena. Whereas the intervention was conceived as being helpful only to those with early-stage dementia, many recipients actually had entered a later stage of dementia while the intervention was still ongoing. Perhaps the worsening dementia exacerbated depression symptoms to a degree that made them resistant to the intervention. Maybe the worsening had a deleterious impact on the way those living with and caring for the recipients related to the recipients, which compounded the tendency for the recipients to become more depressed as their cognitive functioning deteriorated. Perhaps the decline in cognitive functioning made it harder for the recipients to complete the posttests or at least to complete them in a valid manner.

The process findings in this fictitious illustration could imply the need to change to a measurement instrument that has been shown to be more appropriate (valid) for people whose dementia is no longer in an early stage. Or they might imply the need to analyze the intervention's outcome separately for those recipients who are still at an early stage of dementia at posttest. Or they might imply the need to extend the study to increase the number of recipients whose dementia does not move beyond the early stage during the course of the intervention. Finally, they might imply the need to modify the intervention to make it more applicable to those recipients whose dementia worsens. Box 1.4 provides another illustration of a process evaluation.

Chapters 3 and 4 will discuss some of the key skills and methods involved in formative and process evaluations. If you have learned how to conduct unbiased, non-directive, probing interviews, you already have some of those skills. Also, if

---

Box 1.4   Process Evaluation Plan for an AmeriCorps Program[1]

The AmeriCorps program engages volunteer adults in public service positions to help individuals or communities in need. One such program in Cincinnati aimed to help low-income, retired, and young people learn skills in saving and managing their money. The planned process evaluation addressed the following questions.

- Is the program being implemented in a consistent manner across its ten sites spread throughout the greater Cincinnati area?
- Are the volunteers receiving adequate training needed to effectively help their clients?
- Are the site supervisors adequately trained to supervise the volunteers and troubleshoot with clients?

The process evaluation plan used a mixed-methods approach that incorporated quantitative performance measurement instruments and qualitative interviews with volunteers and supervisors from each site as well as qualitative focus groups with volunteers. In addition, the evaluator planned to observe directly the volunteer orientation and training sessions. The results of the evaluation would be used to recommend improvements in volunteer and supervisor training, site resources, and other factors bearing on inconsistencies among the sites.

[1]Source: www.volunteerflorida.org/wp-content/
uploads/2017/02/example_process_evaluation_
plan_annotated-2.12.15.pdf.

---

you are not already sufficiently culturally sensitive, you'll also need to enhance your cultural sensitivity. Chapter 2 will help you do that with regard to conducting culturally sensitive evaluations.

Performance Measurement Systems. Another type of evaluation involves the use of performance measurement systems. These systems are commonly used by managers for administrative purposes rather than program evaluation purposes, such as to establish expectations of different organizational units and to determine whether the expectations are being met. However, the information in these systems can be examined as part of an empirical evaluation of program implementation or outcome, perhaps in a time-series design (see Chapter 7). The measures might include things like the number of clients served, the proportion of clients who complete treatment or prematurely terminate it, the number of family reunifications, the percentage of school dropouts or graduates, the percentage of clients who find jobs or permanent housing, and so on.

Evaluating One's Own Practice. With an additional type of evaluation, direct service providers can evaluate their own practice. This type of evaluation involves the use of single-case designs to track client progress toward attaining their treatment goals. The progress (or lack thereof) can be measured and graphed chronologically – commonly on a daily or weekly basis. Sudden shifts in the graph that coincide with changes in service provision or in the client's outside life might indicate what intervention components or life events appear to be having a helpful or harmful impact on the client. Although this type of evaluation pertains more to evaluating clinical practice than to evaluating programs, an agency can aggregate the findings from its practitioners who evaluate their own practice to identify what types of agency interventions appear to be most or least effective as well as the proportion of successful outcomes being achieved by agency clients. Chapter 8 of this text focuses exclusively on this type of evaluation.

Accreditation. As mentioned earlier, in this book the term *evaluation* will be limited to an empirical context involving the use of research methods to develop evidence about the operations and results of social welfare and human service policies, programs, or interventions. However, you should know that some organizations are content with other forms of evaluation that emphasize expert opinions and management priorities. For example, national accrediting organizations exist to ensure that agencies are in compliance with a set of standards regarding service provision. Accreditation can be much more important to agency administrators and other personnel than being evaluated empirically. Accreditation legitimizes an agency to the public, which in turn can influence prospective clients and sources of funding. Likewise, accreditation is a prerequisite for seeking governmental reimbursement for an agency's clients who are recipients of Medicare or Medicaid.

Accreditation is provided by a national accrediting agency that typically requires that the agency seeking accreditation conduct a self-study and undergo a site visit by volunteer experts. Those site visitors will examine the agency's self-study and various service records, conduct interviews and meetings with agency personnel and clients, and – on the basis of those activities – submit a report to an accreditation commission of the accrediting agency. Accreditation in the field of human service agencies is provided by the Council On Accreditation (COA), which was founded in 1977 by the Child Welfare League of America and Family Service America, now called the Alliance for Strong Families and

Communities. The COA's website (https://coanet.org/) states that it accredits more than 2200 organizations and programs providing services in child welfare, behavioral health, and community-based social services. Standards for accreditation in accrediting bodies like the COA are developed consensually and change over time, depending on the expertise of its accreditation board members in light of advances in the knowledge base.

1.11   Chapter Main Points

- Reasons to evaluate include funding reasons, such as (1) to seek new or continued funding for an agency; and (2) to seek new or continued funding for a new unit or intervention
- More altruistic reasons to evaluate include answering the following questions. (1) Are we really helping people? (2) What needs of our clients or prospective clients should we be addressing? (3) Are staff members implementing the program as intended? (4) Are clients satisfied with our program, and if not, why not?
- Empirical program evaluation involves using research methods to develop evidence about the operations and results of social welfare and human service policies, programs, or interventions.
- Evidence-informed practice involves including the best available evidence among the things that inform practice decisions.
- Four paradigms that can influence the way evaluations are conducted are contemporary positivism, interpretivism, empowerment, and constructivism.
- Empowerment evaluation can use a participatory action design in which participants are members of disadvantaged or oppressed populations and make decisions about the goals and design of the evaluation with the aim of educating the participants, raising their consciousness about social injustice, and mobilizing them for action.
- Quantitative evaluation methods aim to produce findings that are precise and generalizable. They emphasize using data collection procedures that are highly structured and specified in advance; measurement procedures that are reliable and valid, unbiased, and that mainly use closed-ended questions; and deductive data analyses focusing on statistics.
- Qualitative evaluation methods aim to generate tentative discoveries and understandings rather than statistics that test hypotheses or can be generalized to a population. They emphasize using flexible procedures that

can change during the course of an investigation, less structured and more open-ended measurement procedures with more probing, and inductive data analysis procedures that involve fewer statistics.

- The terms *program* and *policy* refer to *a set of rules, resources, or activities that aim to improve the well-being of a target population in need*. Although the terms *policies* and *programs* are closely related, they are not synonymous.
- The term *intervention* refers to *a service delivery or treatment approach that aims to improve the well-being of service recipients*.
- Stakeholders are people who have an interest (i.e., a stake) in a program and can include funders, public officials, community residents, program administrators or managers, board members, program practitioners who provide services, other program personnel, businesses affected by the program, referral sources or recipients of referrals from the program, and service recipients and their families.
- Most evaluations have one or more of the following three purposes: (1) to assess the ultimate success of interventions, programs, or policies; (2) to assess problems in how interventions, programs, or policies are being implemented; or (3) to obtain information needed in planning or developing interventions, programs, or policies.
- Summative evaluations aim to assess the success of interventions, programs or policies.
- Formative evaluations aim to help programs that are still in their *formative* phases. As such, they are more likely to draw upon a variety of more flexible designs that seek to identify or understand potential problems in the way a program is being implemented.
- Process evaluations can be used to describe a program or to monitor its implementation. The main distinction between process evaluations and formative evaluations is whether the evaluation is conducted early during a program's formative phase or later on.
- Performance measurement systems are commonly used by managers for administrative purposes rather than program evaluation purposes, such as to establish expectations of different organizational units and to determine whether the expectations are being met. However, the information in these systems can be examined as part of an empirical evaluation of program implementation or outcome.
- An additional type of empirical evaluation involves individual practitioners evaluating their own practice by using single-case designs to track client progress toward attaining their treatment goals.
- A non-empirical form of evaluation includes the process of accreditation.

1.12   Exercises

1. Interview an administrator or program evaluator at a social welfare or human service program with which you are familiar. Learn about the evaluations that have been completed there. Take notes and share what you have learned with your classmates.

2. Using your school's literature database find a report of a program evaluation. Try to identify all of the evaluation's stakeholders, the type of evaluation, what reasons prompted it, what kind of methods it emphasized, and its main findings and implications. Write down the things you've identified and a brief summary of the evaluation to discuss with your instructor and classmates.

1.13   Additional Reading

- Aikin, M. C., & Vo, A. T. (2018). *Evaluation Essentials* (2nd ed.). New York, NY: Guilford Press.
- Alexander, L. B., & Solomon, P. (2006). *The Research Process in the Human Services: Behind the Scenes*. Belmont, CA: Brooks/Cole.
- Dimidjian, S. (Ed.). (2019). *Evidence-Based Practice in Action: Bridging Clinical Science and Intervention*. New York, NY: Guilford Press.
- *Formative Evaluation Toolkit*, Children's Bureau, www.jbassoc.com/wp-content/uploads/2019/01/Formative-Evaluation-Toolkit.pdf.
- Rubin, A., & Babbie, E. R. (2017). *Research Methods for Social Work* (9th ed.). Boston, MA: Cengage Learning.

Chapter 2

Ethical and Cultural Issues in Program Evaluation

> **WHAT YOU'LL LEARN IN THIS CHAPTER**
>
> In this chapter you'll learn about the ethical and cultural issues that influence program evaluation. You'll learn about Institutional Review Boards (IRBs) that often have to approve of program evaluations that use research methods with human participants. After you learn about the kinds of questions you'll have to answer should you ever need the approval of an IRB, the chapter will turn to cultural issues that bear on recruiting and retaining evaluation participants and collecting and analyzing data in a culturally sensitive fashion. Finally, you'll examine some key concepts that pertain to developing your own cultural competence.

2.1   Introduction

As mentioned in Chapter 1, program evaluation involves the use of research methods. Consequently, the same ethical and cultural issues that pertain to research studies also pertain to program evaluations. If you have taken a research course, you have probably already examined these issues, so this chapter will just briefly review some issues and guidelines that are the most prevalent in program evaluation research. If you would like to read about more of the details and nuances regarding those issues and guidelines, you can examine a research methods text such as Rubin & Babbie (2017).

2.2   Ethical Issues

Because research methods are used in conducting program evaluations, evaluators need to comply with the same ethical guidelines that pertain to other forms of research in which people participate. To begin, the people participating in the evaluation should be informed in advance of the nature, purpose, and potential consequences of their participation in the evaluation, and they must consent to participate voluntarily and without any coercion. This guideline is known as *voluntary participation and informed consent*. A second guideline is that *participation in the evaluation should not harm participants*. As a future helping professional, you might wonder about the need for this second guideline. After all, practitioners in social work and human service agencies seek to help people, not harm them. But although we don't harm people intentionally, sometimes we do so unintentionally. In Chapter 1 we saw how some programs or interventions that seem like reasonable ways to help people can harm them unintentionally. The same applies to program evaluation.

It is not always easy to anticipate the risk of harm posed by participating in an evaluation. For example, you might care very deeply about the problem of domestic violence and be dedicated to protecting its potential victims. Your noble efforts might involve interviewing people about the possible need for a shelter for victims of domestic violence. If perpetrators – or potential perpetrators – of domestic violence overhear part of the interview or learn about it, that might trigger a violent eruption.

Sometimes, however, the risk of harm in an evaluation is unescapable. But if the potential benefits of the evaluation far outweigh the risk of harm the risk might be justified, especially if the harm seems to be minor and very unlikely and the potential benefits are significant. Consider, for example, the risk of harm in a summative evaluation that I designed which is summarized in Box 2.1.

Box 2.1   Benefits versus Risks in a Clinical Outcome Evaluation

During the 1990s I designed an evaluation to assess the effectiveness of a new and previously untested therapeutic intervention for traumatized youths residing in a residential treatment center. There was reason to believe that the new therapy would be more effective than existing treatment approaches. As part of the evaluation of the intervention's effectiveness, I wanted to record videos of some of the treatment sessions so that two nationally renowned experts on the therapy could watch the videos and rate the extent to which the therapy was being implemented properly. I was willing to conduct the evaluation pro bono rather than spend months seeking funding for it. The two expert raters lived in New York and Denver, both of which were hundreds of miles away from me. Therefore, I needed to Fedex the videos to the experts. Two members of my institution's Institutional Review Board (IRB) were unwilling to approve my proposal because of the remote possibility that a video could fall out of a damaged Fedex mailer. They surmised that a Fedex employee might then watch the videos and might recognize one or more of the youths. Consequently, they insisted that I travel to New York and Denver and hand over the videos in person and then wait (who knows how long) for the busy experts to watch the videos and rate them. That seemed unreasonable to me in light of my lack of funding and the slim possibility of the harm occurring. Although that possibility seemed quite unlikely, I could not be absolutely certain that it was impossible. I had to appear at a meeting of my IRB to make the argument that the potential benefits of learning whether the new therapy is very effective outweighed the remote risk of the harm they feared resulting from a damaged Fedex envelope. I was unable to persuade the two board members who had initially voiced concerns about the potential harm, but, fortunately, the IRB chairperson persuaded the other board members that the potential benefits outweighed the risks. My proposal was then approved by a vote of nine to two.

We'll discuss IRBs soon, but first let's briefly review some other ethical guidelines. A third ethical guideline involves the *protection of sensitive information*. The privacy of sensitive information can be protected either by having participants provide it anonymously or by storing the information in such a way that it cannot be connected to the participant who provided it. A common way to do the latter would be to assign a code number to each participant's information and to store those code numbers in a file that is separate from the main data file. It might not be possible to be 100 percent certain that a violation of privacy is impossible, but an IRB can judge whether the likelihood of that risk is outweighed by the potential benefits of the evaluation.

A fourth ethical issue involves *analysis and reporting* of the evaluation's results. During my career I occasionally completed a summative evaluation of an intervention in which the results did not offer the degree of support for the intervention's effectiveness that some program stakeholders had hoped for. Sometimes one or two stakeholders with vested interests in the intervention tried to persuade me to change my findings or interpret them in a way that portrayed the effectiveness of their intervention more favorably. It would have been unethical for me to do so because evaluators are just as obligated to report negative outcomes as they are to report positive outcomes. If they report only positive outcomes, service providers would not learn about programs or interventions that are ineffective. Instead, they would see only reports of positive findings about programs and interventions and thus would be unable to differentiate the programs or interventions that have the best prospects of helping their clients from those with worse prospects. Ultimately, then, clients would not be protected from receiving ineffective (and perhaps harmful) interventions.

In one case, after I had completed an evaluation that produced mixed findings, the administrator of the child welfare program evaluated told me that unless I changed my report to her liking she was not going to submit it to her federal funding source. She justified this on the basis that she believed that her program was effective and therefore wanted to protect its funding and thus its ability to help people. Was she being unethical? I'll let you be the judge.

But what if an evaluation with mixed or negative findings has so many methodological weaknesses that its findings are misleading? In that connection, another ethical imperative in analysis and reporting is to identify the methodological limitations of the evaluation so that those decision-makers who utilize your evaluation can decide whether to be influenced by your results. I have yet to see a program evaluation that is immune from all possible limitations. Sometimes the limitations seem to be minor. At other times they seem so serious that they wreck the credibility of the evaluation and its findings. If the vested interests of stakeholders lead them to fear the findings, they are likely to criticize any minor limitations very harshly, whereas if they like the findings they may be predisposed to overlook or minimize the seriousness of egregious limitations. We'll examine this political aspect of program evaluation more closely in Chapter 9.

2.3   Institutional Review Boards (IRBs)

In response to some notoriously unethical research studies in the past, Institutional Review Boards (IRBs) were created to review and approve (or disapprove of) research proposals in which people participate in light of whether the study's potential *benefits outweigh its ethical risks*. Perhaps the most flagrant and horrific examples of unethical research were the depraved Nazi medical experiments during the Holocaust. A notorious and egregiously inhumane example in the United States was the Tuskegee syphilis study, which began in Alabama in 1932. Several hundred African American men diagnosed as suffering from syphilis were not informed of the diagnosis. Instead, the medical researchers told them that they had "bad blood." The researchers then studied the disease's progress over a long time without treating it – even after penicillin was discovered as an effective treatment for syphilis. The study continued uninterrupted until a social worker, James Jones (1981), exposed it to the press in 1972. If you conduct an evaluation involving human participants, you probably will need to submit an evaluation proposal to an IRB. You might even need to obtain IRB approval if you merely want to analyze existing datasets. The IRB might be affiliated with your agency, a federal funding source, or some other organization. If you are a university faculty member or student, you'll need to submit your proposal to your university's IRB. As was illustrated in Box 2.1, some IRB panelists might disagree about whether an evaluation's potential benefits outweigh – and therefore justify – its potential risks. In their proposals to an IRB, evaluators might be biased toward overestimating the benefits and underestimating the risks of the evaluation that they propose to conduct. Having a board of neutral experts judge whether the benefits really do outweigh the risks is a way to obtain an impartial, expert ruling on the matter and thus better protect evaluation participants from potential harm. Box 2.2 illustrates the many kinds of questions you are likely to need to answer in an IRB application.

Box 2.2   Common IRB Questions

Objectives

Describe the purpose, specific aims, and/or objectives of this study.

Inclusion and Exclusion Criteria

Indicate specifically whether you will include or exclude each of the following special populations. (You may not include members of the populations listed below as subjects in your research unless you indicate this in your inclusion criteria.)

- Adults unable to consent (such as those with physical or mental impairments
- Individuals who are minors (infants, children, teenagers)
- Pregnant women
- Prisoners
- Students for whom you have direct access to/influence on grades
- Economically and/or educationally disadvantaged persons

Vulnerable Populations

If the research involves individuals who are vulnerable to coercion or undue influence, describe additional safeguards included to protect their rights and welfare.

Recruitment Methods

Describe when, where, and how potential subjects will be recruited.
Describe the source of subjects.
Describe the methods that will be used to identify potential subjects.
Describe materials that will be used to recruit subjects.

Procedures Involved

Describe and explain the study design.
Provide a description of all research procedures being performed and when they are performed.

- Describe all interventions, drugs, devices, and biologics used in the research, the purpose of their use, and (for drugs, devices, and biologics) their regulatory approval status
- Describe the source records that will be used to collect data about subjects. (Attach all surveys, scripts, and data collection forms to the SmartForm.)

What data will be collected, including long-term follow-up?

Risks to Subjects

List the reasonably foreseeable risks, discomforts, hazards, or inconveniences to the subjects related the subjects' participation in the research. Including as much detail as may be useful for the IRB's consideration, describe the probability, magnitude, duration, and reversibility of the risks. Consider physical, psychological, social, legal, and economic risks.

If applicable, indicate which procedures may have risks to the subjects that are currently unforeseeable.

If applicable, indicate which procedures may have risks to an embryo or fetus should the subject be or become pregnant.

If applicable, describe risks to others who are not subjects.

Describe procedures being performed to monitor subjects for safety.

Describe procedures performed to lessen the probability or magnitude of risks.

Potential Benefits to Subjects

Describe the potential benefits that individual subjects may experience from taking part in the research. Include, in as much detail as may be useful for the IRB's consideration, the probability, magnitude, and duration of the potential benefits. Indicate if there is no direct benefit. Do not include benefits to society or others. Note that remuneration for research participation should not be included as a benefit to the subjects.

Costs/Payments to Subjects

Describe any costs that subjects may be responsible for due to their participation in the described research.

Describe the amount and timing of any payments or inducements to subjects.

- Include the mode of payment (gift card, check, extra credit, etc.). If using a gift card, the gift card type(s) must be stated.
- If a physical gift is provided (for example, a coloring book for child participants), estimate its monetary value.
- Indicate if subjects will need to complete all measures/procedures prior to receiving any remuneration, or if the payment will be pro-rated.

Confidentiality

Describe the local procedures for maintenance of confidentiality.

Describe what direct identifiers will be obtained and any coding systems that will be used for study data (and specimens, if applicable). Note the following.

- The key to the code should be stored separate from the consent forms and study data.
- Audio is considered an identifier.
- Only indicate that the study is anonymous if no identifying data (including consent forms, contact information, etc.) will be collected and subjects will not be seen in person.

Will anyone outside the research team have access to the identifiers?

How long will the key to the study code be maintained? If it will not be destroyed following data collection, provide justification for maintaining it.

If audiotaping is conducted, will the recordings be destroyed upon transcription? If not, provide justification. Will they be stored in a lock file? Who will have a key?

Informed Consent Process

Informed consent must be obtained from all subjects, unless a waiver or alteration is approved by the IRB (see below).

Indicate whether you will be obtaining consent, and if so describe

- Where and when the consent process takes place
- Any waiting period available between informing the prospective subject and obtaining the consent
- Any process to ensure ongoing consent.

Non-English-Speaking Subjects

- Indicate what language(s) other than English are understood by prospective subjects or representatives.
- If subjects who do not speak English will be enrolled, describe the process to ensure that the oral and written information provided to those subjects will be in that language. Indicate the language that will be used by those obtaining consent.

Non-English-speaking should be included in the inclusion/exclusion criteria.

Consent documents must be submitted to the IRB.

Subjects Who Are Not Yet Adults (Infants, Children, Teenagers)

Delete section if not applicable.

- Describe the criteria that will be used to determine whether a prospective subject has or has not attained the legal age for consent to treatments or procedures involved in the research under the applicable law of the jurisdiction in which the research will be conducted (e.g., individuals under the age of eighteen years.)
- Describe whether parental permission will be obtained from
    both parents unless one parent is deceased, unknown, incompetent, or not reasonably available, or when only one parent has legal responsibility for the care and custody of the child; or
    one parent even if the other parent is alive, known, competent, reasonably available, and shares legal responsibility for the care and custody of the child.
- Describe whether permission will be obtained from individuals other than parents, and, if so, who will be allowed to provide permission.
- Describe the process used to determine these individuals' authority to consent to each child's general medical care.
- Indicate whether assent will be obtained from all, some, or none of the children. If assent will be obtained from some children, indicate which children will be required to assent.
- When assent of children will be obtained, describe whether and how it will be documented.

Cognitively Impaired Adults

- Describe the process to determine whether an individual is capable of consent.

Adults Unable to Consent

- List the individuals from whom permission will be obtained in order of priority (e.g., durable power of attorney for health care, court -appointed guardian for health care decisions, spouse, and adult child).

Process to Document Consent in Writing

If you will document consent in writing, attach a consent (and/or parental permission/assent) form.

If your research presents no more than minimal risk of harm to subjects and involves no procedures for which written documentation of consent is normally required outside of the research context, the IRB will generally waive the requirement to obtain written documentation of consent. In most cases, a cover letter (consent information with no signature requirement, or an online "checkbox" acknowledgment) should still be utilized.

If you will obtain consent, but not document consent in writing, attach a cover letter or verbal consent script

Data Management

Describe the data analysis plan, including any statistical procedures.

Describe the steps that will be taken to secure the data (e.g., training, authorization of access, password protection, encryption, physical controls, certificates of confidentiality, and separation of identifiers and data) during storage, use, and transmission.

Where will data be stored?

How long will the data be stored?

Who will have access to the data?

Who is responsible for receipt or transmission of the data?

Resources

Describe the qualifications (e.g., training, experience, oversight) of you and your staff as required to perform your/their roles. When applicable, describe their knowledge of the local study sites, culture, and society. Provide enough information to convince the IRB that you have qualified staff for the proposed research.

2.4   Culturally Sensitive Program Evaluation

Many current or prospective clients served by social welfare and human service agencies are members of a minority culture. Consequently, it is imperative that evaluation procedures be sensitive to those cultures (Box 2.3).

2.4.1   Recruitment

One reason why culturally sensitive procedures are needed is to enhance efforts to recruit members of minority populations to participate in the evaluation and to

---

Box 2.3   Why Evaluation Should Be Culturally Sensitive

- To recruit members of minority populations and retain their participation in the evaluation
- To enhance the collection of data from members of different cultural groups
- To take into account cultural differences in analyzing and interpreting evaluation findings
- To ensure that the data are equivalent across cultural groups
- Being on the receiving end of cultural insensitivity can be painful
- Culturally insensitive evaluations in a minority community can discourage the members of that community from participating in evaluations in the future

---

retain their participation in it. The barriers to recruiting and retaining the participation of members of minority populations will differ depending on the nature and purpose of the evaluation. For example, because the clients are already participating in the program in a summative evaluation that assesses clients' well-being after participating in a program, recruiting participants is likely to be less of a challenge than in a formative, planning evaluation that does not yet have people participating in the program. Suppose, for example, that a formative evaluation seeks to assess the needs of Native Americans who are members of a tribe. Prospective participants might decline to be interviewed unless they know that you secured permission for your evaluation from the tribal council. Recruitment of prospective clients in many ethnic minority neighborhoods can also be enhanced by obtaining support for the evaluation study by an esteemed community leader. Such support can make potential participants less suspicious of interviewers and more motivated to participate in interviews. Likewise, prospective participants might be more likely to consent to be interviewed if recognizable members of their community have been employed to conduct the interviews.

Your recruitment can also be enhanced if you learn about places where it is possible to look for potential participants in a culturally sensitive manner. Relying exclusively on traditional social and human service agencies, for example, would not be a very culturally sensitive approach. Again, you can learn about alternative, more culturally sensitive ways to look by talking to community leaders and community residents (some of whom, it is to be hoped, are on your staff). If you are seeking participants who might need mental health services, for example, you might be advised to contact local members of the clergy or primary care physicians. This does not mean that you are culturally insensitive if you include traditional service agencies in your search. It just means that you should not rely on them *exclusively*.

Once you have established connections with key people in traditional as well as culturally sensitive non-traditional referral sources, you should nurture your relationship with them. It will help if you can have many interactions with them and establish rapport with them before you ever mention your evaluation. It might help if you attend their meetings and perhaps volunteer your assistance to them and continue to do so even after your evaluation begins and throughout its duration. Continuing to nurture the relationship, combined with occasional updates on the progress of the evaluation and any preliminary findings will help maintain their awareness of your need for referrals and foster a continued willingness to supply them. At the time when you first mention your evaluation to them, be sure to point out its advantages both in terms of implications for improving services and in terms of any benefits that participants might receive in return for participating. The latter might include some modest financial compensation or perhaps free provision of a promising intervention that you are evaluating. Box 2.4 lists the procedures that have been discussed in this section.

2.4.2   Retention

If your evaluation requires that participants attend multiple sessions – perhaps to receive an intervention being evaluated or to complete longitudinally collected measures – your culturally sensitive recruitment efforts need to be followed by culturally sensitive retention efforts. How best to make those efforts culturally sensitive will depend on the culture of your participants. With low-income Latinx participants, for example, some researchers who have worked with the community recommend regular phone calls by warm and friendly research assistants. In addition to reminding participants about upcoming evaluation sessions, the assistants can inquire about the well-being of the participants and their families (Alvidrez *et al.*, 1996; Miranda, 1996). That recommendation probably applies

---

Box 2.4   Culturally Sensitive Recruitment Procedures

- Obtain approval of evaluation from community leaders
- Employ members of the minority community for data collection
- Learn where to look (don't rely exclusively on traditional referral sources)
- Seek advice from community leaders and other community members
- Build rapport with and nurture culturally sensitive referral sources

to low-income members of other cultural minority groups, as well. Other suggestions include the following.

- Provide transportation to and from each assessment session
- Provide coffee, cold drinks, and snacks at the sessions
- Make reminder calls before the sessions, a day or two in advance AND a week or two in advance

Homeless and residentially transient participants will need special retention efforts. One suggestion is to use *anchor points* and *tracking*, which include gathering information about the various alternative places where you might be able to contact a participant and then using that information to stay in touch with them and remind them of impending interviews or other evaluation sessions. Anchor point information for a homeless participant might include the following:

- where they usually hang out, eat, or sleep;
- how to contact any nearby family members or friends;
- whether there are any human service personnel who know how to locate them or an address where they pick up their mail, other messages, or perhaps a financial assistance check; and
- any nicknames or aliases they might have.

You should be sure to update your anchor point information with each subsequent tracking contact with the participant or someone who knows about them. With homeless and residentially transient individuals, you should remember that it is important to be persistent in trying to contact them. You might need to seek out numerous anchor points to learn where to try to contact the participant, make numerous attempts to contact them, and then continue to schedule interviews despite their repeatedly not showing up for them (Hough *et al.*, 1996; Rubin & Babbie, 2017).

2.4.3 Data Collection

Culturally sensitive procedures that enhance recruitment and retention can also enhance data collection from members of different cultural groups. For example, having bilingual interviewers might be essential in communities where English is not the preferred language. If the evaluation is summative and requires having clients come to your agency to attend treatment sessions or measurement sessions, you might need to provide transportation and childcare services to facilitate their attendance, especially in those communities with high rates of poverty. It might also help to choose a setting that is more accessible and more familiar to them than your office. Some people might be intimidated by offices. The site should be convenient and safe. A neighborhood community center or place of worship might seem like a good choice, but some residents might be uncomfortable attending at a place of worship for a religion other than their own. A nearby university or local library might work better. You might want to talk to some community leaders to help you select a good site for collecting data. If you have residents of the community on your evaluation staff, they might be able to advise you on selecting a culturally sensitive site.

If evaluation data are being collected via interviews, the interviewers should be of the same ethnicity as the interviewees if feasible. For some populations, being of the same gender is also important. According to Nandi (1982), for example, Asian women tend to perceive even relatively non-aggressive white male interviewers as overly aggressive. Likewise, Muslim women might be more comfortable being interviewed by women. Although matching interviewer and interviewee ethnicity makes sense and is preferable, it does not guarantee that the data will be free from culturally related bias. Some members of oppressed minority groups, for example, "might exaggerate their feelings of anger or resentment about racism" when interviewed by members of their own ethnicity in an effort to say what they assume that the interviewer wants to hear (Rubin & Babbie, 2017, p. 126).

2.4.4   Analyzing and Interpreting Evaluation Findings

It is important to bear in mind cultural differences when analyzing and interpreting evaluation findings. Rather than lump all the participants' data together and just report one summary statistic, you should look to see if the findings are different for different subgroups. For example, the need for a particular service or resource might be much higher for one ethnic group than for others. Likewise, a particular intervention might appear to have a much greater impact on some subgroups than on others. Even if an intervention appears to be very effective on average for the entire group of recipients, it might be ineffective with members of one or more particular minority subgroups. Finally, you should be sensitive to potential differences within the same category of ethnicity rather than assume that any particular minority group is monolithic. The needs of and program effects on undocumented Hispanic immigrants, for example, might differ a lot from those of Hispanic citizens. The same applies to potential differences between those who are recent immigrants and those who immigrated long ago and have become acculturated to the majority culture.

2.4.5   Measurement Equivalence

Finally, you should ensure that your measurement approach is equivalent across different cultural groups. Measurement equivalence is especially important if you are asking participants to complete scales that measure some abstract concept like depression, caregiver burden, quality of life, or some such. You should make sure that participants from different cultural groups have the same, accurate, understanding of what they are being asked. This requires not only translating scales – or the questionnaires you devise – accurately from English to a different language, but also checking to see if the translated words or phrases have the same conceptual meaning in the translated version. For example, suppose the English version of a scale that measures the quality of the relationship between a parent and child asks the child if his parent gets on his nerves and then the scale is literally translated into the Asian wording for "gets on my nerves." Unless the child knows that the intended conceptual meaning of the *gets on my nerves* idiom pertains to whether their mother bothers them in some emotional way, they might think that they are being asked about some physical, touching phenomenon. Thus, you should be sure to select a scale that has already been shown to have linguistic and conceptual equivalence across the cultural groups participating in your evaluation. You should examine the research on the scale to see if it has been tested for and shown to have linguistic equivalence as well as conceptual equivalence. Linguistic equivalence is tested by having one bilingual person translate the scale – or your devised questionnaire – from English into the other language and then having another bilingual person back-translate the translated version back to English. The back-translated version should match the wording of the original, English, version of the scale. If it does, then the scale or questionnaire has linguistic equivalence.

Conceptual equivalence is assessed by testing the reliability or validity of the translated version of a scale among a sizeable sample of members of the minority culture for whom the translated version is intended. The concepts of reliability and validity are explained in basic research methods texts. Validity pertains to whether a scale really measures what it intends to measure. Reliability pertains to whether people are responding in a consistent manner. For example, suppose some respondents score in the severely depressed range on half of the items on a scale measuring depression and as not at all depressed on the other half of the items on the same scale. That would be inconsistent (unreliable) and would suggest that perhaps respondents are having difficulty understanding the scale's wording. Research methods texts also identify benchmarks for what is considered acceptable levels of reliability. If the translated version has an acceptable level of reliability, that would indicate that participants understand not only the language of the scale items, but also what the language means conceptually.

If the measurement instrument is a questionnaire you have constructed just for your evaluation, the notion of testing its reliability or validity before using it in your evaluation is probably not feasible. However, you should at least administer it in a dry run to one or two handfuls of members of the relevant minority culture in your target population and discuss with them whether they understand

Table 2.1 *Illustration of linguistic and conceptual equivalence*

English	Spanish with linguistic equivalence only (not valid)	Spanish with conceptual equivalence (valid)
"I feel blue"	"Me siento azul"	"Me siento triste"
	Meaning: "I feel the color blue"	Meaning: "I am sad"

the wording to mean what you intend it to mean. You can try to avoid problems regarding conceptual equivalence with idioms by using an online translator. For example, Google Translator translates "I feel blue" into Spanish as "Me siento triste" which is "I feel sad" in English. It does not translate it into "Me siento azul" which would lose the idiomatic meaning and convey a person's color being blue. Table 2.1 illustrates linguistic and conceptual equivalence with regard to translating into Spanish a scale item on which respondents can agree or disagree with the statement "I feel blue."

Finally, because there are many ways in which your evaluation can be insensitive in one culture or another, you should learn all you can about being sensitive to the minority cultures of the people you hope will participate in your evaluation, especially those cultural aspects bearing on participation and measurement in evaluation. You should also be aware that the same language might be spoken differently in different countries that speak that language. For example, if the target population is Mexican, then a Mexican translator should be used, and if the target population is from a different Latin American country, then a translator from that country should be used.

2.5   Developing Cultural Competence

Before you design an evaluation which will involve participants from an ethnic minority you should become well-read in the literature that describes the culture, its values, and issues regarding the participation by its members in research and evaluation studies. You should make sure that you learn about the culture's historical experiences with prejudice and oppression and how those experiences might affect whether and how its members participate in your evaluation. For example, if you expect Native Americans to participate in your evaluation, you should know about their feelings about having their lands taken from them, and the importance of their tribes in their lives and how their tribes can influence their participation in your evaluation (Norton & Manson, 1996; Rubin & Babbie, 2017). If you are conducting a mental health needs assessment among African Americans you should know that some of their responses might be affected by the relatively high degree of stigma many attach to the concept of mental illness

(Thompson *et al.*, 1996). If you become well-read about Latinx attitudes and utilization of mental health services, you will learn that their underutilization of mental health services has less to do with a preference for faith healers (a misconception) and more to do with inadequate outreach efforts to them by those services (Miranda, 1996). If you expect participation by lesbian, gay, bisexual, and transgender (LGBTQ) individuals in your evaluation, you should make sure you have read about culturally sensitive research and evaluation with them. Ferguson-Colvin & Maccio (2012), for example, have authored a toolkit for working with LGBTQ youths that can be found online at https://capacity.childwelfare .gov/states/focus-areas/workforce/agencies-serving-lgbtq-toolkit/.

2.5.1 Acculturation and Immigration

An important part of being culturally sensitive is understanding acculturation-related differences among ethnic minority participants (as opposed to thinking that their cultures are homogeneous). Recent immigrants from Central America, for example, are likely to have different service needs and different attitudes about participating in an evaluation than those who came to the United States decades ago. The ones who have lived here longer are likely to be more acculturated to the North American culture, which means that they are more likely to speak English and share the values, attitudes, and lifestyle preferences that are prevalent in the United States. Assessing level of acculturation can involve asking how long they have lived in the United States, whether they or their parents were born in the United States, and what language they prefer to speak.

Likewise, recent immigrants from Central America who have experienced the trauma and stress caused by a policy in which parents and their young children are separated and detained for weeks or longer in squalid facilities are apt to have a very different reaction to an evaluation than immigrants who arrived before that separation policy was implemented and who thus were treated more humanely upon entering the United States. A Latino or Latina who has experienced that trauma is apt to have a very different reaction to an evaluation than one who has not been so traumatized.

2.5.2 Subgroup Differences

Being culturally sensitive also means understanding that no ethnic minority group is homogeneous. Subgroup differences related to acculturation and immigration are not the only ways that ethnic minority groups can be heterogeneous. For example, people born in Mexico, Cuba, Honduras, Puerto Rico, Brazil, and Spain are all Hispanic, but there are important differences in the cultures of those countries. Also, economically affluent Latinos are likely to have different cultural characteristics than those who are poor.

2.5.3 Culturally Sensitive Data Analysis and Interpretation

In light of the subgroup differences discussed above the analysis of evaluation data should not just lump everyone together under one ethnicity label. For example, if you are assessing the degree of client satisfaction with your program, it would be better to compare the mean satisfaction scores for recently immigrated Latinxs with the mean scores of those who are not recent immigrants, than to just report one score for an undifferentiated category of Latinxs. Likewise, immigrants from Central America should not be lumped with others of Hispanic origin under the label *Hispanic*. At the end of this chapter you'll see some books that might help you become more culturally sensitive.

2.6   Chapter Main Points

- Ethical guidelines in program evaluation pertain to the following: (1) ensuring voluntary participation and informed consent; (2) ensuring that no harm is done to participants; (3) protecting sensitive information; and (4) analysis and reporting of the evaluation's results, even when the results are disappointing.
- Sometimes the risk of harm in an evaluation is unescapable. But if the potential benefits of the evaluation far outweigh the risk of harm, the risk might be justified, especially if the risked harm seems to be minor and very unlikely and the potential benefits promise to be significant.
- Institutional Review Boards (IRBs) review and approve or disapprove of proposals for program evaluations involving human participants in terms of whether the evaluation's potential benefits outweigh its ethical risks. If you conduct an evaluation involving human participants, you probably will need to submit an evaluation proposal to an IRB.
- Many current or prospective clients served by social welfare and human service agencies are members of a minority culture. Consequently, it is imperative that evaluation procedures be sensitive to those cultures.
- Because there are many ways in which you can be insensitive in evaluating one culture or another, you should learn all you can about being sensitive to the minority cultures of the people you hope will participate in your evaluation.
- Before you design an evaluation which will involve participants from an ethnic minority, you should become well-read in the literature that describes the culture, its values, and issues regarding the participation by its members in research and evaluation studies.

- Reasons to ensure that an evaluation is culturally sensitive include (1) to recruit members of minority populations and retain their participation in the evaluation; (2) to enhance the collection of data from members of different cultural groups; (3) to take into account cultural differences in analyzing and interpreting evaluation findings; and (4) to ensure that the data are equivalent across cultural groups.
- Culturally sensitive ways to enhance recruitment efforts include obtaining approval of the evaluation from community leaders, employing members of the minority community for data collection, learning where to look (not relying exclusively on traditional referral sources), seeking advice from community leaders and other community members, and building rapport with and nurturing culturally sensitive referral sources.
- Culturally sensitive ways to enhance retention include the making of regular phone calls by warm and friendly research assistants, providing transportation to and from each assessment session, providing coffee and snacks, making reminder calls, and (with homeless and residentially transient participants) using anchor points and tracking.
- When a scale is translated from one language to another, measurement equivalence requires conceptual equivalence in addition to linguistic equivalence.
- An important part of being culturally sensitive is understanding acculturation-related differences among ethnic minority participants (as opposed to thinking that their cultures are homogeneous).
- Being culturally sensitive also means understanding that no ethnic minority group is homogeneous.
- The analysis of evaluation data should not just lump everyone together under one ethnicity label.

2.7   Exercises

1. Go to the website of the National Institutes of Health (NIH) at https://phrp .nihtraining.com/. Take their free online tutorial on protecting human participants in research. Jot down a summary of what you learn there to discuss with your classmates and instructor. Those who complete the tutorial receive a certificate that they would need later if they want to be a research assistant on a study requiring IRB approval. Some instructors grant extra credit for earning the certificate.

2. Read the following book: Jones, J. H. (1981). *Bad Blood: The Tuskegee Syphilis Experiment*. New York, NY: Free Press. Identify the ethical guidelines violated by that experiment and discuss what the experience of social worker

Peter Buxton implies regarding why practitioners working in the field of social welfare or human services are obligated to engage in efforts to promote social justice. Share your notes with your instructor and classmates.

3. Using your school's literature database, enter the search term *culturally sensitive program evaluation*. Click on one or more of the links until you find new information about the topic or something that provides an interesting illustration of it. Summarize what you learn to discuss with your instructor and classmates.

4. Using your school's literature database, find the article "Korean social work students' attitudes toward homosexuals" (*Journal of Social Work Education*, fall, 2001). Critically appraise how the study dealt with measurement equivalence.

5. Using your school's literature database, find the article "Ethnic pride, biculturalism, and drug use norms of urban American Indian adolescents" (*Social Work Research*, June 2002). Summarize and critically appraise how the study illustrates cultural sensitivity.

6. Read the following toolkit and identify a few things in it that you did not know and that you think are particularly important: Ferguson-Colvin, K. M., & Maccio, E. M. (2012). *Toolkit for Practitioners/Researchers Working with Lesbian, Gay, Bisexual, Transgender, and Queer/Questioning (LGBTQ) Runaway and Homeless Youth (RHY)*. New York, NY: National Research Center for Permanency and Family Connections, Silberman School of Social Work. Discuss this with your instructor and classmates.

2.8   Additional Reading

- Cuellar, L., & Paniagua, F. A. (Eds.). (2000). *Handbook of Multicultural Mental Health: Assessment and Treatment of Diverse Populations*. San Diego, CA: Academic Press.
- Fong, R., & Furuto, S. (Eds.). (2001). *Culturally Competent Practice: Skills, Interventions, and Evaluations*. Boston, MA: Allyn & Bacon.
- Hernandez, M., & Isaacs, M. R. (Eds) (1998). *Promoting Cultural Competence in Children's Mental Health Services*. Baltimore, MD: Paul H. Brookes.
- Jones, J. H. (1981). *Bad Blood: The Tuskegee Syphilis Experiment*. New York, NY: Free Press.
- Potocky, M., & Rodgers-Farmer, A. Y. (Eds.). (1998). *Social Work Research with Minority and Oppressed Populations*. New York, NY: Haworth Press.
- Rubin, A., & Babbie, E. R. (2017). *Research Methods for Social Work* (9th ed.). Boston, MA: Cengage Learning.

PART II

QUANTITATIVE AND QUALITATIVE METHODS FOR FORMATIVE AND PROCESS EVALUATIONS

As mentioned in Chapter 1, formative evaluations and process evaluations are similar in that they use similar evaluation methods and aim to help programs make improvements. The key distinction between the two is that formative evaluations focus on improving programs while they are still in their *formative* phases, when they are still being developed and improved, while process evaluations focus on needed improvements after programs are more established. In a sense, this distinction is somewhat vague because programs should always be monitoring how well they are being implemented and always be vigilant about needed improvements. Nevertheless, the literature on program evaluation continues to refer to formative and process evaluations as two types of evaluation. Although these two approaches to evaluation share many similarities, one thing is clear: a summative evaluation should not be conducted until

a program has been fully developed and had an evaluation completed to identify and correct its implementation problems. This section will delve into the methods used in formative and process evaluations. Methods commonly used by both types of evaluation include surveys and individual and group interviews.

At some point in your career – perhaps earlier than you expect – you are likely to be involved in a formative or process evaluation. The chapters in this section will discuss competencies in two key areas that you will need for such evaluations: needs assessment and client surveys.

Chapter 3 will examine these methods in regard to needs assessment. It will look at the various purposes of conducting a needs assessment, alternative ways to define needs, and different needs assessment approaches. Special attention will be given to skills in conducting qualitative focus group interviews.

Chapter 4 will attempt to prepare you to conduct surveys and interviews of clients or staff members. The chapter will review alternative sampling approaches; examine the advantages, caveats, and guidelines for conducting client satisfaction surveys; and review alternative survey modalities and their relevant research methods. Special attention will be given to constructing survey instruments and to conducting qualitative interviews.

Chapter 3

Needs Assessment

WHAT YOU'LL LEARN IN THIS CHAPTER

You'll learn about some of the complexities in trying to define the unmet needs of a program's clients and prospective clients. You'll learn about the process of assessing client needs, six different approaches for doing so, and the advantages and disadvantages of each approach and what they imply regarding the desirability of triangulating approaches. You'll also learn how to conduct a qualitative focus group interview.

3.1   Introduction

Before resources are expended on any new human services program, a careful study should be conducted to assess the need for the program. Such a study is called a *needs assessment*. The purpose of a needs assessment is to learn not only about a target population's most important *needs*, but also about the *characteristics of the target population*. What are its socioeconomic characteristics? What kinds of needs are most pervasive in what parts of the community, and in what parts are the unmet needs most problematic? The answers to questions like these will guide the planning of what services to offer, where to locate them, and how to maximize their use by members of the target population.

Although needs assessment is a key part of formative evaluation – as a basis for planning what a new program should offer – even well-developed programs at times should conduct a needs assessment. That is because the characteristics and needs of the target population may have changed, as is illustrated in Box 3.1, which discusses this in regard to the deinstitutionalization movement near the end of the twentieth century. That box also illustrates why formative evaluations do not necessarily precede process evaluations. For example, Box 3.1 describes how the deinstitutionalization movement discharged state hospital residents en masse into communities where community mental health programs were serving clients with very different needs than those of the discharged residents. Suppose that some process evaluations at that time found that the practitioners in a community mental health program were not serving discharged residents (Rubin & Bowker, 1986). That process evaluation might spawn the development of a new intervention by the program to serve the deinstitutionalized residents. If that intervention is a new programmatic effort by the established community mental health program, then one way to look at its needs assessment with the new kind of clients is as a formative evaluation in a new program spawned as part of an established program.

Box 3.1 An Illustration of Why Well-Developed Programs Should Assess Needs: The Case of Deinstitutionalization

During the 1960s, community mental health (CMH) programs sprang up all over the United States as part of national legislation that aimed to help people with psychiatric disorders get the treatment they needed while residing in the community and thus avoid the need to institutionalize them in state hospitals. After the programs had been operating for about a decade – serving clients already residing in the community, many of whom were not afflicted by the severe and persistent psychotic disorders associated with institutionalization – advances in psychotropic medications combined with state budget cuts led many states to begin discharging residents of state hospitals en masse into the community. This deinstitutionalization movement reduced the cost of institutionalization, but the states by and large did not use the cost savings to improve services for the deinstitutionalized population now residing in the community. The many needs of that population were unlike the needs of most of the existing community mental health program clientele in that they included things like getting humane housing, learning basic independent living skills, and case management services to support proper use of medications. But those needs were not being met, as exposés emerged decrying transferring people from the back wards of state hospitals to homeless back wards in the community (Morrissey & Goldman, 1984).

It could be reasonably argued that CMH programs should have tried to meet those needs in light of the fact that providing an alternative to institutionalization was a prime reason for funding the CMH programs. Some praiseworthy programs did try to meet those needs. One, for example, developed and provided an intervention called Assertive Community Treatment (ACT) (Bond et al., 2001). This new initiative emerged as part of a well-developed CMH program that recognized and tried to meet the needs arising from the changes in its target population. On the one hand, assessing those needs could be deemed to be part of a formative evaluation in the new ACT program. On the other hand, the ACT initiative can be viewed as a response to an assessment of needs by a developed program. So, when an established program creates a new initiative in light of the changing needs of its target population, must the assessment of those needs be viewed as part of a formative evaluation by a new initiative or part of a process evaluation by a developed program? One might argue that it is a semantic distinction that doesn't matter – that what matters is that a program assessed and recognized unmet needs and tried to meet them.

As is the case with many other kinds of decisions made in the human services, however, decisions about implementing new services – and about the nature of those services – are often made without any a priori systematic, empirical investigation as to the need for them. Programs are often developed solely according to the biases or noble intentions of influential program staff members or community leaders.

Regardless of how noble a program's mission might be, it is not enough to be on the side of the angels. Of course, we should all want to be on that side, but our noble perspective or good intentions will not ensure that we are guided by accurate information regarding what services people really need, what services they think they need, or what services they will actually utilize. Unless we supplement our noble aims with an empirical assessment of needs, not only will we not know the answers to these questions, but also we will not know the segments of the target population that have the most and least need, where they are located, their socioeconomic circumstances, how best to tailor the services to fit their circumstances, and what barriers might impede their utilization of what we have to offer.

For example, suppose your first position after graduation is in a new program to deal with homelessness in a particular community. In early staff meetings for program planning purposes the program director opines that the program's focus should be on developing a shelter for the many homeless folks in the community. Especially if most of your colleagues in the program are early in their careers like you, a "group-think" dynamic might discourage staff members from expressing any skeptical questions about the director's shelter idea or from advocating a careful, systematic, empirical investigation of its merits. Let's suppose that you have the idealistic courage to ask such questions or advocate for such an investigation. What concerns might you express? Perhaps, given your familiarity with the empirical literature regarding homelessness, you might wonder about the need to assess how the homeless people in your community feel about shelters. You might wonder about the ages of the homeless population. How many of them are runaway youths, and are those youths much less likely to go to a shelter than are older folks? How many of them were kicked out of their homes because of their gender identity or some family dysfunction? To what extent might it make more sense to provide outreach services to those youths to help them better cope with their problems and perhaps encourage a rapprochement with their families? And how do the older homeless folks feel about shelters? Do they fear that shelters are unsafe? Do the women especially feel that way, and what proportion of the homeless individuals are women? Where should the shelter be located to make it most accessible to the people who want to use it? These are just some of the important questions to ask, even if you believe it would be inhumane to not provide shelters for the homeless. Let's now look at alternative ways to assess needs. We'll begin by returning to the difference between normative need and felt need.

3.2   Defining Needs: Normative Need versus Felt Need

You can't always get what you want
But if you try sometime you'll find
You get what you need

The Rolling Stones

When considering the assessment of needs for human services, the above lyrics by the Rolling Stones rock band can apply, but so can they be reversed to say "You can't always get what you need but sometimes you get what you want." These lyrics pertain to the difference between *normative need* and *felt need*. *Normative needs* are defined in terms of what service providers *think* people in their target population need. As an example of normative need, suppose a substantial increase in the prevalence of substance abuse among teens in a community has prompted most of the members of the advisory board of a local church to open a teen-oriented storefront coffee house in which a young, junior pastor will build an empathic relationship and employ motivational interviewing techniques with the youths who drop in and who mention abusing drugs or alcohol. Motivational interviewing is considered to be an evidence-based intervention to help people realize that they need to make behavioral changes for mental or physical health problems or substance-use disorders – perhaps by seeking treatment that they previously thought they did not need (Miller & Rose, 2009). If the members approve the storefront coffee house idea without first assessing the extent to which local teens would come to the coffee house – especially those teens using drugs or alcohol – then the decision would be based only on *normative* need. Despite the reasonableness of the idea, the program would fail if the youths don't attend it or if the only youths who do come are ones not at risk for substance abuse. This would be an example of a program that was inadvisable without an assessment of *felt* need. *Felt needs* are defined in terms of what members of a target population say they need.

Some decisions based on normative need might be warranted without an assessment of felt need. One example might be a decision to provide free and nutritious school lunches to children in high-poverty communities. Some decisions based on normative need might even be warranted *despite* findings showing little to no felt need. For example, try to recall how you felt about being required to take a research methods course, or perhaps even a course on program evaluation. If you aspired to be a service provider – as opposed to a researcher or evaluator – you probably felt that you did not need such a course. You might have even resented being required to take it. Requiring such a course typically is based on *normative need*, not *felt need*. Curriculum decision-makers probably thought that they knew best what students need, believing that if they only required the courses that students wanted, or that were popular, then future practitioners would be ill-prepared to ask about or look for evidence as to whether the right services are being provided or whether those services are effective. If you agree with those decision-makers, you probably believe that requiring such a course is an appropriate decision based exclusively on normative need. Of course, however, if the decision pertains not to whether to *require* such a course, but rather to whether to offer it as an *elective*, then it would be essential to assess *felt* need. Despite how much some professors might love to hear themselves talk, most (perhaps not all) of them would probably agree that having them speak to an empty classroom is an undesirable deployment of scarce resources. For another example of normative versus felt need you can examine Box 3.2.

Box 3.2   Example of Normative versus Felt Need: Evidence-Informed Practice

Suppose practitioners in a statewide mental health agency are surveyed to assess what areas of in-service training they need the most. They respond to a questionnaire that lists a variety of in-service training alternatives, including treatment options such as family therapy, cognitive-behavioral therapy, and so on. Another option – for which virtually no need is expressed – is the evidence-informed practice process. The evidence-informed practice process training would teach them about how to search for and critically appraise research evidence regarding what intervention has the best effects for one's clients and how to evaluate one's own effectiveness in providing a chosen intervention. Assuming that attending the in-service training sessions on evidence-informed practice is mandatory, what decision should be made regarding whether to provide training? If you believe in the importance of evidence-informed practice, you might endorse requiring that training even if it is unpopular and based only on normative need. If, on the other hand, attendance is voluntary, you might *not* want to offer the training because of the lack of felt need (and consequent poor attendance) regardless of how much you think that practitioners need that training.

3.3   Felt Need versus Service Utilization

Just because people express the need for something doesn't necessarily mean that they will utilize the service you offer to meet that need. One reason for this possible discrepancy is the difference between what people say and what they do. For example, it is a lot easier for young or prospective parents to anonymously check a survey questionnaire box asking whether they need more information about healthy child-rearing than it is for them to actually attend child-rearing training sessions. Even if the sessions are easily accessible and free, it takes a great deal more time and effort to attend the sessions than to check a questionnaire box. Moreover, the sessions might be hard to attend. There might be transportation difficulties, conflicts with work hours, childcare barriers, not wanting their neighbors to see that they need to learn about child-rearing, and so on. Consequently, it would be a mistake to assume that people who say they have a need that your service will address will actually use the service when you offer it. Assessing needs therefore involves assessing not only what people say they need but also how likely they are to utilize the service you plan to offer and under what circumstances they would be more or less likely to utilize the service.

3.4   Needs Assessment Approaches

Early in your career you are likely to be in a meeting where someone suggests the need to develop a new program or service to address some problem in the community. That someone might be your program director, a coworker, a community resident, or some other stakeholder. Let's assume that the need pertains to "latchkey" children who are left alone after school because of parental job requirements and inability to pay for a nanny or other childcare possibilities. Let's imagine that the program being proposed to meet this need involves mobilizing retired residents to volunteer at places of worship, playgrounds, and other community facilities where they can supervise the children in recreational activities. Recognizing that the person who expressed this idea might be responding to their own pet issue and idiosyncratic circumstances, suppose you speak up and, after acknowledging the merit of this idea, you tactfully pose several needs assessment questions. Good for you! One question might be "Do we know how many children in our community actually are latchkey kids in need of a program like this?" Another might be "Is there a sufficient number of retired residents in the community who would volunteer?" Also, "How many children would attend the activities?" "Are there enough community facilities that are willing and able to participate?" "How would the parents feel about this? Might they worry about potential abuse by some volunteers?" Or, "This sounds like a great idea, but are there other great ways that other communities have tried to address this problem that we should learn about? And, if so, what can we learn from their experiences?"

Chances are that the reaction to your questions will be to assign you the task of conducting the needs assessment to answer them. Before you accept that assignment, you should inquire about the resources that will be allocated to it. Will others collaborate with you on it? How much of your time and their time will be freed up for it? Is there a deadline for completing the assessment? What budgetary resources will be allocated to it? How these questions are answered will influence your inclination to accept the assignment as well as the potential scope, complexity, and sophistication of the eventual assessment.

There are six broad categories of needs assessment approaches: (1) social indicators; (2) rates under treatment; (3) key informants; (4) community forums; (5) focus groups; and (6) community surveys. The different approaches are not mutually exclusive; that is, they can be combined. Which approaches you use and the specific details and methods that you use with them will be influenced by the resources and time you have for completing the needs assessment. Before you embark on a resource-heavy approach that involves gathering data from people, you might start with an approach that draws on data that are already readably accessible to you. One such approach examines *social indicators*. Another looks at *rates under treatment*. Let's now examine each of these approaches before moving on to approaches that gather data from people.

3.4.1   Social Indicators

The social indicators approach to needs assessment examines available statistics on the conditions of – or prevalence of problems in – a target population. Depending on the nature of the target population or the type of needs being assessed, examples of the kinds of social indicators that might be examined include infant mortality rates, rates of reported child neglect or abuse, school dropout rates, and so on. Regarding our latchkey children example, some census data you might look at include the following:

- the number of school-age children residing in a community, the number of them living in poverty, and the census tracts where most reside;
- the number of adults aged sixty-five or older in the community; and
- the number of employed women in the community who are the parents of young children.

Advantages/Disadvantages. The advantages of the social indicators approach are that it does not require collecting information from people and thus is inexpensive and unobtrusive and can be done quickly. Potential disadvantages include the possibility that the existing data might not have been collected carefully, might not adequately pertain to the needs on which you are focusing, and, even if they do pertain to those needs, might not reflect the extent to which the people with those needs will actually use the program or service that you are planning to provide.

3.4.2   Rates under Treatment

The rates under treatment approach looks at the number and characteristics of people who participate in a program or service similar to the one you have in mind. That program or service should exist in a community that is demographically like your community. If it is, you can assume that the number and types of people who eventually participate in the program or service that you are planning probably will parallel the number and types of people participating in the comparison community. Implementing the rates under treatment approach requires obtaining and analyzing the rates under treatment data from the comparison community.

Advantages/Disadvantages. The advantages of the rates under treatment approach mirror the advantages of the social indicators approach. It is quick, easy, unobtrusive, and inexpensive. However, a disadvantage is that it might underestimate normative need, especially if resource limitations in the comparison program make it impossible to serve all the people who want to participate in it or if some aspects of the comparison program make it hard for potential participants to access or make it unattractive for potential participants. Also, as with the social indicators approach, the value of this approach depends on the extent to which the comparison program data are accurate. Careful, accurate, reliable record keeping might be a low priority in resource-strapped human service agencies. Although inaccuracies are often unintentional, some agencies might exaggerate the number of people they serve. They might inflate that number, thinking that doing so will help their search for more funding or make them look better to board members or other stakeholders.

3.4.3   Key Informants

One alternative to relying exclusively on existing data regarding social indicators and rates under treatment for needs assessment is to seek the opinions of people who are thought to have special expertise about the problems and needs of the target population. This alternative is called the *key informants approach* to needs assessment. Key informants can be human service professionals who work with the target population, leaders of organizations that advocate for the target population, or any other people whose work brings them into close contact with the target population. For example, if you are assessing needs related to homelessness, key informants whom you should consider interviewing might include the director of a local homeless shelter or soup kitchen, mental health case managers, community leaders in the neighborhoods where a lot of homeless people are visible, leaders of groups that advocate for homeless people, and law enforcement personnel who deal with the problem. If you are assessing needs pertaining to latchkey children, key informants to interview could include personnel in schools, members of school parent–teacher associations (PTAs), caseworkers in child welfare programs, treatment service providers in child and family service agencies and child guidance centers, juvenile justice personnel, and so on. When you interview the key informants you should ask questions in a non-directive, unbiased, open-ended manner, using neutral probes when seeking elaboration. Box 3.3, which appears later in this chapter, illustrates these interviewing techniques.

Advantages/Disadvantages. As compared with community surveys (to be discussed later), the key informant approach is less costly and less time consuming. As compared with relying on existing data, it offers expert opinions from people who deal with and have special expertise about the target population. Also, it will give your program visibility and build relationships with community resources that can be of value to the program that you eventually develop to address the needs you are assessing. The main disadvantage of this approach is that the value of the information being gathered depends on the accuracy and objectivity of the opinions expressed by the key informants. Directors of homeless shelters, for example, might be biased regarding the conditions of the shelters and lack expertise regarding the many homeless folks who refuse to use the shelters for a variety of reasons, with whom they might never come into contact. Thus, the information you get directly from members of the target population can be very different from the opinions expressed by key informants.

3.4.4   Community Forums

One relatively easy way to seek information directly from members of the target population is to use the *community forum approach*. With this approach a meeting can be held where members of the community can express their needs and their views about existing problems and potential remedies. The forum can be unstructured, encouraging participants to discuss whatever is on their minds, or it can be more structured around a particular type of need or a program or service being considered to address that need.

Advantages/Disadvantages. There are several advantages of the community forum approach in addition to the fact the members of the target population are providing the information. It requires less time and money than community surveys, and, unlike responding to structured survey questionnaires, participants can be stimulated by what others say to consider things that they might otherwise have not thought of. One disadvantage, however, is the potential for the people who attend the forum and what they say there to be unrepresentative of the mainstream members of the community and their most prevalent and most important needs. The people most motivated to attend a forum might have a vested interest in a particular problem or how to deal with it. Regarding homelessness, for example, they might be storeowners concerned about the presence of homeless people nearby dissuading potential customers from shopping in their stores. Even if the attendees at the forum are representative of the community, those participants who have a particular ax to grind and who are the most outspoken might intimidate other participants from expressing more representative viewpoints. If, despite these disadvantages, you opt for the community forum approach, you probably should hold multiple closed meetings, with each targeting a different, preselected, segment of the community. A side benefit of this approach is that with each meeting you hold you will build the visibility of your agency in the community, which in turn can enhance community support for the agency and utilization of its services.

3.4.5 Focus Groups

An approach that shares some of the advantages of the community forum approach but that involves a smaller number of people, can be more structured, and can avoid some of its disadvantages is to engage community members in focus groups. This is a group interviewing approach in which roughly eight to ten participants are selected on the basis of their relevance to the topic of the group interview. If the topic pertains to needs regarding latchkey children, for example, potential participants could be working parents and their neighbors, people whose work involves frequent contact with parents or children, community leaders, and so on.

As with the community forum approach, it is best to convene multiple focus groups because any one group might be atypical. You might opt to have one group for working parents, one for their neighbors, one for people whose work involves frequent contact with parents or children, one for community leaders, and so on. As with the community forum approach, participants can be stimulated by each other's comments to consider things that they might have overlooked in an individual interview or a questionnaire survey. However, having a smaller number of (preselected) participants and a more structured and focused group process led by a skilled group leader can reduce the risk of being misled by people who are the most outspoken, have vested interests, or the biggest axes to grind or the risk of having a meeting in which so many disparate views are vented in a helter-skelter manner that it is difficult to develop a good feel for the most important needs and how to address them.

How to Conduct a Focus Group. If in your professional education you are learning how to be a skillful interviewer with individuals, you have a big head start in becoming a skilled focus group leader. That is, you know the importance of, and are skilled in, asking questions or responding to comments in an unbiased manner, using neutral probes. You need to be flexible and non-directive in responding to comments you did not anticipate, and you need to use neutral probes when seeking further clarification. You can ask questions, but should not let your own predilections influence what you ask, how you ask it, or how to respond or interpret the answer. Box 3.3 illustrates a skillful way to do so. When examining the box, be sure to notice and read its footnotes.

Box 3.3   A (Fictitious) Focus Group Discussion of a Homeless Shelter

HOMELESS PERSON: That shelter is a disaster!

GROUP LEADER: A disaster …?[1]

HOMELESS PERSON: Yeah; it's dangerous.

GROUP LEADER: Dangerous, eh; in what ways?[2]

HOMELESS PERSON: Yadda, yadda, yadda![3]

GROUP LEADER: Are there other ways in which the shelter is a disaster?[4]

ANOTHER HOMELESS PERSON: It's impossible to stay asleep there.

GROUP LEADER: That can be rough! Can you say more about that?[5]

HOMELESS PERSON: Yadda, yadda, yadda!

GROUP LEADER: I wonder if some of the folks who haven't spoken yet would like to share their thoughts.

---

[1] Notice that a neutral probe need not be wordy. Just repeating a key word with an interested tone of voice or facial expression can suffice. Avoid the tendency of inexperienced interviewers to preface their follow-up probes with stilted, wordy responses like "I hear you saying that the shelter is a disaster." Also, do not repeat the words with a tone of voice or facial expression that might convey the notion that you think the person is expressing a weird idea or is not communicating properly.

> [2] Notice the neutrality and non-directiveness of this probe. The interviewer did not try to guess at what the person might have in mind and then ask yes/no questions about the possibilities.
>
> [3] If you are a fan of the syndicated "Seinfeld" TV sitcom, you'll recognize that "Yadda, yadda, yadda" merely implies that the person gave a long response regarding the dangerousness.
>
> [4] This is another neutral, non-directive probe without letting one's predilections narrow the focus of the probe.
>
> [5] It's not a bad idea to preface the neutral probe with some brief empathy, but be sure that the empathy is not too wordy and does not narrow or bias the probe.

Types and Sequence of Focus Group Questions. Although focus group interviews should emphasize open-ended questions and neutral probes, they should not be completely unstructured. The leader should make sure that the group does not wander too far from the reason for convening the group, such as the need to learn about the service needs of participants that a particular agency is equipped to provide. For example, if the focus group discussion strays off into irrelevant topics such as dissatisfaction with the local football team coach, the group leader might ask, "How do you feel about police–community relations here?"

Another aspect of focus group structure involves having a plan for the sequencing of different types of questions. For example, Krueger and Casey (2015) recommend using what they call *opening questions*, *introductory questions*, *key questions*, *ending questions*, and *summary questions*. They suggest starting off with an *opening question* that they portray as a community-building *icebreaking question*. One such question might be, "Can you each briefly introduce yourselves, where you live, and how you like to spend your time?" After everyone has responded briefly to that opening question, the leader should – in an open-ended fashion – introduce the focus for the discussion, such as by asking a *key question* such as "What is it like to live in this neighborhood?" Or, "What do you think is most needed to make this neighborhood an even better place to live?" Most of the neutral probes by the group leader should follow answers to the key question. If the agency has a specific interest in learning about the community's feelings about a particular service or resource that it is considering, the leader might ask a narrow key question that focuses sharply on that service or resource, perhaps asking something like "What do you think about the recreational facilities for youths in this neighborhood?" If there are multiple specific resources or services being considered, then the leader might ask a narrowly focused key question about each resource or service and spend up to about 15 minutes with neutral follow-up probes about each one.

As the focus group nears the end of its allotted time – which is probably about an hour – the leader should pose an *ending question* that asks participants to think about the most important aspects of the discussion. For example, the leader might ask, "Of all the things [or needs] that have been mentioned, are there one or two that are the most important to you?" After the responses to the ending question have been expressed, the leader should summarize the overall discussion's main points and then ask a *summary question* like "Is my summary accurate?" Or, "Did I miss anything?"

An example of the kinds of key questions that guided a focus group assessment of the long-term care needs of LGBT older adults is presented in Box 3.4.

Box 3.4   Long-Term Care Needs of LGBT Older Adults

A focus group assessment of the long-term care needs of LGBT older adults was reported by Stein *et al.* (2010). The assessment utilized two focus groups. One group included twelve participants at a non-residential community-based facility in New York City, and the other included four residents living in a long-term care facility in New Jersey. The following five key questions guided each group interview (Stein *et al.* 2010, p. 427).

1. How comfortable do you feel being openly gay in your neighborhood (or long-term care setting)?
2. What are your thoughts as a gay senior about retirement communities?
3. What thoughts do you have about assisted living residences or nursing homes?
4. Do you think you would be (or are now) comfortable as a gay senior in a residential setting?
5. How can health care providers be more responsive to gay people?

Participants' responses to the five questions emphasized a preference for gay-friendly care and expressed various fears associated with being in a facility that is not limited to LGBT participants. The things being feared included rejection or neglect from health care providers, rejection and lack of respect from straight peers, and, consequently, having to return to the closet. On the basis of what they learned in the focus groups, Stein *et al.* recommended that long-term care facilities should train their providers to understand the needs of LGBT older adults and be more respectful of them. In order to ensure this sensitivity and respect, they also recommended dedicating special floors, units, or complete facilities to members of the LGBT community.

Advantages/Disadvantages. Focus groups have several advantages over other needs assessment approaches. For example, unlike community surveys (an approach that we'll examine shortly) or analyzing existing social indicators or rates under treatment data, focus groups provide the flexibility for in-depth probing to gain a better understanding of the needs and views of the target population. Unlike surveys, the group dynamics that occur in focus groups provide a synergy that can elicit aspects of the topic that designers of survey questionnaires might not think to ask about. As to disadvantages, evaluators and focus group leaders need to be wary of the possibility that those who opt to participate in a focus group might be atypical and unlike most members of the target population. (Convening multiple focus groups, instead of relying on just one, might alleviate this concern.) Also, the focus group leaders need to understand group dynamics and know how to deal with situations where certain excessively vocal participants might dominate the discussion. Likewise, they need to know how to help shyer participants feel safe in expressing their views, especially views that might disagree with views that have already been expressed. The leader also needs to resist being overwhelmed with voluminous data and should be able to synthesize the discussion and summarize the main points. The recommendations emanating from a focus group needs assessment can be misleading if the groups are led by leaders who lack these skills or who impose their own views on the discussion.

An excellent YouTube demonstration of how to skillfully moderate a focus group interview can be viewed at www.youtube.com/watch?v = xjHZsEcSqwo.

3.4.6 Community Surveys

Unlike focus groups or community forums, the **community survey** approach to needs assessment asks individuals about their needs, characteristics, and circumstances. Individual community members typically respond in the privacy of their own homes. If the questions are being asked in a mailed or online questionnaire (as opposed to an individual interview), their responses can be anonymous. Conducting a community survey that will provide valid information about the needs and characteristics of the target population requires expertise in survey research methods and in questionnaire construction, and the next chapter will be devoted to those topics. Before we move on, however, let's summarize the advantages and disadvantages of this approach, some of which we will reexamine in Chapter 4.

Advantages/Disadvantages. The advantages and disadvantages of the community survey approach mirror those of research surveys in general. If the sample of survey respondents is chosen properly – perhaps using probability (random) sampling techniques – one advantage is that this approach can instill more confidence in the representativeness of the respondents and the views they express. If the survey is administered anonymously, another advantage is that respondents can be less influenced about the social desirability of their answers and less intimidated about disagreeing with other – perhaps intimidating – people. As with focus groups and unlike analyzing existing data about social indicators or rates under treatment, another advantage is the opportunity to hear directly from the people you are seeking to serve.

One disadvantage, however, is the possibility that many people will not respond to the survey and that those who do respond might be unlike the non-respondents in important ways. For example, they might be more motivated to respond because they feel more strongly about certain needs or prospective programs. Consequently, if the response rate to a survey of households is very low – say about 20 percent – and 70 percent of the respondents say that they will attend weekly meetings on avoiding or dealing with domestic violence – it would be a mistake to conclude that attendance at such meetings will be anywhere near 70 percent of the target population. Also – as with focus groups – the advantages of the community survey approach depend on the expertise of the people designing and conducting it. For example, questionnaires need to be constructed in a user-friendly format and use unambiguous and unbiased wording. A sampling approach is needed that will minimize the chances of unrepresentativeness. And even with the best sampling procedures, proper efforts are needed to deal with the potential for non-response bias.

3.5   Triangulation

As you have seen, none of the alternative approaches to needs assessment is immune from yielding misleading findings and recommendations. Consequently, resources permitting, you should employ more than one approach – perhaps several. If the different approaches are yielding similar findings, then you can have more confidence in the plans you make based on those findings. If the findings are dissimilar, you can consider the advantages and disadvantages of each approach in trying to decide which set of findings is the most trustworthy. You might even choose to replicate that approach with a different group of participants to see if the same findings and implications emerge. Although no methods of program evaluation guarantee foolproof results, **triangulating** methods – which means employing more than one method to see if the different methods yield comparable results – can be a helpful way to try to avoid being misled.

3.6   Chapter Main Points

- The purpose of a needs assessment is to learn about a target population's most important needs and the characteristics of the target population.
- Normative needs are defined in terms of what service providers *think* people need.
- Felt needs are defined in terms of what members of a target population say they need.
- Just because people express the need for something doesn't necessarily mean that they will utilize the service you offer to meet that need.
- There are six broad categories of needs assessment approaches: (1) social indicators; (2) rates under treatment; (3) key informants; (4) community forums; (5) focus groups; and (6) community surveys.
- More than one needs assessment approach can be used. Which approaches you use and the specific details and methods that you use with them will be influenced by the resources and time you have for completing the needs assessment.
- The social indicators approach to needs assessment examines available statistics on the conditions of – or prevalence of problems in – a target population.
- The rates under treatment approach to needs assessment looks at the number and characteristics of people who participate in a program or service similar to the one you have in mind.
- The key informants approach to needs assessment seeks the opinions of people who are thought to have special expertise about the problems and needs of the target population.
- With the community forum approach to needs assessment, a meeting is held, where members of the community express their needs and their views about existing problems and potential remedies.
- The focus group approach to needs assessment is a group interviewing approach in which roughly eight to ten participants are selected on the basis of their relevance to the topic of the group interview.
- The community survey approach to needs assessment asks individuals about their needs, characteristics, and circumstances. Individual community members typically respond in the privacy of their own homes. The questions might be asked in a mailed or online questionnaire or in individual interviews.
- The different needs assessment approaches have different advantages and disadvantages. None can guarantee foolproof results. Consequently, triangulating methods – which means employing more than one method to see if the different methods yield comparable results – can be a helpful way to try to avoid being misled.

3.7   Exercises

1. You have been asked by a community organization to conduct a needs assessment that will guide program planning aimed at reducing crime and drug abuse by juveniles in a low-income neighborhood with which you are familiar. Possible ideas being considered by the organization include increasing youth recreational facilities, convening police–community dialogues, providing a youth counseling program, and installing an outpatient drug treatment facility in the community. Keeping in mind the different ways to define needs:

    a. Which needs assessment approach(es) would you choose, and why?
    b. What would you do to minimize the disadvantages of your choice(s)?
    c. How would budgetary considerations influence your choice?
    d. If you chose the key informants approach, identify the key informants in your community whom you would want to interview.

2. Form focus groups with your classmates, with about eight to ten members per group. Have one person per group volunteer to conduct a focus group interview with their group about the strengths and weaknesses of your program's curriculum and student needs for revisions. Another student should volunteer to be the recorder for the group and should write down the main needs identified by the group. Each focus group interview should last approximately 50–60 minutes, followed by a discussion within each group lasting approximately 10–15 minutes regarding the strengths and limitations of the process. The recorder should write down the main strengths and limitations identified. After a break the class should reconvene, and each recorder should present a summary to the class of the main needs identified and the main strengths and limitations of the process. A class discussion should ensue after each recorder has completed their summary.

3.8   Additional Reading

- Altschuld, J. W., & Kumar, D. D. (2009). *Needs Assessment: An Overview, Book 1*. Thousand Oaks, CA: Sage Publications.
- Wambeam, R. A. (2015). *The Community Needs Assessment Workbook*. Chicago, IL: Blackstone.

Chapter 4

Survey Methods for Program Planning and Monitoring

> **WHAT YOU'LL LEARN IN THIS CHAPTER**
>
> In this chapter you'll learn about surveying and interviewing clients and staff members. The survey content will consist mainly of quantitative evaluation methods. The interview content will be largely qualitative and will cover various do's and don'ts. You'll learn some of the key concepts of sampling, with an emphasis on sampling techniques and issues for surveying low-income or hard-to-reach populations. You'll see that although probability samples are the most representative in survey research, social and human service agencies often must use non-probability samples. You'll learn how those surveys can be valuable and how to maximize their value. You'll also learn about constructing survey questionnaires, including doing so online.

4.1   Introduction

Chapter 3 ended with a discussion of the community survey approach to needs assessment. If you have taken a course on research methods, you probably learned that a *survey* is a way to collect data that most commonly involves attempting to describe the characteristics of a population on the basis of responses from a sample of people from that population to a series of written or oral questions about their characteristics and views. When surveying needs, those views typically pertain to how people feel about what they need or what their community needs. Surveys also can be used to assess views regarding how satisfied clients feel about the services an agency provides or does not provide, but should provide. Early in your career you may well be involved in planning or carrying out such surveys.

4.2   Samples, Populations, and Representativeness

You may have already learned that the value of survey findings depends largely on the extent to which the *sample* of people who participate in your survey is truly representative of the larger population. The term *population* does not necessarily refer to a very large population, such as all the residents of a city, state, or country. The survey population can include all of the clients served by your agency, all of the residents of a particular neighborhood, all of the homeless people in a community, all of the students in a high school, and so on. It can even be restricted only to members of a small population who have certain characteristics. For example, if your needs assessment survey is focused on the needs of undocumented immigrants in your community, then those immigrants, and not all of the community's residents, comprise your population. But if you are interested in how all of the residents of your community feel about undocumented immigrants and how the community can best help them, then all of the community residents would make up your population.

Probability Sampling. You may have learned from a research methods course that the best way to try to maximize the representativeness of a sample – and thus avoid sampling bias – is to use probability sampling methods which involve using random procedures for selecting the people who will comprise the sample. Random procedures are akin to blindly drawing names out of a bin or using random numbers to select people from a numbered list of names. Although probability sampling might be ideal, it is often not feasible in program evaluation surveys.

Non-probability Samples. When participation in your survey is influenced by other than a purely random process, you have a non-probability sample. One risky type of non-probability sample involves *reliance on available subjects*. As discussed in research methods texts, this method is risky because the people who happen to be available can have markedly different characteristics, needs, or views than those who are not available. The needs of the clients already participating in your agency might be quite unlike the needs of people who refuse your services or are unable to access them. Likewise, the needs or views of the people who respond to your survey might differ from the needs and views of the non-respondents. Sometimes, in fact, you don't even select a sample; instead you can try to include all of the members of your target population in your survey, such as by inviting all of your agency's current and/or previous clients to respond to a survey of their satisfaction with your agency's services or their unmet needs. Or you might invite all of the child welfare workers in your county to respond to a survey about their views regarding evidence-informed practice or the extent to which they try to learn about or employ interventions that have the best evidence regarding their effectiveness. Another non-probability sampling approach is called *snowball sampling*, which is often used in surveys of homeless people and other hidden or hard-to-reach populations, which will be discussed below.

4.2.1 Non-response Bias

Regardless of which sampling approach you use – and even if you try to include an entire population in your survey – your ultimate sample of participants will be a non-probability sample if a lot of people whom you invite to participate in your survey decline your invitation. These people are called *non-respondents*. Even if you use probability sampling methods in attempting to obtain your sample, your actual sample will be limited to the people who actually participate in your survey. Suppose you use probability (random) sampling procedures to determine which 60 of the 600 residents of a neighborhood you will attempt to interview, and only 20 (33 percent) of the 60 chosen residents agree to be interviewed. Your sample size would be 20, not 60. With so many chosen people refusing to participate in your survey, you would not have a probability sample. That's because the purpose of probability sampling is to eliminate sampling biases by relying solely on random procedures as the determinant of who will participate in your survey. If some randomly selected people actually refuse to participate, then something other than random procedures affected who will actually provide your survey information and who will not do so. And, it is reasonable to suppose that the non-participants might have needs or views that are very different from the needs or views of the people who agree to participate. That means there is a sampling bias; in this case it is called *non-response bias.*

Suppose, for example, that you distribute a client satisfaction questionnaire to all of your agency's clients, that only 30 percent of them respond, and that the mean (average) satisfaction rating of the respondents is 4 on a scale from 1 (very dissatisfied) to 5 (very satisfied). Assuming that 4 on the scale represents "satisfied," it would be quite risky to infer that the population of your agency's clients is, on average, satisfied. Chances are that the more dissatisfied clients were less motivated to take the time to respond to your survey because they feel more negatively about your agency. It's also conceivable that the most dissatisfied clients would be the most motivated to respond so that they could vent their dissatisfied feelings. Thus, if the mean rating is 2 (dissatisfied), it would be risky to infer that your client population is, on average, dissatisfied.

Some survey methodology purists might scoff at drawing any conclusions based on a 33 percent response rate. But, think for a moment about what you would be certain to know if the average rating of that 33 percent was 2 (dissatisfied). You would know that *at least* one-third of your agency's clients are, on average, dissatisfied. You would know that a sizeable portion of your clients are dissatisfied, even in the (perhaps unlikely) event that every client who did not respond is satisfied. Knowing that at least one-third of clients are, on average, dissatisfied would probably motivate your agency administrators and service providers to try to improve their services, especially if the survey respondents specified those agency or service aspects with which they are most dissatisfied.

So, am I suggesting that you not worry about how a sample is selected or its representativeness? Not at all! Instead, I am recognizing that it is very hard in evaluation surveys to end up with a truly representative sample and that, although you should strive to get an ideal sample, you should not automatically dismiss the possible value of your findings because of sampling imperfections. This is especially applicable to evaluation surveys in modestly resourced service-oriented agencies.

4.2.2   Sample Size

Another possible source of sampling error pertains to having a sample that is too small. There are two main ways in which a sample can be too small. One is when you want to look for similarities or differences among subgroups in your sample. Suppose your agency has served 1000 clients and that only 30 of them are Native Americans. If you randomly select 100 (10 percent) of your population to be interviewed, you are apt to have only a few Native Americans in your sample. Just due to the luck of the draw, you might even end up with no Native Americans being selected. You probably would not want to generalize to all of your Native American clients on the basis of the responses of only a few of them. One way to try to avoid this problem is to increase the size of your sample. Another way depends on knowing in advance the ethnicities of all of the client population. If you do have that advance information, you can select your desired percentage from the Native American clients. If there are only 30 of them, for example, you might opt to select 50 percent of them while selecting 10 percent of the remaining population. That would be called *disproportionate sampling*. Suppose you did so and found that the mean satisfaction score of the 15 Native American respondents was very different from the mean of the rest of the respondents. To calculate an overall mean score for your sample of 100 (assuming that everyone selected agrees to participate), you would have to make an adjustment so that the influence of the 50 percent of Native Americans was proportional to that of the 10 percent of the other ethnic groups. How to do that is explained in the sampling chapter of Rubin & Babbie (2017, pp. 369–371).

You might also want to oversample in anticipation of a low response rate. If you hope to have at least 100 respondents from your population of 1000, but anticipate only a 33 percent response rate, you'll probably want to select 300 clients to invite to participate – instead of 100 – to have a good chance of winding up with a sample size of 100.

Another way that a sample size can be too small is when it leaves too much room for random error (as opposed to error based on sampling *bias*). A simplified way to understand how random sampling error can occur is to imagine that your needs assessment survey pertains to predicting what proportion of your target population will oppose the development of a homelessness program in their neighborhood. Further imagine that 50 percent of the population will do so. Next, suppose that only 10 people respond to your survey. Just due to random error, it is not too far-fetched to imagine that maybe 7 or 8 of them reply that they would welcome such a program. "Wonderful!" you might say, adding that "only 20 to 30 percent (2 or 3 out of 10) of the neighborhood residents will oppose the program." You would be mistaken because, with 50 percent opposed in the population, the possibility of getting only 2 or 3 opposed in a sample of 10 is not too remote. It would be like flipping a coin 10 times and getting 7 or 8 tails or 7 or 8 heads. Unlikely, but not far-fetched just due to random error. Imagine how much more unlikely it would be to get 70 or 80 heads or 70 or 80 tails when flipping a coin 100 times. Or, to make the point even clearer, imagine getting 700 or 800 heads or tails out of 1000 flips. In other words, the more the size of a randomly selected sample increases, the more likely it is that the sample characteristics will resemble the population characteristics. The technical statistical term for that tendency is the central limit theorem. If you want to learn more about this, you can visit the following website: www.surveysystem.com/sscalc.htm.

At that site you can enter the size of your population and different sample sizes that fit your resources and the site will calculate how much sampling error you would be risking for each sample size. For example, if your community has 5000 households, and you want to randomly select 100 heads of households to be interviewed about whether they would oppose having a homelessness program in their neighborhood, it will tell you that – assuming the actual approval percentage is 50 percent – you are likely to get a result showing that somewhere between 45 and 55 percent oppose the program, which would mean that your result would likely be within 5 percentage points less or 5 percentage points more than the true population percentage. In other words, your *margin of error* would be plus or minus 5 percentage points. If you plug in figures asking how big your sample would need to be in order to be within 3 points above or below the true population percentage, it will tell you that for a population of 5000 your sample would need to be as large as 536 to have a 95 percent probability of getting a result that close to the true percentage. Interviewing that many people probably would not be feasible, so if it is important to you to have a probability sample with that little margin of error, you'll probably want to conduct a mailed survey or an online one. However, remember that if not everyone responds to your survey, you do not have a probability sample. Consequently, feasibility issues will probably have the most influence on your sampling decisions.

As discussed earlier, you might be able to get useful findings even with a substantial proportion of non-responders. For example, if you get a 50 percent response rate in which the majority of responders say that by far the greatest need in the community is for an opiate addiction program, even if most of the other 50 percent don't feel so strongly, you would still know that a fairly large segment of the population feels a great need for that program.

Maximizing Response Rates. There are several things you can do to try to motivate people to respond to your survey and thus mitigate the non-response bias problem. One method is to introduce your survey with a strong **cover letter**. The cover letter should explain the purpose and importance of the survey and how its results will be of value to the target population, assure respondent anonymity, indicate how the sample was selected (or that everyone in the specified population has been sent the survey), mention how long it will take to complete the survey (the quicker, the better – preferably not more than about 10 minutes or so), and explain briefly why it is important to have a high response rate. If feasible, you also should provide some tangible incentive and reward for taking the time to respond, such as a gift card for an online shopping site. It might also help to make the survey results accessible to respondents. Box 4.1 provides a guide for ou when your time comes for constructing a cover letter.

Follow-ups. Many potential survey respondents will not respond immediately. Many will set the mailed materials aside and perhaps forget about them under a pile of more pressing materials. If the survey invitation is sent by email, the email can disappear below subsequent emails waiting for replies in the inbox. Consequently, a vital part of increasing response rates is sending follow-up reminders to respond. If the survey is being conducted online, the follow-up email invitation can repeat the online link to the survey. Otherwise, it is best to include a new copy of the survey questionnaire with the follow-up letter.

A good time to send the follow-up reminder is about 2 to 3 weeks after the first invitation is sent. About 2 to 3 weeks after that another follow-up reminder should be sent. In each follow-up you should remind respondents of the importance of the survey and their response, perhaps repeating the contents of the original cover letter. However, the reminder should begin by letting respondents know that if they have already responded you thank them and that they therefore can disregard the follow-up reminder.

Box 4.1   A Sample Cover Letter[1]

[Agency letterhead]

Dear Veteran:

   This survey aims to assess the needs that recently discharged military veterans have when transitioning from military service to civilian life. It is being sent to all recently discharged veterans who have contacted our agency.

   Your response to the survey will provide useful information that can help us improve services to veterans in transition. Your participation in this survey is very important. The value of our survey results will depend on how many

---

[1] If this letter is sent as an email invitation for an online survey, it also should specify the online link to the survey website.

veterans respond. The greater the response rate, the more confidence we can have that the results accurately portray the most important and most common needs of the population of recently discharged veterans.

Your responses to the survey questions are completely anonymous. We will not know whom the responses are coming from, and there is no way to connect you to your responses.

We expect that you will be able to complete the survey in about 10 minutes or less.

To thank you for your time, after you complete the survey you will have the opportunity to enter into a raffle to win a $25 gift card. After the survey has been completed and the report written we will send you an online link so that you can read the survey report.

Thank you in advance for participating. And thank you for your service.

Respectfully,

[your name and title]

[your contact information]

4.3   Recruiting Hard-to-Reach Populations

Recruiting survey participants from some populations is a lot more challenging than just sending a letter or email. Homeless people, for example, lack an address, and comprise one type of *hidden population*. Other hidden populations may try to conceal their group identity because they fear legal consequences or social stigma. Thus, if your survey is targeting the special needs of people who are homeless, newly arrived immigrants, migrant laborers, illegal drug users, LGBTQ people who still fear coming out, and so on, just reaching potential participants – not to mention obtaining a representative sample – can be quite a challenge.

It is often necessary to use *snowball sampling* with these populations. This method relies on finding some initial participants, asking them to help you find others whom they know, and then repeating that referral process with each of the people to whom you are referred and whom you find. As you might imagine, snowball sampling is highly vulnerable to a *selection bias* in which outsiders not connected to the social network are under-represented in the sample. The personal attributes and needs of outsiders who are not well connected with a social network might differ dramatically from those of the insiders.

One offshoot of snowball sampling that aims to reduce selection bias is called *respondent-driven sampling (RDS)*. It involves such procedures as paying for participation and for recruiting peers, capping the number of additional participants that each new participant can recruit, and using a mathematical formula involving weighting to compensate for the lack of randomness (Heckathorn, 1997). Various other approaches for improving snowball sampling are discussed by Kirchherr & Charles (2018).

Tactics for Reaching and Recruiting Millennials. Millennials (young adults born shortly before or shortly after the start of the twenty-first century) commonly don't check for any messages that aren't sent by texting. They also tend to be heavy users of social media. Guillory *et al.* (2018) report a study demonstrating novel strategies for recruiting LGBT millennials via Facebook and Instagram ads or intercept in social venues such as LGBT bars and nightclubs. They concluded that social media methods are faster and less costly than intercept methods but have more data-quality issues.

4.4   Survey Modalities

The two main alternative ways to administer a survey are (1) with a *self-administered questionnaire* or (2) by *interview*. If a self-administered questionnaire is used, the respondents can complete it at home, in a meeting, or perhaps while waiting to be seen at an agency. If they complete it at home, there are two main ways for them to receive the survey and complete it: (1) using a hard copy of a questionnaire (and cover letter) mailed to them; or (2) receiving the cover letter by email along with a link to a survey website where they can complete the questionnaire online.

4.5   Interviews

If the survey is being administered in an interview, the interview can be in person or by phone. Interview surveys with a target population can be more problematic than self-administered questionnaires for several reasons. First, they are much more time consuming, and harder to make anonymous. Without anonymity, survey respondents are less likely to respond in ways that they feel make them seem more emotionally unstable, more prejudiced, more needy, more negative, and so on. Research texts refer to this tendency as a *social desirability bias*. Telephone surveys are less time consuming and can be conducted anonymously, but we now live in an age of cell phones, caller ID, and computer-generated robocalls, which make it hard to get people to answer calls and agree to be interviewed. In my house, for example, we refuse to answer about a handful of calls each evening as our caller ID tells us the calls are coming from people or organizations we've never heard of. And when we succumb and answer, more often than not we are either listening to a computer or some sleazy sales gimmick. "No, we do not want to buy a warranty extension on our TV or a time share in Swamp Island! Stop calling us; I need to concentrate. My wife is beating me in Scrabble!"

You might recall that interviews were discussed in Chapter 3. But that was in the context of group interviews in focus groups, not by traveling for individual interviews at people's homes or by trying to get them to answer their telephone. Aside from focus groups, another purpose for which interviews can be both feasible and desirable is when you are interviewing agency staff members to monitor progress and problems in program implementation. Early in your career, in light of your limited experience in your agency, you are unlikely to be assigned the task of interviewing other practitioners regarding issues or problems in program implementation. But in case you eventually do have that task, let's briefly examine some important interviewing do's and don'ts. As we do, keep in mind that our focus is on *survey* interviewing, which, unlike qualitative research or focus group interviewing, means using a structured interview questionnaire.

Be Prepared. The interview should take place in a relaxed, comfortable setting. Before you commence any interviews you should thoroughly understand the questionnaire that guides the interview. This means understanding the overall purpose of the questionnaire and each question on it. You should know which questions are the most important and be sufficiently rehearsed that you can state the questions naturally, comfortably, and smoothly, without stumbling over words. Even if the questions are written out for you in an interview schedule, you should have practiced reading them aloud, so that respondents are not turned off by someone who is wasting their time by being ill-prepared or appearing unsure of the task. When you ask the questions, use the exact words that are in the questionnaire. Unlike qualitative interviewing, survey interview questionnaires are constructed and pretested in dry runs in an effort to ensure that respondents will interpret items precisely as intended. Even slight changes in the wording can convey an unintended meaning to the question or perhaps even introduce an unintended bias.

Professional Demeanor. Although you should be confident and well prepared regarding understanding the purpose and wording of the questions and your ability to ask them skillfully, you should not come across as a superior, all-knowing person. Instead, you should project a casual, pleasant, and curious professional demeanor, neither appearing too familiar and too personal nor seeming cold or insecure. Another part of professional demeanor concerns your attire. It should be consistent with your agency's norms for professional attire. Even if the interview is taking place on a casual Friday, do not dress in an excessively casual manner. Wearing torn jeans and a Freddy Krueger tee shirt probably would not be the ideal way to make a first impression.

Be Punctual. Arrive early. Being even a minute late conveys disrespect for the interviewee and the importance of the interview. A traffic jam is an unacceptable excuse. You would not risk a traffic delay if you were commuting to an interview for a job you craved; you would leave early. Your attitude should be the same when commuting to a survey interview.

Starting the Interview. Introduce yourself (unless the respondent is a colleague you already know) and thank the respondent for the interview. If you want to record the interview, ask permission. If permission is granted, after turning on the recorder thank the respondent aloud for permission to record. If permission is denied, don't argue; just casually mention that you'll take notes instead. Unlike mailed or online surveys, interviews are not anonymous. Therefore, instead of assuring anonymity, you should assure confidentiality. If the respondent says something that you'd like to quote in your report, ask for permission to use the quote in your report, and ask the respondent if they would like to be credited for the quote (Newcomer *et al.*, 2015).

Note Taking. When you cannot use a recorder and therefore need to write down responses by hand, your notes should record responses exactly as given. This is especially important with open-ended questions. Suppose you are evaluating the implementation of a latchkey recreation program led by retired senior citizen volunteers. One open-ended question on the interview schedule might pertain to what the volunteer does when a fight breaks out between two kids. One volunteer says, "I break it up; I get in the middle and calmly try to have the kids talk to me about what's going on. Then I try to help the two of them understand the other's feelings, shake hands and make peace with each other." Another says, "I break it up by grabbing whoever is about to throw the next punch and pulling them out of the game." If you record both responses as "breaks it up," you would miss an important difference in the responses.

Some of your notes might require more time to jot down than others. When you need to take extra time you might tell the respondent, "I want my notes to be complete regarding what you just said. Please excuse me for a moment while I make sure I record it accurately." Saying that is not only polite, it might make you feel more comfortable about taking the time and might make respondents proud that they have said something important.

Use Neutral Probes. Even when answering a closed-ended survey question, sometimes respondents will reply ambiguously or inappropriately. For example, a question might ask the volunteers in the recreational latchkey program whether they strongly agree, agree somewhat, disagree somewhat, or strongly disagree with an item that states "When engaging the children in a sport, volunteers should emphasize teaching the children how to win in that sport." Suppose a respondent answers "I wouldn't do that." Such an answer does not differentiate between *strongly disagree* and *disagree somewhat*. Moreover, the answer just mentions what the respondent would do, not whether they think the behavior is desirable. Maybe they wouldn't do that because they are not athletic or competitive themselves, while believing it is okay for others to do it. Therefore, the interviewer should probe by saying "Would you say you strongly disagree or disagree somewhat?" Of course, the question might have been better worded as "When *you* engage the children in a sport, do *you* emphasize teaching the children how to win in that sport?" But when you are conducting an interview, you have to use the exact wording. If different interviewers tried to improve the questions in different ways, the resulting data would be indecipherable.

Probes are needed more often with answers to open-ended questions. For example, an open-ended question regarding children fighting might be "What do you do when some of the children you are supervising start fighting?" The respondent might say "I won't stand for that!" You would need to probe for what that means behaviorally. Even if the respondent says "I break it up," you would need more behavioral specificity. As discussed in Chapter 3, there are different acceptable ways to probe neutrally. Sometimes remaining silent with a curious look on your face will suffice. Alternatively, you might ask "In what ways?" Or, "Can you say more about that?" Whichever choice you make, the key is to be completely neutral and non-directive. You should not, for example, respond "Would you discipline the kids?" Or, "Sounds like you'd be angry." If you are involved in constructing the interview questionnaire, you should provide interviewers with examples of one or two useful neutral probes next to the questions that you anticipate might require some probing. Remember to be tactful and non-threatening at all times. When probing about a vague response do **not** ask something like "What do you mean?" A question like that can make the respondent feel criticized for not communicating more clearly.

4.6   Interview Guides

Some evaluations give interviewers more flexibility than is the case with survey questionnaires that require the high degree of structure described earlier in this chapter. If so, interviewers can use an interview guide, which allows them to adapt the sequencing and wording of questions to each particular interview. An interview guide will attempt to ensure that the same topics and issues are covered in each interview, while giving the interviewers more latitude to communicate in a more conversational style and to feel freer in how to probe into unanticipated

responses. How much latitude will depend on factors such as interviewer experience and skill and the extent to which evaluators who design the guide feel they
can anticipate in advance the kinds of issues and topics that are likely to arise in
the interviews (Patton, 2015).

Technically speaking, interview guides are not a survey method. Surveys fall
under the rubric of quantitative evaluation, which implies using highly structured
questionnaires, whereas interview guides, being less structured, are deemed to
be part of qualitative evaluation. But if you design an evaluation, you probably
will care a lot more about how best to obtain the information you need than
about whether a research professor will say you are using the correct quantitative or qualitative label. If you feel that you cannot adequately anticipate in
advance all the specific questions you need to ask and likely avenues for probing,
and if you feel that your intended respondents will neither feel comfortable nor
respond well to a highly structured interview format, you probably will opt for
an interview guide approach even if you are calling your data-gathering method
a survey. Box 4.2 displays what an interview guide might look like for an interview of trainees regarding the pilot testing of the implementation of an in-service
training program on the areas of interviewing knowledge and skills that have
been discussed so far in this chapter.

**Box 4.2   An Interview Guide Illustration for an Implementation
Evaluation of a Piloted in-Service Training Program on
Interviewing**

1. Overall impression of the training
   a. Strengths?
   b. Weaknesses?
   c. Likes/dislikes?
   d. Suggested modifications?
2. In what areas of interviewing did the training do well or need to
   improve on?
   a. Starting the interview?
      i. Meeting/greeting/introductions?
      ii. Explaining purpose?
      iii. Confidentiality?
      iv. Recording/permission?
      v. Professional demeanor?
      vi. Making respondent feel comfortable?

> b. Note taking?
>   i.   How to take good notes?
>   ii. Respondent and interviewer comfort with note taking?
> c. Using neutral probes?
>   i.   With closed-ended questions?
>   ii. With open-ended questions?
> d. Interview guides?
>   i.   Using one?
>   ii. Constructing one?
> 3. Training room
>   a. Comfort?
>   b. Able to hear speaker and other trainees?
>   c. Suggested improvements?
> 4. Trainer characteristics and teaching style
>   a. Strengths?
>   b. Weaknesses?
>   c. Suggested improvements?

4.7   Client Satisfaction Surveys

If you have ever looked at Yelp ratings online before choosing a medical professional or a consumer goods product, you can understand the importance of consumer satisfaction ratings to both the consumer and the provider of goods or services. From the standpoint of the service provider, there are both idealistic and pragmatic reasons to conduct a client satisfaction survey. Idealistically, we want our clients to feel that we are helping them and interacting with them in a respectful, caring manner. After all, you are not preparing for a social work or human service career so you can get rich! And, if our clients are dissatisfied with our services, knowing why will help us improve them. From a pragmatic standpoint, if our clients do not feel positively about those things, they are apt to stop using our services and to dissuade others from using them. That would not be good for our budget, not to mention the kind of consumer feedback provided to accreditation site visitors.

When designing a client satisfaction survey, we should not limit the focus to satisfaction with the professional practitioner to whom a client's case has been assigned or to the kind of service they provide. We should also ask about how long they usually have to wait after arriving before the provider sees them, the comfort of the waiting room and its provision of things for them to read and toys or games to occupy their children, whether the receptionist is friendly, how long they get put on hold when they try to telephone, and so on.

Limitations. As discussed by Royse *et al.* (2016), there is a big problem with client satisfaction surveys. The problem is the tendency of most respondents to report a high level of satisfaction with the services that they received. This tendency was found consistently in numerous client satisfaction studies. Many reasons have been postulated in the literature for this phenomenon, including non-response bias in which less satisfied clients are less likely to respond to the survey; client gratitude for receiving any help at all; and the cognitive dissonance that would result from feeling dissatisfied after investing so much time, energy, and hope into the services. In light of this problem, Royse *et al.* offer various recommendations for conducting client satisfaction studies, including the following.

- Conduct the satisfaction survey on repeated occasions. Then, even if the results are positive each time, the times when it is less positive than others can indicate a drop in the level of client satisfaction.
- Use some open-ended questions for respondents to indicate the specific areas of service that respondents were less satisfied with than others. For example, you can ask two questions pertaining to what they liked best about the program and what they liked least. Or you can ask about any aspect of the program that they think needs to be improved.
- Use the survey methods discussed in this chapter for minimizing non-response bias.
- Triangulate your survey with a qualitative effort to obtain feedback on satisfaction and needed areas of improvement, such as focus groups and in-depth interviews.
- Use an established, already-tested, and highly regarded client satisfaction survey instrument with good reliability, such as the CSQ-8 questionnaire displayed in Box 4.3, instead of trying to develop one yourself. You can learn more about the scale and obtain permission to use it by entering CSQ-8 as your search term.

Box 4.3   Overview of the Client Satisfaction Questionnaire (CSQ-8)

After a brief introductory statement about the purpose of the CSQ-8 that encourages responses to all questions, the questionnaire[1] asks eight questions followed by a 4-point scale in which clients can circle a number to rate the following:

---

[1] The actual version of the scale can be seen on p. 198 of Royse *et al.* (2016).

1. The quality of service received?
2. Getting the service the client wanted?
3. Has the program met their needs?
4. Would they recommend the program?
5. Satisfaction with the amount of help received?
6. Did services help you deal more effectively with your problems?
7. How satisfied are you overall with the service?
8. Would you come back to our program?

4.8   Survey Questionnaire Construction

If you have already completed a research methods course, you probably learned about constructing a survey questionnaire. But in case you have not learned that or have forgotten much of what you learned, let's review some of the key points, as discussed by Rubin and Babbie (2017). Let's begin with some key guidelines for wording the items on a questionnaire. After that we'll examine guidelines regarding the formatting of questionnaires.

4.8.1   Guidelines for Item Wording

- **Make items clear.** Avoid ambiguous words or phrases. For example, instead of asking "How big is your family?," ask "How many people (including yourself) live in your household?" Likewise, instead of asking "How often do you drink?," ask "How many days during the last seven days did you consume enough alcohol to get high or drunk?"
- **Use mutually exclusive and exhaustive response categories.** For example, when asking about ethnicity, if your three response categories are White, Black, and Hispanic, the categories are not exhaustive because they do not include other categories of ethnicity. If virtually everyone being surveyed is of one of those three categories, then at least you should add an "other" category for the exceptions. Neither are the three categories mutually exclusive, because some Hispanic individuals consider themselves to be Black, and some consider themselves to be White. Another example of categories that are not mutually exclusive is when the upper or lower limit of the range for one response category overlaps with that of another, such as in the following flawed example regarding age in which a person who is exactly 20, 30, 40, or 50 would not know which box to check:

  20 or younger

  20 to 30

> 30 to 40
>
> 40 to 50
>
> 50 or older

- **Avoid double-barreled questions.** For example, instead of asking "Can you afford your monthly rent and utility bills?," ask a separate question about each cost. Instead of asking "Did your parents attend college?," ask separately about each parent. Instead of asking caregivers "Do you have a need for more social support and respite?," ask separate questions about respite and about support.

- **Ask questions that respondents are able to answer.** For example, don't ask people with moderate to severe dementia to remember how often they get lost wandering off; it is better to ask their caregiver.

- **Short items are best.** Questions that are long and complicated can confuse respondents, frustrate them, and make them less likely to respond carefully or at all.

- **Avoid biased items and words.** When the Affordable Care Act was proposed during President Obama's administration to make health care more affordable, some of its political opponents called it *Obamacare*. When public opinion polls asked whether people felt favorably or unfavorably about it, the results were more favorable when the question asked about the *Affordable Care Act* than when it asked about *Obamacare*. Apparently, the term *Obamacare* had a biasing influence on many respondents (Obernauer, 2013). Similarly, if a poll asked respondents whether they shared President Trump's view of Obamacare, the results might be heavily influenced not only by the term Obamacare, but also by how respondents felt about Donald Trump. Likewise, if you want to learn how community residents feel about a new opiate treatment facility in their community, you should not ask whether they agree with prominent clergy about it.

- **Questions should be culturally sensitive.** Asking culturally sensitive questions was discussed in Chapter 2. Being culturally sensitive requires more than a question of language translation, it also requires taking into account unique cultural values and social desirability issues. For example, caregivers from an Asian culture when asked about how burdened they feel taking care of a parent with dementia might indicate less expressed degree of felt burden or need for respite than most American caregivers would indicate.

- **Pretest the questionnaire.** No matter how confident you may be in the appropriateness of your items in conforming to the above guidelines, there are sure to be some people in your target population who don't understand or struggle with the wording of some items. Consequently, you should debug your questionnaire in dry runs with a handful of people like the ones you intend to survey, asking them to indicate if they have difficulty with the wording of any items as they complete the questionnaire. After each dry run you should revise the wording accordingly, and then repeat the process of dry runs and revisions until you have a version that needs no more revising.

4.8.2   Guidelines for Questionnaire Format

- Provide clear and prominent instructions.
- Keep the questionnaire spread out and uncluttered. If you try to shorten a questionnaire by squeezing too many items on the same page, your efforts are likely to backfire by making it more difficult for respondents to distinguish one question from another and to recognize exactly where to enter their responses. This, in turn, is apt to frustrate respondents and make them less likely to respond carefully or at all.
- Use adequately spaced boxes or circles for checkmarks. For example:
  - o   Have you ever been employed as a social worker after earning your MSW degree?
  - o   Yes, always or usually full-time
  - o   Yes, always or usually part-time
  - o   No, never

- Use contingency questions. For example:
  - o   Do you ever use texting to communicate with people?

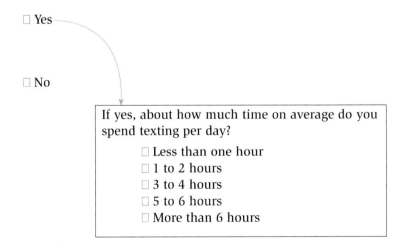

- Order questions logically. For example, if you ask several questions about physical health care needs and several questions about mental health care needs, ask the physical health questions consecutively and the mental health questions consecutively. Don't intermingle the physical with the mental.

4.9   Online Survey Questionnaire Preparation

If you conduct your survey online you can use an online service like Qualtrics[XM] or Survey Monkey[TM] to format your questionnaire and thus save you a lot of time regarding formatting with proper spacing, contingency questions, and so on. You can Google either of those two services if you want to use them. If you want to learn more about them, you can register for free and then monkey around to get a feel for how they work.

4.10   Chapter Main Points

- The best way to try to maximize the representativeness of a sample – and thus avoid sampling bias – is to use probability sampling methods which involve using random procedures for selecting the people who will comprise the sample. Random procedures are akin to blindly drawing names out of a bin or using random numbers to select people from a numbered list of names.
- Although probability sampling might be ideal, it is often not feasible in program evaluation surveys. When participation in your survey is influenced by other than a purely random process, you have a non-probability sample.
- One risky type of non-probability sample involves reliance on available subjects. The people who happen to be available can have markedly different characteristics, needs, or views than those who are not available.
- Snowball sampling, another type of non-probability sampling, is often used in surveys of homeless people and other hidden or hard-to-reach populations.
- Regardless of which sampling approach you use – and even if you try to include an entire population in your survey – your ultimate sample of participants will be a non-probability sample if a lot of people whom you invite to participate in your survey decline your invitation. This can create a non-response bias in which the respondents might be markedly different than the non-respondents regarding the focus of the survey.
- You can try to maximize response rates by preparing a strong motivational cover letter and by sending follow-up reminders.
- Another possible source of sampling error pertains to having a sample that is too small.
- The two main alternative ways to administer a survey are (1) with a self-administered questionnaire or (2) by interview.

- Survey interviews should be conducted in a relaxed, comfortable setting and by interviewers who thoroughly understand the questionnaire that guides the interview.
- The interviewer should be punctual, project a casual, pleasant, and curious professional demeanor – neither appearing too familiar and too personal nor seeming cold or insecure, should dress with attire that is consistent with their agency's norms for professional attire, and should use probes that are neutral when seeking more elaboration from the interviewee.
- Qualitative interviews are more flexible than survey interviews and can use an interview guide that allows the interviewer to adapt the sequencing and wording of questions to each particular interview. The interview guide will attempt to ensure that the same topics and issues are covered in each interview, while giving the interviewers more latitude to communicate in a more conversational style and to feel freer in how to probe into unanticipated responses.
- A major problem with client satisfaction surveys is the tendency of most respondents to report a high level of satisfaction with the services that they received.
- Guidelines for the wording of survey questionnaire items include making items clear, using mutually exclusive and exhaustive response categories, avoiding double-barreled questions, asking questions that respondents are able to answer, keeping items short, avoiding biased items and words, using questions that are culturally sensitive, and pretesting the questionnaire in dry runs to correct for wording bugs.
- Guidelines for formatting questionnaires include providing clear and prominent instructions, keeping the questionnaire spread out and uncluttered, using adequately spaced boxes or circles for checkmarks, using contingency questions, and ordering questions logically.
- When conducting an online survey you can use an online service like Qualtrics^{XM} or Survey Monkey^{TM} to expedite formatting your questionnaire.

4.11   Exercises

1. Go to the website of the state of Washington's Department of Social and Health Services at www.dshs.wa.gov/search/site/satisfaction%20survey. In the search bar at the top right of that site, enter "satisfaction survey" or "client satisfaction." Next, click on the link to the 2013 client survey. Summarize the ways in which the results of that survey reflect some of the key points mentioned in this chapter about client satisfaction surveys. Discuss your summary with your classmates and instructor.

2. What is wrong with the formatting and wording of each of the items on the following fictitious questionnaire to be administered to fourth- through sixth-grade clients in a Child Guidance Center?

   1. Do your parents drink? __ Yes __ No
   2. Are your parents nice? __ Yes __ No
   3. Do your parents work? __Yes __ No
   4. How many alcoholic beverages did your father drink last week? ___
   5. Do you cheat in school? __Yes __ No
   6. What do you want to do when you grow up?

   _____

3. Construct a client satisfaction questionnaire to be administered to your classmates asking about their demographic characteristics (age, sex, ethnicity), how satisfied they are with various aspects of your social work or human services curriculum, the strongest and weakest aspects of the curriculum, and needed improvements in it.

4. Go online and try to create your above questionnaire on Qualtrics[XM] or Survey Monkey[TM]. Jot down notes about the ways the site made the questionnaire construction easier and about any difficulties you encountered. Discuss your notes with your instructor and classmates.

5. Find online, read, and critically appraise the following evaluation study: Eady, A., Dobson, C., & Ross, L. E. (2011). Bisexual people's experiences with mental health services: A qualitative investigation. *Community Mental Health Journal*, 47(4), 378–389. Discuss your appraisal with your instructor and classmates.

4.12 Additional Reading

- Guillory, J., Wiant, K. F., Farrelly, M. *et al.* (2018). Recruiting hard-to-reach populations for survey research: Using Facebook and Instagram advertisements and in-person intercept in LGBT bars and nightclubs to recruit LGBT young adults. *Journal of Medical Internet Research*, 18(6), 20–26.
- Heckathorn, D. D. (1997). Respondent driven sampling. *Social Problems*, 44(2), 174–199.
- Rubin, A., & Babbie, E. R. (2017). *Research Methods for Social Work* (9th ed.). Boston, MA: Cengage Learning. Chapters 10 and 16 on constructing measurement instruments and on surveys.
- Thyer, B. A., & Pignotti, M. G. (2015). *Science and Pseudoscience in Social Work Practice*. New York, NY: Springer Publishing Co.

PART III

EVALUATING OUTCOME IN SERVICE-ORIENTED AGENCIES

With the chapters in this section, this book moves from formative and process evaluations to summative evaluations. As you may recall from Chapter 1, summative evaluations aim to assess the success of interventions, programs, or policies. In other words, they evaluate their outcomes. Chapter 5 will examine how to select and measure outcome objectives. In it you will see that determining what outcome indicators to measure and how to measure them can be complicated, but I hope the chapter will prepare you well for the challenge.

Chapter 6 will discuss the logic involved in inferring whether the outcomes that are measured were caused by the program (or policy or intervention) being evaluated. If you have taken a research methods course, you may recall that the ideal design for drawing conclusive inferences about treatment causality is a randomized clinical trial (RCT), in which participants are randomly assigned to different treatment conditions, with one group receiving the

treatment hypothesized to be effective and one or more other groups not receiving that treatment. Recognizing how difficult it is to have RCTs approved and implemented feasibly in service-oriented agencies, however, Chapter 6 will focus on the logic of more feasible, albeit less ideal, evaluation designs in those agencies. If you conduct an outcome evaluation in a service-oriented agency, you are likely to have to use one of those less ideal but more feasible designs, and I hope the discussion in Chapter 6 will help you feel better about their value.

Chapter 7 will build on Chapter 6 by delving into the various outcome designs that are more feasible than RCTs, how to choose the most appropriate design, and how to improve the plausibility of any tentative causal inferences that can be drawn from them. Part of Chapter 7 will show how a user-friendly statistical technique can help improve the value of even the most basic, inferentially limited outcome evaluations – those that merely measure client change from before participating in a program to after they have completed their participation. If you have any aversion to statistics, you might want to do some deep breathing stress reduction exercises when you get to that part, although I think that might not be necessary in light of how user-friendly I think it is.

Chapter 8 will be devoted to single-case designs, which are a type of outcome design that can be used not only if you are conducting an agency-wide outcome evaluation, but also if you want to evaluate the outcome of your services to a particular client or group of clients. The chapter will examine different types of single-case designs, their logic, and how plausible causal inferences can be drawn just by visually eyeballing a graph that plots client progress (or lack thereof) without having to analyze any statistics.

Chapter 9 will discuss the many practical and political pitfalls that you might encounter when trying to conduct an outcome evaluation. You'll see how being a successful evaluator of outcome requires more than expertise in the various outcome designs and their logic; it also requires understanding and being prepared for the many practical realities in service-oriented settings that can undermine even your best-laid plans. One particularly worrisome political pitfall involves the vested interests that different stakeholders might have in the results of an outcome evaluation. You will see how those vested interests represent a potential pitfall not only regarding how stakeholders might react to findings that they don't like, but also regarding how they can interfere with the implementation of your evaluation.

Chapter 5

Selecting and Measuring Outcome Objectives

WHAT YOU'LL LEARN IN THIS CHAPTER

In this chapter you will begin to learn how to design outcome evaluations, beginning with selecting and measuring outcome objectives. Four sources for identifying outcome objectives are the program's funding contract, its mission statement, its logic model, and its stakeholders. Using those sources as a starting point, you will learn how to specify outcome objectives in observable terms and how to do so using self-report outcome measures. You'll also learn about the principle of triangulation, which means using more than one measurement option when each option has some disadvantages.

5.1   Introduction

Assessing whether a program has a successful outcome requires being able to identify and select the most appropriate indicators of outcome that you will measure and then defining those indicators in measurable terms. The process of doing so, however, can be challenging. This chapter will prepare you for the challenge. To begin, you should examine whether any funding contracts specify any intended outcomes. Outcome objectives might also be specified in the program's mission statement. But you'll have to decide what a program's mission statement really means.

5.2   Mission and Vision Statements

A mission or vision statement briefly states why an organization exists, what its overall goal is, what service it provides, its primary intended consumers, and its geographical target region. For example, the website of the Jackson State University School of Social Work posts its mission statement as follows:

> The School of Social Work provides educational opportunities for a diverse group of students to earn degrees at the baccalaureate, master's, and doctoral levels. Students learn the knowledge, skills, values, and ethics of the profession of social work in a supportive academic environment. The School produces graduates who apply their knowledge and skills to improve the urban quality of life in Mississippi, the nation, and the world. Through their work, graduates empower vulnerable individuals, families, groups, organizations, and communities. Graduates are expected to demonstrate serious concern for economic, political, and social justice through practice, continuing education, and research.

Some mission and vision statements are worded in vague and perhaps grandiose terms that sound great and can perhaps enhance a program's image and its ability to secure funding, but offer the evaluator no clear path to ascertaining what specific outcome objectives to measure. If you are a student in a school of social work, for example, you might want to go to your school's website and search for its mission statement. Chances are it emphasizes preparing its students to achieve social justice. But what does that really mean? Is the school claiming that its graduates will be prepared to become charismatic leaders of social movements? Or is a more modest aim involved? Is the focus on economic aspects such as poverty and health insurance? Or is it on identity-based aspects associated with discrimination against women, ethnic minorities, and LGBTQ individuals? Or might it be all of the above, as in the case of the University of Houston's Graduate College of Social Work website's "vision to achieve social, racial, economic, and political justice, local to global." Likewise, consider a mission statement that aims to improve the mental health of a community. Does that imply alleviating the symptoms of people suffering from severe psychiatric disorders or helping people cope with the normal stresses of life?

Here is another example. A "Families First" program website mission statement at www.familiesfirstindiana.org/about states that its mission is "To create healthier communities by strengthening families and individuals during life challenges and changes." What outcome objectives does that imply? Are they connected to the Family First Prevention Services Act enacted into federal law on February 9, 2018 which spends child welfare funds with the aim of preserving families at risk of child neglect or abuse and of preventing foster care? Or do the objectives have a more ambitious connotation regarding the well-being of families in general?

5.3   Logic Models

Perhaps the first step you should take in trying to decipher what outcome objectives are implied by a program's mission statement is to find out if the program has a logic model. A logic model graphically depicts a program's components and shows the short- and long-term objectives that the components attempt to achieve. If the program being evaluated has submitted a funding grant application, you might be able to find the program's logic model in that application. There are different forms of logic models. Some are theory-based and might word outcome objectives in broad terms that do not specify measurable indicators. Others are outcomes-oriented, and they will provide you with more specific options regarding what outcome objectives you might want to select and measure. For example, an outcomes-oriented logic model for a Family First program might look like the skeletal one displayed in Table 5.1.

Table 5.1 *Skeletal possible template for an outcomes-oriented logic model for a Family First program*

Program resources	Core program components	Indicators of program implementation and participation	Evidence of change	
			Intermediate outcomes	Long-term outcomes
Inputs	Activities	Outputs		
Funds	Engage families	Extent of family participation in program activities	Improved positive parenting as observed during home visits	Decreased incidence of child neglect or abuse
Staff (number/ type)	Assess family needs and refer to community services and resources	Number of families using community services	Improved scores on self-report scale measuring knowledge and attitudes about parenting	
Staff training		Number of home visits made		Decreased incidence of foster home placements
Training	Home visits (three per week)	Increased involvement by fathers in parenting	Improvement in child behaviors and emotional well-being	
Materials	Parent education classes	Number of parents attending parent education classes	Family satisfaction with program services	

As discussed by Newcomer *et al.* (2015), logic models serve other functions in addition to helping to identify outcome objectives, such as

- helping stakeholders develop a common understanding of the program and its components, how the program works, and the expectations of program staff members and units;
- helping design or improve programs;
- Helping in reconsidering the program goals and activities in light of changing circumstances over time.

Also, a logic model might be required by a funding source as part of a grant application to secure funding for your program. If you would like to learn more about logic models and how to build them, you can examine the online resources listed in Box 5.1.

Box 5.1   Online Resources for Understanding, Using, and Building Logic Models

Alternative Logic Model Formats

YouTube presentation at www.youtube.com/watch?v=bZkwDSr__Us.

Building Logic Models

1. W. K. Kellogg Foundation Logic Model Development Guide at www .wkkf.org/resource-directory/resource/2006/02/wk-kellogg-foundation-logic-model-development-guide.
2. United Way Logic Model Training Manual at www.unitedwayofyc .org/sites/unitedwayofyc.org/files/UWYC%20Logic%20Model%20 Training%20Manual.pdf.
3. YouTube presentation on designing a logic model at www.youtube .com/watch?v=GtMv11bClMU.

5.4   Stakeholder Goals

Another early step you can take in trying to determine what outcome indicators to assess in your evaluation is to interview stakeholders regarding their views of the program's key goals. A problem is that different stakeholder groups can have competing views regarding the most important goals. In a faith-based Family First program, for example, ultra-religious board members might say that preserving families – and thus preventing foster care – is a more important goal than reducing the incidence of child maltreatment. That view might deem a program to be successful if out-of-home placements of children in foster care decrease even if the incidence of abuse or neglect increases. Other stakeholders – who prioritize child safety – might deem the program unsuccessful if the latter were to happen. Patton (2008) identified additional ways in which stakeholders in human service settings might clash over goals. In sex education programs, for example, should the aim be to promote safe-sex practices or to promote abstinence? In welfare reform programs, should an increase in parental employment indicate program success even if the family poverty rate does not change or if parental absence from home has a deleterious impact on children? Regarding homelessness, should the goal be increased usage of shelters versus improving the availability and use of low-income housing?

5.5   Triangulation

One way to handle the uncertainty regarding what objectives to choose is to select more than one. For example, if you measure *both* the incidence of child abuse and neglect as well as the incidence of foster care placements, you might find a desirable decrease in both, which would provide a much stronger and more conclusive depiction of program success than finding a decrease in only one of those alternative outcome indicators. For example, if you found a decrease in the incidence of foster care placements but did not assess the incidence of neglect or abuse it would be conceivable that perhaps your program staff – in their zeal to keep families together – too often opted to leave children in situations where the risk of maltreatment was too great. If you found a decrease in the incidence of child maltreatment but did not assess the incidence of foster care placements it would be conceivable that your program staff – in their zeal to protect children – were breaking up families when they did not need to, and thus were failing to meet the program objective of family preservation.

Another reason to triangulate the selection of outcome indicators is to cast a wide net to decrease the risk that you might miss some of the ways a program is being successful. For example, suppose a restorative justice program for incarcerated juveniles aims to prevent future criminal acts with a group-treatment intervention. The intervention might be successful in improving the youths' empathy for victims of crime or in improving their motivation to resist criminal behavior. Despite that success, however, when the youths are discharged they might return to communities where antisocial peer pressures and other pathogenic family or community influences outweigh the before-discharge effects of the treatment. If the only outcome indicator you measure involves the incidence of criminal acts after discharge, you would miss the ways that the program is succeeding. If you measure the pre-discharge outcome indicators, on the other hand, you might end up deeming the program to be successful in some important ways while noting that the undesirable incidence of criminal acts might have more to do with pathogenic community influences than with the effectiveness of the pre-discharge interventions.

A caveat is in order here. It is possible to cast a net of outcome indicators that is so wide that you can find a successful outcome on one indicator just due to chance. For example, if you pretested and posttested the youths on about ten or twenty self-reported attitudinal or personality measures – for example, attitudes about crime, empathy for victims, self-esteem, motivation to change, quality of relationship with parents, and so on – you might find that one of those indicators improved not because of the program, but just due to the fact that you looked at so many things that one was apt to show improvement due to mere luck, alone.

In order to understand this statistical phenomenon without getting into statistics, imagine that you are at a casino that has a roulette wheel with numbers ranging from 1 to 20. You think about what number to bet on. You think the winning number will be between 1 and 10, but you can't decide which of the first ten numbers to bet on. So, you bet on all ten – one per spin – picking them in order from 1 to 10. Suppose on the tenth spin the wheel stops on the number 10. You win, but is that because your roulette judgment is savvy or because you cast such a wide net that the chances were pretty good that you would get one successful outcome just due to the laws of probability? You should remember this roulette analogy if you ever "bet" on ten different outcome indicators in an evaluation and only one or two have a "successful" result.

5.6   How to Write Good Program Outcome Objectives

If the program that you are evaluating has not already specified its outcome objectives, perhaps in a logic model, or if they have stated their objectives in ambiguous terms, you might have to figure out how to specify the outcome objectives that your evaluation will assess on the basis of your examination of program materials and interviews with program stakeholders. As you do this, you should bear in mind the difference between *process objectives* and *outcome objectives*. Process objectives refer to the services, interventions, or other activities that a program will provide with the aim of achieving its outcome objectives. For example, an objective that says "We will train and supervise twenty family caregivers to provide six life-review sessions to their parent or spouse with early stage dementia" is a process objective. (Life-review sessions help older adults recall details of the various stages of their lives in an effort to help them feel better about and see meaning in their lives.) It can only be an outcome objective if the sole purpose of the grant proposal is to test the *feasibility* of finding twenty caregivers who will complete the training and provide the life-review sessions. And even then there would be the question of how well they learned how to provide life review and how appropriately they implemented it. If the objective were stated in terms of whether the recipient of the life-review sessions had an improvement in their depressive symptoms or satisfaction with their life, then it would be an outcome objective. But it would not be a well-stated outcome objective if it did not specify the *observable indicator(s)* of the improvement. To be more specific about the indicators of improvement, the objective might mention the particular measurement instrument(s) to be used to quantify degree of life satisfaction or depression.

The website of the United States Centers for Disease Control (www.cdc.gov/dhdsp/evaluation_resources/guides/writing-smart-objectives.htm) recommends a *SMART* mnemonic to help you remember the attributes of a well-stated objective. The *S* stands for being *specific* regarding who will achieve what. The *M* stands for stating the objective in *measurable* terms. The *A* stands for *achievability*. The objectives should be stated in terms that are realistic for the program to achieve in light of its resources. The *R* stands for the *relevance* of the desired outcome to the program processes or services. The *T* stands for *time-bound*, which requires stating when the objective will be achieved.

For example, a well-stated outcome objective of a Family First program that commences on January 1, 2020 might read as follows: "There will be a 20 percent decrease in the incidence of out-of-home foster care placements between the 2019 calendar year and the 2022 calendar year as indicated in the records of the Harris County Department of Child Protective Services." Note that the objective statement not only specifies what will be achieved and how it will be measured, but is also more realistic about achievability than aiming to achieve the 20 percent reduction by 2021, which would be after the program had been operating for only one year. By instead specifying 2022, the objective takes into account start-up difficulties that programs often encounter before those implementation glitches are identified and corrected in a formative or process evaluation.

5.7   Operationally Defining Objectives

If you learned about operational definitions in a research methods course, you might recognize the resemblance between the SMART mnemonic and an operational definition. That's because, to be operational, a definition must be stated in observable terms. It must specify the indicators that will be observed to determine if an objective is being achieved. Before being operationally defined, the aims of social work and human service programs are commonly expressed as abstract concepts that offer no clue about how change in them will be observed – concepts like marital satisfaction, quality of life, depression, self-esteem, and so on. For example, suppose a Family First program aims to improve positive parenting in an effort to avoid foster care placement among families referred for child maltreatment (see Table 5.1). A first step toward operationally defining how the outcome objective of improved positive parenting observed during home visits might include identifying the behavioral indicators of positive parenting, such as praising, encouraging, modeling, consistency of discipline, and so on. Likewise, you could identify undesirable parenting behaviors, such as hitting, threatening, bribing, angry outbursts, and so on. The next step would be to specify how you will observe the extent to which the parents who receive the Family First service are exhibiting the desirable and undesirable behaviors. The three main options for specifying how abstract objectives will be observed in the evaluation of social services are

- direct observation
- self-report
- examining available records

Let's now look at the advantages and disadvantages of each of the three options with respect to the positive-parenting outcome objective.

5.7.1 Direct Observation

The most direct way to observe something, obviously, is to look at it. Thus, if you want to know the extent to which parents are exhibiting desirable or undesirable parenting behaviors, one possible direct observation method is to watch them in the act of parenting. You could watch them in their homes or in a playroom at your agency and count the number of instances when they exhibit a positive-parenting behavior and the number of negative instances. Subtract the number of negative marks from the number of positives to give them a score. An advantage of direct observation is not having to rely on parents telling you the unbiased, accurate truth about how they behave with their kids. But the flip side of that advantage is that if they are aware that you are watching, they can try to impress you with what wonderful parents they are – doing only positive-parenting things your program taught them and being vigilant not to lose their cool or do any of the negative things that they might often do in their everyday lives when no child welfare professional is watching them. If you took a research methods course, you might recall that the term for this phenomenon is *social desirability bias*, which refers to people acting in a way other than how they typically behave so as to make a good impression on researchers. Another disadvantage is the cost of this observational approach, which would require an extreme amount of staff hours to conduct.

5.7.2 Self-Report

Imagine how much less time would be required if instead of directly observing the parents you asked them to complete a self-report scale in which they indicated how often – during a recent time period or on average – they exhibit each of the positive or undesirable behaviors on your list. For example, one item on the scale might read "How often do you raise your voice in anger when your kids misbehave? □ Often; □ Rarely; □ Never." Or, if you think that the use of subjective, imprecise terms like *often*, *rarely*, and *never* is too vulnerable to a social desirability bias, you might ask something like "How many times did you raise your voice in anger at your kids during the past week? □ Never; □ Once or twice; □ At least three times." Although the latter option has the advantage of specificity, it is limited to a relatively short recent time frame, and respondents may not remember accurately.

Despite the greater efficiency of the self-report approach, a disadvantage is that – like direct observation – it is also vulnerable to a social desirability bias. However, vulnerability to that bias is just as great, if not greater, when parents know you are actually watching them. What if you had all the parents who completed your program complete your scale *anonymously*? Having them anonymously self-report might decrease the vulnerability to a social desirability bias, but it does not eliminate it entirely. That's because people might not want to admit even to themselves that they have imperfections. Thus, someone who often erupts in anger at their child might honestly say that they rarely do so. They would be being honest despite being biased and misleading if they truly believed in what they were saying. Thus, a social desirability bias might influence some people to lie, but it also can influence them to truthfully report a desirable but inaccurate view that they have about themselves.

When considering the issue of anonymity and social desirability biases involved in using self-report instruments, it is important to bear in mind that some self-report instruments are designed to be administered orally by an interviewer. The presence of an interviewer negates the possibility of anonymity and increases the vulnerability to a social desirability bias. For example, a commonly used scale for measuring the extent of depression symptoms is the Hamilton Depression Rating Scale (also known as the HDRS or the Ham-D). It is administered in an interview format by a clinician with hospital inpatients, nursing home residents, or others for whom a written format could be too difficult to complete (Hamilton, 1960). Another is the Clinician-Administered PTSD Scale (CAPS) that is administered via interview to assess the severity of PTSD symptoms (Blake *et al.*, 1995).

5.7.3   Available Records

An even more expedient way to operationally define an outcome objective is according to indicators of the objective that can be seen in available records. A child's improvement in behavioral problems, for example, can be observed as a reduction in the number of disciplinary reports on the child in school records. But the available records option is not relevant to outcome objectives for which there are no available records. County government records, for example, might show whether a parent has an incident of documented child abuse or neglect, but they won't show how often a parent has praised, encouraged, or yelled at their child. So, if your Family First outcome objective is to improve positive parenting, and not to prevent future incidents of abuse or neglect, there may be no available records. However, if improving positive parenting appears in a logic model as a short- or intermediate-term objective, with preventing future incidents of abuse or neglect as the long-term objective, then available county records can be of use to your evaluation. But even then, you might want to use an anonymous self-report approach to operationally define and measure your shorter-term objective regarding positive-parenting behaviors. If you do so, it will be important for you to understand the criteria for selecting a good self-report measure as well as how to find the best outcome measures.

5.8 How to Find and Select the Best Self-Report Outcome Measures

There are four main ways to try to find an existing outcome measure that fits the objective you want to assess. One way is to find a reference volume that reports on various existing scales that might pertain to your objective. If you saved the textbook from your research methods course, chances are it will list various reference volumes. Rubin & Babbie (2017, p. 183), for example, lists twenty-eight such volumes with titles like *Outcome Measures for Child Welfare Services*, *Family Assessment*, *Outcomes Measurement in the Human Services*, *Behavioral Assessment of Childhood Disorders*, and so on.

Another way is to do an internet search using a search term that asks for outcome measures pertinent to the area of service being evaluated. For example, if you Google the search term *child welfare outcome measures*, you can find the following links:

- Child Welfare Outcomes/Children's Bureau/ACF
- Selecting outcome measures for child welfare settings …
- Outcome measures for Child Welfare Services: Theory and …

A third option is to use a search term about a specific target problem. For example, if you Google the search term *instruments to assess positive parenting*, you will see links such as the following:

- Assessing parenting and family functioning measures
- Measuring positive parenting using the RRFSS
- Assessing parenting behaviors to improve child outcomes

A fourth option would be to access the website of a national organization that focuses on your target problem and check to see if it lists outcome measures or reference volumes for finding outcome measures. For example, if you Google the search term *National Child Traumatic Stress Network*, you will find detailed reviews of seventy-two measures of trauma-related problems in children. Likewise, the website of the California Evidence-Based Clearinghouse for child welfare lists and describes twenty-three assessment measures related to child welfare. Box 5.2 illustrates how a reference volume might describe an existing scale.

> **Box 5.2   How a Reference Volume Might Describe an Existing Scale: A Fictitious Example**
>
> **Name of Scale**: Fictitious Positive Parenting Scale
>
> **Target Population**: Parents of Young Children (Newborns through Age 10)
>
> **Purpose**: To provide a score representing the extent to which knowledge, attitudes, and self-reported behaviors about parenting are desirable.
>
> **Description**: The development and validation of this scale were reported by Smith & Jones (2011). It can be completed in paper-and-pencil by parents, perhaps before and after training in positive parenting. The scale contains 25 statements to which parents can indicate their degree of agreement or disagreement on a 5-pont Likert scale (from Strongly Disagree to Strongly Agree), yielding a possible range of scores from 25 (least desirable) to 125 (most desirable). Alternate versions of the scale are available in English and Spanish. The Spanish version was translated from English to Spanish and then backtranslated to English by bilingual child psychologists for use with people living in or emigrating from Central America.
>
> **Psychometric Properties**: The reliability and known groups criterion validity of the English version of the scale was assessed with a sample of 50 parents who were on a waiting list to be trained in positive parenting after being investigated and found to have had at least one incident of child neglect or abuse and 50 comparison parents who were child development faculty members (Smith & Jones, 2011). The latter group of parents had a mean score of 100, which was significantly more desirable than the waitlist parents' mean score of 33. High internal consistency reliability was reported (alpha = 0.94). Smith and Jones are currently investigating the sensitivity of the English version and the psychometric properties of the Spanish version.
>
> Contact Information: Hieronymus Smith, Department of Child Development, Somewhere State University, 1600 Schmensylvania Ave., Somewhere, SM 99999. HQ.smith@Nomail.com

5.9   Criteria for Selecting a Self-Report Outcome Measure

If you have taken a research methods course, you might recall studying about some of the key attributes of a good measurement instrument, such as reliability and validity. An instrument that you select for an outcome evaluation should have those attributes. It also should be feasible for your study to use this instrument, and it should be sensitive both culturally and in terms of being able to detect small improvements over time in the targeted objective. Reference volumes that list various existing scales might tell you whether a scale in which you are interested has these desirable attributes. If the volume does not provide that information, or if the information is unclear or skimpy, you may need to search for the studies that assessed whether the scale has these attributes. Let's now look at each of the attributes that comprise the criteria for your selection and what you should be sure to find out about each.

5.9.1 Relevance

The scale should be clearly relevant to your target group's characteristics, problems, attention span, language, and reading level. For example, scales that measure severity of trauma symptoms would be more relevant than scales that measure level of depression if your aim is to evaluate the effectiveness of a treatment for PTSD. Likewise, if the treatment participants are young children who have been traumatized, a scale developed for use with traumatized children would be better than one for traumatized adults. If the traumatized children are recent immigrants from Central America, then you'll need a scale in Spanish.

5.9.2 Feasibility

You might need to obtain permission and perhaps pay for the use of some scales. You might also need to cover the costs of scoring some scales and training assistants to administer them properly. You'll need to see if your evaluation budget covers that. The scale you choose should not be too complicated for your evaluation participants. For example, short and simply worded scales probably will be preferable if your participants have cognitive impairments.

5.9.3 Reliability

The responses to the scale items should be consistent across the items or over time. As mentioned in Chapter 2, reliability pertains to whether people are responding in a consistent manner. For example, suppose some respondents report being extremely satisfied with their marriage on half of the items on a scale measuring marital satisfaction and dissatisfied on the remaining items. That would be inconsistent (unreliable) and would suggest that perhaps respondents are having difficulty with the complexity, layout, or wording of the scale. Being consistent across the items means that the scale has *internal consistency reliability*, which usually is depicted by a statistic called *coefficient alpha*. Alphas at or above 0.80 depict good reliability, and at least 0.90 is considered to be excellent. Lower than 0.80 alphas should make you wary about a scale's reliability, and much lower than 0.80 – say below 0.70 – should make you particularly skeptical. Most assessments of a scale's reliability will focus on its internal consistency reliability because it only requires having one administration of the scale to a sample of respondents and thus is a lot more feasible to look at than studying consistency over time, which requires administering the scale at least twice to the same sample of respondents to see if their scores on the first test correlate with their scores on the retest. That approach assesses the scale's *test–retest reliability*, also known as its *stability*. If the scale that seems to fit your objective has good internal consistency reliability, that should suffice even if its stability has not been tested. That is because stability is reported more rarely than is internal consistency reliability and because the scale's validity is a more important selection criterion.

5.9.4   Validity

The term *validity* refers to whether an instrument really measures what it intends to measure. A scale cannot be valid unless it is reliable, but it can be reliable without being valid. For example, suppose you want to measure improvement in positive parenting among parents referred for child abuse or neglect. If the measurement scale you select is highly vulnerable to a social desirability bias, even parents who have not improved at all from before to after receiving your intervention are likely to answer the scale items in ways that depict themselves as wonderful parents who consistently exhibit positive-parenting behaviors and rarely do the wrong thing. Their answers would be internally consistent in that they would score in the socially desirable direction across the scale items, but the scale would not be valid because, instead of measuring the extent to which the parents engage in positive parenting, it would merely be providing a false portrayal of the quality of their parenting. Consequently, parents who did not receive your intervention but are biased to convey a socially desirable impression might score about as well on the scale as the parents who did receive the intervention. Likewise, if the intervention is ineffective, the parents who received it might nonetheless want to portray themselves as having improved even if they did not.

   There are four main kinds of measurement validity, two of which should count as criteria for selecting a scale, and two that hardly matter. The two that do matter are known as *criterion validity* and *construct validity*. Both of these forms of validity are based on testing the scale out with people and seeing if their scores on it correlate well with other, independent indicators of the concept being measured. For example, parents who have never been referred for child maltreatment should have much better scores on the scale than parents who have been investigated and found to have maltreated their children. That would indicate a form of criterion validity known as *known groups validity*. Construct validity is more complicated than criterion validity and is much less frequently reported. When it is reported, its distinction from criterion validity is not always clear. But it can be a more sophisticated form of validity – one that incorporates criterion validity but goes beyond it. Consequently, if you find a scale that is reported to have *either* criterion or construct validity then that scale probably meets the validity criterion for use in your evaluation. But if the only validity information supplied pertains to the other two forms of validity, you should not be impressed – at least not *favorably* impressed. Those two forms of validity are called *face validity* and *content validity*. Both of those forms refer only to whether some supposed experts look at the scale and say it looks fine to them. Big deal! Experts – even if they really are experts – can make mistakes, and there have been instances in the history of psychometric scale construction when their verdict that a scale had face or content validity was not supported when the scale was actually tested out with real respondents.

5.9.5 Sensitivity

An occasionally overlooked but very important criterion for selecting an outcome measure is its ability to detect small improvements that participants might make from the time they begin receiving program services until they finish. A measure's ability to detect those subtle differences is called its *sensitivity*. If an instrument is not able to detect modest improvements – that despite being small are meaningful enough to show that your program is successful – then that instrument should not be selected no matter how impressive its validity might be. For example, some instruments have been found to have known groups validity because people who have never needed treatment for a problem score much better on it than do people experiencing severe difficulties with that problem. But that does not mean that the instrument will detect small, but meaningful, improvements among people who move from having severe difficulty to having moderate difficulty.

You might understandably wonder if there is an incongruity between expecting an instrument to be stable over time (that is, to have good test–retest reliability) while also expecting it to be sensitive to detecting subtle, modest improvements over time. Two reasons explain why those two expectations are not incongruent. The first reason is that the time lapse between the test and the retest should be quite brief, perhaps no longer than two weeks, allowing little time for sizeable changes to occur. The second involves understanding the concept of correlation. Suppose 100 people complete the test–retest assessment. Suppose 50 of them score very low on the first test and then improve slightly on the retest. Despite the slight improvement, their retest scores will still be relatively low. Suppose the other 50 people score much higher on the first test and then – despite a slight change in either direction – score relatively high on the retest. There would be a strong correlation between the first test scores and the retest scores because relatively low scores on the first test would be associated with relatively low scores on the retest, and relatively high scores on the first test would be associated with relatively high scores on the retest. This correlation is illustrated with the scores of eight respondents in Table 5.2 and Figure 5.1. In Table 5.2 notice how each person improved slightly on the scale, but that didn't change the fact that low scorers at Time 1 were low scorers at Time 2. Each person's scores need not be identical at Time 1 and Time 2 for there to be a strong correlation. The only requirement is that the relatively low scorers at Time 1 be the relatively low scorers at Time 2, and vice versa for the high scorers. To further illustrate this concept, Figure 5.1 displays a graphical depiction showing the correlation.

Table 5.2 *An illustration of strong test–retest reliability on a scale measuring self-esteem despite sensitivity to slight changes*

Name of respondent	First test score (Time 1)	Retest score (Time 2)
Ann	20	22
Dan	22	24
Jan	24	26
Han	25	27
Beau	50	51
Flo	51	52
Joe	52	53
Moe	53	54

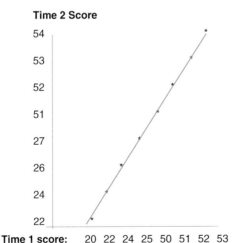

FIGURE 5.1 A graphical depiction of the correlation in Table 5.2.

Returning to the concept of sensitivity, imagine, for example, two instruments that measure level of depression. One asks yes/no questions like "Do you feel sad?" or "Do you feel hopeless?" The other instrument asks the same questions but, instead of limiting response options to yes/no, the response options are "All the time," "Most of the time," "Occasionally," "Rarely," or "Never." Someone who starts off severely depressed but ends up moderately depressed is likely to answer yes to both questions in the yes/no instrument after completing the program but might move from all to most of the time or from most to occasionally in the other, more sensitive, instrument.

Even if you find an instrument that is known to have excellent sensitivity, however, you need to consider whether its time frame matches your program's time frame. Many years ago a child guidance center contracted with me to analyze their data regarding whether their three-month summer intervention was successful in helping children who were diagnosed as having behavioral problems. For many years the center routinely administered a child behavioral checklist scale to all the parents of the children it served at intake and then again at the completion of treatment. The scale measured the degree of behavioral problems by asking parents to indicate how frequently the child exhibited each behavior *during the past six months*. As you might expect, a comparison of the scale scores upon entering the three-month program with the scores three months later did not support the program's effectiveness. If a child very often exhibited a negative behavior during the three months before the program commenced and then improved somewhat toward the end of the three-month summer program, the parent would nevertheless be likely to answer "very often" in regard to the six-month time frame. That scale was (and still is) highly regarded in the literature for its validity and sensitivity. But its sensitivity was in the context of a six-month time frame and thus did not fit the agency's three-month time frame. Consequently, it was a poor choice for evaluating the program's outcome despite its validity and *six-month* sensitivity.

The foregoing child guidance center summer program evaluation is just one example of how choosing a good operational definition can be difficult. Box 5.3 presents another daunting example.

Box 5.3   Should Child Welfare Practitioners be Required to Have a Social Work Degree? An Illustration of Problematic Operational Definitions

Many years ago the Texas branch of the National Association of Social Workers (NASW) contracted with me to conduct a review of the literature to look for evidence that job applicants with social work degrees should be preferred over job applicants with other degrees when hiring practitioners to provide services in public child welfare agencies. The NASW staff members were hoping that I could supply them with evidence that they could use in persuading state legislators to enact a provision that would call for requiring child welfare workers to have a social work degree.

My literature review found some studies that used retention and burnout rate as the operational definition for comparing the outcomes of the binary degree categories (social work versus non-social work). Other studies used supervisory ratings of practitioner performance as the operational definition. The studies with the retention/burnout-rate definition were conducted by social work faculty members. Some found that social workers had longer retention rates and, in turn, lower burnout rates, and therefore recommended that preference be given to social workers in hiring – if for no other reason than at least to save the state the costs associated with the process of hiring and training new workers. Others found that the social workers had worse retention and burnout rates. Guess what those social work researchers recommended? If you guessed the very same recommendation as in the other studies you are pretty savvy. Their argument was that the social workers were leaving the child welfare system because its bureaucratic rules and regulations and exorbitantly high caseloads were inconsistent with their superior preparation for and ideals about effective child welfare practice. In other words, the fact that they were unwilling to tolerate the conditions that prevented them from providing the higher quality of service that they had been prepared to and expected to provide, coupled with their higher ideals regarding the characteristics to be desired in child welfare agencies, was a reflection of their superior preparation. Conversely, they argued that the willingness of non-social workers to abide those conditions reflected that they had not been prepared as well and consequently were less likely to advocate for needed improvements in child welfare services.

The studies that used practitioner performance ratings as the operational definition found that the social workers tended to get worse performance ratings than the non-social workers. Guess how some social work faculty members (who did not conduct the studies) interpreted that finding? If you guessed that they interpreted it to mean that the social workers were better prepared and should be preferred in hiring then you are super savvy. They argued that because of their superior preparation the social workers were more likely to make waves in advocating for bureaucratic reforms – waves that rankled their bureaucratically oriented non-social worker supervisors, who gave higher performance ratings to less prepared, less idealistic workers who just abided by the rules and did not try to change the system.

My report to the NASW therefore was inconclusive. I suggested that the operational definitions used in the studies that I found were problematic and that if we really want good evidence about whether social workers should be preferred we would need to compare the outcomes of cases served by a sample of social workers with the outcomes of cases served by an equivalent sample of non-social workers. The next chapters of this book will examine pragmatic ways to design such outcome studies and their logic.

Before leaving this chapter, it is important to remember that many objectives can be operationally defined in more than one way. In fact, some definitions can be operational without making any sense. For example, I could propose an operational definition for ascertaining whether the readers of this book are intelligent. The very intelligent ones are wearing jeans while they read this book. The very unintelligent ones are wearing something else or nothing at all. What are you wearing? Kudos to you if it's jeans. Just kidding! The point is that whether you are wearing jeans is definitely observable and thus operational. But it would be a nonsensical way to define intelligence. A more serious example of alternative operational definitions would be to ask stakeholders how best to operationally define positive parenting. Some might recommend asking parents how regularly they pray with their children or take them to religious services. Others might recommend observing how many times they praise and encourage their children. Although each definition is operational, they are not necessarily equally appropriate for your evaluation.

5.10   Chapter Main Points

- Mission and vision statements are often worded in vague and perhaps grandiose terms that sound great and can perhaps enhance a program's image and its ability to secure funding, but offer the evaluator no clear path to ascertaining what specific outcome objectives to measure.
- A logic model graphically depicts a program's components and shows the short- and long-term objectives that the components attempt to achieve.
- Some logic models are theory-based and might word outcome objectives in broad terms that do not specify measurable indicators. Others are

outcomes-oriented and will provide more specific options regarding what outcome objectives to select and measure.

- Different stakeholder groups might have competing views regarding the most important goals of a program.
- One way to handle the uncertainty regarding what objectives to select is to triangulate, which means selecting more than one objective.
- Another reason to triangulate the selection of outcome indicators is to cast a wide net to decrease the risk that you might miss some of the ways a program is being successful. However, it is possible to cast a net of outcome indicators that is so wide that you can find a successful outcome on one indicator just due to chance.
- Process objectives refer to the services, interventions, or other activities that a program will provide with the aim of achieving its outcome objectives.
- A well-stated objective should be specific regarding who will achieve what, be stated in terms that are realistic for the program to achieve in light of its resources, be relevant to the program's processes or services, and state the time period for achieving the objective.
- Outcome objectives should be defined in operational terms; the operational definition must specify the indicators that will be observed to determine if an objective is being achieved.
- The three main options for specifying how abstract objectives will be observed in the evaluation of social services are direct observation, self-report, and examining available records. Each of these three options has advantages and disadvantages.
- To find an existing outcome measure that fits the objective you want to assess, you can examine a reference volume that reports on various existing scales, do an internet search using a search term that asks for outcome measures pertinent to the area of service being evaluated or about a specific target problem addressed by that service, or examine the website of a national organization that focuses on that target problem.
- A good outcome measurement instrument should be relevant to your participants, be feasible, be reliable, have empirical validity (criterion or construct), and be sensitive enough to detect small improvements that participants might make from the time they begin receiving program services until they finish.
- Just because a definition is operational is no guarantee that it is a *good* operational definition or the *best* operational definition. There might be alternative ways to operationally define an outcome objective, and sometimes choosing the most appropriate operational definition can be difficult.

5.11   Exercises

1. Examine the mission statement or vision statement of an agency or program with which you are familiar. Discuss whether that statement is too vague or grandiose and whether it offers a clear path to ascertaining what specific outcome objectives to measure.

2. Prepare a logic model for an agency or program with which you are familiar. If you need to get more information to help you prepare your logic model, you might want to examine the program's website and/or printed materials and speak with some of the program's staff members whom you know. You might also want to examine the online resources listed in Box 5.1. Share your logic model for discussion with your classmates and instructor.

3. A community-based program serving older adults living with dementia and their family caregivers submits a grant proposal to fund a new intervention that aims to alleviate caregiver burden. Complete the following tasks and discuss your answers with your instructor and classmates.

    a. Write a well-stated outcome objective for the proposal.
    b. Operationally define the objective.
    c. Identify at least one alternative way to operationally define the objective and explain why you prefer the definition in your answer to task b above.
    d. Would your operational definition involve direct observation, self-report, available records, or a combination of two or more of those three options?
    e. Explain the rationale for your choice in task d above.
    f. Using your school's online literature database (such as PsycINFO, PubMed, ProQuest, HAPI, etc.), go online to find and select a good self-report scale for measuring your outcome objective.
    g. Explain the rationale for your selection in task f above.

4. In response to a recent increase in the number of homeless people sleeping and hanging out in public places in your agency's neighborhood, your agency wants to submit a grant to fund a program to deal with the homelessness problem. As part of preparing the proposal, you convene an advisory committee of community residents. The committee includes representatives from the clergy, the chamber of commerce, parent–teacher associations (PTAs), homeowners' associations, other mental health and human service agencies, and law enforcement officials. Specify in observable terms at least two competing short-term process objectives and at least

two *competing* long-term outcome objectives that might be recommended by different committee members. Explain your reasoning and discuss your answers with your instructor and classmates.

5.12   Additional Reading

- Fischer, J., & Corcoran, K. (2013). *Measures for Clinical Practice and Research*. New York, NY: Oxford University Press.
- Magnabosco, J. L., & Manderscheid, R. W. (Eds.). (2011). *Outcomes Measurement in the Human Services: Cross-Cutting Issues and Methods in the Era of Health Reform* (2nd ed.). Washington, DC: NASW Press.
- Nunnally, J. C., & Bernstein, I. H. P. (1994). *Psychometric Theory*. New York, NY: McGraw-Hill.

Chapter 6

Inference and Logic in Pragmatic Outcome Evaluation: Don't Let the Perfect Become the Enemy of the Good

> **WHAT YOU'LL LEARN IN THIS CHAPTER**
>
> Outcome evaluations in service-oriented agencies typically cannot be designed in a way that provides the same degree of support for causal inferences about program effects as is found in experimental intervention outcome studies that are conducted in research settings. In this chapter, we'll review the criteria for inferring causality and see how a feasible outcome evaluation can have value even if it does not meet all of those criteria in an ideal fashion. In that connection, you'll learn how not letting the perfect become the enemy of the good bears on becoming a pragmatic evaluator and therefore a successful evaluator

6.1   Introduction

If you have taken a course on research methods you probably learned that the gold standard (ideal) design for outcome studies on the effectiveness of interventions involves randomly assigning clients to treatment versus control groups to control for threats to internal validity like history, passage of time, selectivity bias, and regression to the mean. It's good that you learned that because such designs are the best way to determine whether a tested intervention appears to be the *real* cause of any observed outcomes.

Being able to rule out alternative explanations for the results strengthens the value of these designs to practitioners engaged in the evidence-informed practice process of seeking to make practice decisions in light of the best available evidence. At some point in the future, you might be in a position to carry out such gold standard studies and thus be able to obtain sizeable grants for your rigorous research and ultimately have the reports of your studies published in prestigious professional journals. Maybe you'll become a tenured professor at a topnotch research university and become nationally renowned for your accomplishments. Not too shabby! If that is your dream, I wish you well.

But if you are like most of your classmates you are much more likely – especially early in your career – to become involved in outcome evaluations that do not seek to establish causal inferences but instead seek to merely show that a program's goals are being attained. Or, you might be working in an agency that is providing an intervention that has had a lot of research support regarding its effectiveness but where there is uncertainty regarding whether the agency practitioners are implementing the intervention as appropriately and effectively as the practitioners in the research studies were implementing it. In that case, the purpose of the agency's outcome evaluation probably would not be to test the effectiveness of the already-supported intervention, but rather to assess whether the agency's clients are achieving outcomes that are similar to the outcomes achieved in the research studies. An evaluation with that purpose would be worth doing because studies have shown that it is not safe to assume that interventions whose effectiveness has received strong research support will be similarly effective when they are implemented by practitioners in service-oriented agencies that cannot afford the same degree and quality of training and supervision in the intervention as is commonly provided to the practitioners in the randomized controlled trial (RCT) research studies (Embry & Biglan, 2008; Weisz et al., 2011).

The focus of this chapter, therefore, will be on the logic and rationale of some outcome evaluations that lack random assignment to experimental and control conditions but that are more feasible in service-oriented agencies. The chapter will discuss how some evaluations that are more limited regarding generating causal inferences can still be worth doing. We'll begin by examining inferential issues regarding causality in outcome evaluations in general and then look at alternative ways that more limited but more feasible outcome evaluations can be designed and conducted and how to strengthen the inferential value of those evaluations.

6.2   Causality Criteria Revisited

Basic research methods texts identify three criteria for making causal inferences, as follows:

1. Correlation
2. Time sequence
3. Ruling out alternative explanations

Let's examine how these criteria pertain to outcome evaluations.

6.2.1   Correlation

Correlation means that the things that a program seeks to improve should turn out better for those whom the program has served than for those not served by the program. Correlation can be assessed by answering either or both of the following two questions:

1. Do things improve for program recipients after they have participated in the program?
2. Are things better for program recipients than for a comparable group of non-recipients?

Suppose, for example, that the posttraumatic stress symptoms of combat veterans are less severe after receiving treatment for PTSD than they were before treatment. That would show a correlation between two variables: (1) whether PTSD treatment was received; and (2) the severity of PTSD symptoms. Likewise, suppose that some veterans with PTSD received treatment and others did not, and that those who completed the treatment had less severe symptoms than those with no treatment. That, too, would establish the correlation between those two variables.

6.2.2   Time Sequence

Time sequence means that, for the treatment to have caused the difference in level of severity, that level should have improved *after* treatment. If those receiving treatment had less severe symptoms to begin with, and had no improvement after treatment, it would not be logical to conclude that the treatment caused the symptoms to be less severe.

6.2.3   Ruling Out Alternative Explanations

However, even if the symptoms improved after treatment, something else may have happened during the course of treatment that was the real cause of the improvement. That possibility implies the need to *rule out alternative explanations*. For example, perhaps the emotional support of family or friends explains the improvement, or maybe it was simply the passage of time away from the trauma of combat that helped.

When considering the three criteria for causal inference in the context of outcome evaluations that most commonly occur in the practice of program evaluation, it helps to remember that, although all three of the criteria are required for making a conclusive causal inference, any *one* of them, alone, provides *some limited* evidence supporting the *plausibility* of causality.

For an explanation to be plausible, it should be more than just possible. It should be reasonable and not far-fetched. For example, if the PTSD treatment approach is based on some of the fundamental tenets of trauma theory, the treatment would be a more plausible cause of improvement than if the treatment involved snake oil or exorcism.

Therefore, an evaluation that finds a strong correlation between participation in a theoretically reasonable program and a desirable outcome has provided *some, albeit limited*, evidence supporting the notion that the program *might* be effective. Consider, for example, the strong correlation between heavy cigarette smoking and lung cancer. There is abundant biological research showing the impact of smoking on lung cancer (Surgeon General Report, 2014). However, suppose we lacked that biological evidence and knew only of the strong correlation. Without an experimental design that assigned some people to smoke heavily and others to abstain, would the notion that smoking can cause lung cancer be plausible? An affirmative answer to that question would be implied by the strength of the correlation coupled with the theoretical reasonableness of the idea that inhaling so much smoke might damage the lungs.

But would the mere *plausibility* of a causal link – without experimental evidence – warrant policy recommendations? If so, that might imply the need for various public service announcements about the dangers of smoking, higher cigarette taxes, required warnings on cigarette packages, banning ads by tobacco companies, and so on. Suppose some sticklers demeaning evidence based mainly on correlation and not experimental design convinced the public (and legislators) not to take action to reduce smoking because the nature of the evidence was only correlational. A lot more people might die from lung cancer.

So, where does the burden of proof lie when we have strong correlational evidence about a relationship that it would not be unreasonable to suppose might be causal? With those who want to take action to help people on the basis of strong correlational findings and plausible (albeit tentative) causal inferences? Or with those who reject taking such action without experimental findings? If those who want to take action are wrong regarding smoking, what harm is done? Some public service announcements, taxes, and package warnings would be a waste of time and money. And tobacco company profits might decline as cigarette sales drop. If those who reject taking action are wrong, a lot more people get sick and/or die. Unless you think money is more important than public health and death, you'd probably agree that taking the actions to reduce smoking was justified. Likewise, you might argue that, when trying to alleviate serious health or social problems, if an outcome evaluation without a control group finds that recipients of a program fare much better than non-recipients – and there is no evidence that the program causes pain, is harmful, or is financially burdensome to recipients – the prudent implication is to further support the program until and unless future, stronger, evidence emerges with contrary implications. Taking that position, you would not be arguing against conducting better controlled outcome studies. Instead, you might encourage such studies so that, if the actions generated by the correlational studies were misguided and not really helping people, we can find that out and take corrective actions. But until those better controlled studies are completed, and until better evidence comes along, it would be reasonable to support the actions that were taken on the basis of the best evidence we had at the time.

6.3   Implications of Evidence-Informed Practice and Critical Thinking

The foregoing logic is consistent with engaging in evidence-informed practice. Making decisions in light of the best *available* evidence is a core tenet of evidence-informed practice. That does not mean that you should disregard the limitations of the evidence or close your mind to the possibility that better evidence might emerge in the future that might imply that the path you have chosen has been mistaken. In fact, evidence-informed practice encourages being vigilant

---

Box 6.1   What to Do When Using Your Critical Thinking Skills

1. Think for yourself instead of automatically accepting and following blindly traditions or what respected authorities or prestigious publications say.
2. Maintain a stance of healthy skepticism, of questioning whether beliefs or assertions of knowledge are supported by sound and persuasive logic and evidence.
3. Be vigilant to examine whether assertions of fact are based on unstated assumptions and unverified assertions.
4. Be open-minded and willing to consider new ideas and new evidence, even if they contradict currently accepted "knowledge" or long-standing traditions. However, while your mind should be open, it should not be *so* open that your brains fall out. Remember points 2 and 3 above!
5. Be willing to test whether your own cherished beliefs and practices are supported by evidence and be willing to alter them if compelling new evidence implies doing so.
6. Seek the best available evidence to inform the decisions you make.

---

about the limitations of the current evidence and being on the lookout to learn about emerging better evidence.

Thus, evidence-informed practice implies using your *critical thinking* skills. Critical thinkers will not automatically accept the arguments and conclusions they hear from experts and authorities. Instead, they will have a questioning attitude. They will vigilantly seek to recognize unstated assumptions and will use reasoning and logic to think for themselves, distinguish fact from belief, and question whether claims are based on sound evidence. Using critical thinking skills involves doing the things listed in Box 6.1.

6.4   A Caveat

An important caveat is in order here. Recognizing the potential utility of pragmatic, but inferentially limited, outcome evaluations does not imply that anything goes. As a critical thinker, you'll need to skeptically appraise the limitations of the evaluations to determine whether they are so egregious that the evaluation's findings lack credibility and should not influence your practice decisions.

For example, in the history of program evaluation there have been methodologically biased studies that have purported to support the effectiveness of worthless and sometimes harmful interventions. These evaluations have been depicted as *pseudoscience*. *Pseudo* means *fake*, and therefore *pseudo*science means *fake* science. Some pseudoscientific evaluations might use non-experimental designs. Others might use experimental ones that suffer from measurement biases. What makes them *pseudo* is that the claims and implications made by their authors go way beyond what is warranted by their methodologies – especially fatal methodological flaws such as egregiously biased measurement.

Randomized experiments are not immune to fatally flawed measurement. For example, Shapiro (1989) – in the first randomized experimental outcome evaluation of eye movement desensitization and reprocessing (EMDR), a treatment for trauma symptoms that Shapiro created – measured outcome in a way that was very vulnerable to a social desirability bias. She had the recipients of the therapy she had invented and provided tell her if they experienced less stress when recalling the traumatic event after treatment than they did before treatment. You can imagine how difficult it would have been for recipients who were not helped by the treatment to look Shapiro in the eye and tell her that her treatment did not help. That measurement flaw, however, did not prevent some from depicting EMDR as a sort of miracle cure or from marketing books and workshops on it to mental health professionals. During the ensuing decades better studies emerged supporting the effectiveness of EMDR (but not as a miracle cure). But the extravagant claims made about the wonders of EMDR predated those studies and thus were deemed pseudoscientific not because the original evaluation had a serious flaw, but because the exorbitant claims disregarded that flaw and thus went far beyond the more appropriate, more cautious implications of Shapiro's seminal study.

So, if you conduct an outcome evaluation with some important methodological limitations, your evaluation would not warrant the pseudoscientific label unless you disregard those limitations and develop implications that go far beyond what is warranted. For example, you should draw adequate attention to those limitations in your report and explain why your conclusions and recommendations are therefore tentative. Those who utilize your report can then make decisions in light of your report's findings *and* its caveats. Box 6.2 provides an example of an evaluation that has been depicted as pseudoscientific.

Box 6.2   An Outcome Evaluation That Has Been Depicted as Pseudoscientific

Thought field therapy (TFT) uses "mechanical stimulation of points on the body's energy meridians, plus bilateral optical cortical stimulation" to try to alleviate trauma symptoms (Johnson *et al.*, 2001, p. 1239.) Johnson and his

> **Box 6.2   (Cont.)**
>
> colleagues evaluated the effectiveness of TFT by providing it to Albanian victims of torture inflicted by invading Serbian forces in 1999. The report concluded that TFT was extremely effective despite the fact that the evaluation lacked a pretest and despite the fact that the only outcome measure was extremely vulnerable to a social desirability bias in which the Albanian recipients of the TFT told foreigners who had come to help them that the TFT helped them. In addition to the severely biased measurement procedure and other design flaws, the pseudoscientific depiction was based on the report's extreme claims and the lack of plausibility as to why physical stimulation of "energy meridians" would alleviate trauma symptoms. (By the way, articles that severely criticized the TFT study appeared in the same issue of the same journal that published that study.) Adding to the basis for deeming TFT to be pseudoscience, its proponents have been known to expel from the TFT organization members who express doubt about its effects or the quality of the research that has supported it (Thyer and Pignotti, 2015).

6.5   A Successful Evaluator Is a Pragmatic Evaluator

> The perfect is the enemy of the good.

The above-quoted aphorism has been attributed to Voltaire, an eighteenth-century French philosopher. Although it can be interpreted in various ways, one way to think about it is to view people who refuse to do anything that involves some unavoidable imperfections as folks who would rather enjoy the emotional gratification of their own purity than make necessary compromises to get good things done. In the context of outcome evaluations, it can mean that if we insist on conducting ideally designed evaluations, only, we can fail to take advantage of opportunities to conduct imperfect evaluations that have some value and are worth doing despite their flaws. If you are perfectionistic in your approach to outcome evaluation, you'd better have other things to do, because program realities in service-oriented agencies tend to preclude ideally designed evaluations. Therefore, program stakeholders are apt to shun evaluators who insist on ideal designs. For example, consider the scenario depicted in Box 6.3, in which a new agency emerged seeking to provide referral and case management services to US combat veterans who were transitioning to civilian life after deployment in Iraq and Afghanistan. Its director came to my office to brainstorm possible ways to evaluate the agency's impact. Like the agency in Box 6.3, many agencies that focus on linking people with the resources or services that they need might want their outcome evaluation to be limited in scope to simply counting the proportion of the agency's clients that obtain the resources or treatment that matched their assessed needs. Box 6.3 considers how the managers of such agencies might react to an evaluator proposing a randomized experimental design for their outcome evaluation.

Box 6.3   Designing an Outcome Evaluation for a New Referral Service for Recently Discharged Military Veterans

In 2015, at a time when many US military veterans were coming home from deployments in Iraq and Afghanistan, a new program sprang up in Houston, Texas with the goal of helping recently discharged military veterans transition smoothly to civilian life by referring them to the proper resource or service providers to meet the various needs that they might have. For example, some were unemployed and thus needed assistance with finances, housing, employment, or perhaps college education. Some needed medical help. Some had lingering alcohol or drug-use problems. Some suffered from PTSD or depression and thus needed mental health treatment. Some were having difficulty reconnecting with their family and thus in need of family counseling or therapy. Others simply felt lonely, isolated, or lacking a sense of purpose in their life. While the program was still in its start-up phase its director sought my advice regarding possible outcome evaluation ideas.

He mentioned that he merely hoped to show that, several months after receiving the program's referral services, the needs of the veterans that were unmet upon discharge are now being met. I mentioned that I was in the process of developing a self-report scale that his clients could complete upon intake in their program (the pretest) and then again at a later date (the posttest). Scale scores would represent the extent to which the veterans felt that their needs were being met in various economic, health, and psychosocial areas. A meaningful degree of improvement in scale scores from pretest to posttest would provide evidence supporting the value of the program. (See Weiss *et al.*, 2019, if you want to see or learn more about that scale.) I knew better than to recommend using an experimental design. In fact, I don't know if he ever followed through with any outcome evaluation. Perhaps the prospect of having to track down the veterans for a posttest was itself too daunting.

Suppose, however, that he took my advice, completed the evaluation as recommended and found that the veterans' needs were being met at posttest. Would those needs have been met without the referral

Box 6.3   (Cont.)

service? Perhaps. Maybe other supports in the community made the difference. Or, maybe it just takes a little time for the veterans to figure out how to get what they need. But the impetus for the evaluation was not to demonstrate that the agency's services were the *only* plausible cause of the improvement. Therefore, it did not require a control group to satisfy potential funding sources or other stakeholders and thus have some value. An evaluation with a control group would have had more inferential value regarding the *causal* impact of the program, but it was not necessary to meet the agency's needs. Moreover, delaying service to some veterans in order to form a control group most likely would be unacceptable to the agency's administrators and service provision staff members. Not to mention the difficulty of finding an agency that could serve as a comparison group in a quasi-experimental design – such as an agency serving newly discharged veterans without trying to help them to get the assistance they urgently needed. Indeed, any evaluator who suggested that the start-up agency use a randomized experimental design with a waitlist control group might strike the agency's stakeholders as being out of touch, unfeeling, or incompetent. That evaluator might never hear from that agency again, unless they were an in-house evaluator, in which case their reputation (and perhaps job security) in the agency might be damaged.

Program administrators are unlikely to approve of a randomized experimental evaluation design unless it is required as part of a grant to fund a new program. Proposing such a design without such a grant would not be the best way to impress an administrator. However, I do not want to understate the importance and value of randomized experimental designs, which in clinical outcome evaluations are called randomized controlled trials (RCTs). They are the best way to establish causality, and the risks associated with using less rigorous but more feasible designs are important. So, whenever it is feasible for you to conduct a randomized experiment, I encourage you to do it. This chapter has merely sought to show the rationale for using alternatives to that kind of design in light of pragmatic, feasibility obstacles. Now that you have seen the logical and practical rationale for designing and conducting outcome evaluations that lack randomized experimental designs when RCTs are not feasible – as well as the need to be careful with how you interpret and make recommendations based on the more limited evaluations – the next chapter will examine some pragmatic alternative outcome design options, their strengths and limitations, and how they can be improved.

6.6   Degree of Certainty Needed

Patton (2008) discussed the theme of this chapter in terms of the degree of certainty that the primary intended users of an evaluation need in order for them to use the findings and recommendations of the evaluation. For example, Patton cited a study (Kristof, 2007) that found that 82 percent of children in the Congo have hookworms, which makes most of them anemic, causes diarrhea, and in turn affects their school attendance. Guided by the theoretical plausibility of the notion that deworming children will increase school attendance, Patton (2008, p. 493) asks "Does one need a randomized controlled experiment to establish the linkage between deworming and school attendance and the cost–benefit of spending 50 cents per child per year?" Patton suggests that the answer is "no," especially if students, parents, teachers, and health professionals all view hookworm symptoms as a major cause of the poor school attendance. Suppose that an evaluation with no control group finds that after children receive worm medicine there is a meaningful increase in school attendance. That level of evidence would be sufficient to influence decision-makers to implement a deworming program – especially if the parents report that taking the worm medicine and being relieved of the symptoms (such as diarrhea) is the reason for the increase in attendance. Thus, the decision-makers in this example would not need an RCT level of certainty as a basis for taking appropriate action. Theoretical plausibility, a strong correlation, and the low cost of deworming – along with the risks arising from inaction outweighing the risks of deworming (assuming the deworming medicine is safe) – provide a sufficient basis for implementing the deworming program.

6.7   Chapter Main Points

- The gold standard (ideal) design for outcome evaluations of the effectiveness of interventions involves randomly assigning clients to treatment versus control groups. Such evaluations are called randomized controlled trials (RCTs). But those designs are not often feasible when evaluating programs in service-oriented agencies.
- Three criteria for inferring causality are correlation, time sequence, and ruling out alternative explanations such as history, passage of time, selectivity bias, and regression to the mean.
- Although all three of the criteria are required for making a conclusive causal inference, any *one* of them, alone, provides *some*, albeit limited, evidence supporting the *plausibility* of causality.
- Assuming that the notion of a causal link seems theoretically reasonable, if an outcome evaluation without a control group finds that recipients of a program fare better than non-recipients – and there is no evidence that the program

causes pain, is harmful, or is financially burdensome to recipients – the prudent implication is to further support the program while continuing to be on the lookout in case future, stronger, evidence emerges with contrary implications.

- Evidence-informed practice implies using your critical thinking skills, which involves being open to new ideas but not so open that you forget to appraise them skeptically.

- In the history of program evaluation there have been methodologically biased studies that have purported to support the effectiveness of worthless and sometimes harmful interventions. These evaluations have been depicted as *pseudoscience.*

- If you conduct an outcome evaluation with some important methodological limitations, your evaluation would warrant the pseudoscientific label if you disregard those limitations and develop implications that go far beyond what is warranted. You should be sure to draw adequate attention to those limitations in your report and explain why your conclusions and recommendations are therefore tentative.

- The phrase "the perfect is the enemy of the good" in this context means that if we are faced with situations in which the ideal outcome evaluation design is not feasible and yet insist on conducting only an ideally designed evaluation, we can fail to take advantage of opportunities to conduct imperfect evaluations that have some value and are worth doing.

- As long as we remain mindful of the limitations of an imperfect outcome evaluation design, the mere *plausibility* that a new program caused a desired and important change can be grounds for continuing to fund and provide the program, especially when the humanitarian implications of being wrong in discontinuing the program are much worse than the implications of being wrong in continuing the program. The idea here – consistent with the concept of evidence-informed practice – is that you make decisions based on the best available evidence you have at the time and remain prepared to change those decisions if and when better evidence comes along.

- Whether an outcome evaluation requires an experiment that controls for the various threats to internal validity (such as history, passage of time, etc.) depends on the degree of certainty that the primary intended users of an evaluation need in order for the findings and recommendations of the evaluation to be of use for them.

6.8   Exercises

1.   Meet with an administrator of a service-oriented agency and see how they react to the idea of conducting a randomized experimental control group

outcome evaluation of a program or intervention that their program provides. Summarize in writing a description of their reaction and discuss it with your peers and instructor.

2. Ask the same administrator as in exercise 1 above what alternative design they would prefer for an outcome evaluation. Summarize their answer and why they would prefer it. Ask why they think that their alternative would have value, and in what way. Discuss your notes with your peers and instructor.

3. Shortly after George W. Bush was elected president of the United States in 2000, the national news media were abuzz about his interest in funding faith-based social services. The director of a bible studies program that operated in various prisons soon appeared on several cable news programs and extolled the effectiveness of his faith-based program, reporting that only 14 percent of the prisoners who participated in it got re-arrested after release from prison, as compared to a re-arrest rate of 41 percent among the non-participants. None of the news moderators asked him tough questions about the research design that produced those rates.

    a. If you were the moderator, what questions would you have asked regarding his design's ability to imply causal inferences about the effectiveness of bible studies in preventing future crimes by prisoners?

    b. Explain why, from an internal validity standpoint, you might be suspicious about the effectiveness of his program in preventing re-arrest, despite the impressive figures he cited.

    c. Discuss how this example illustrates the importance of a selectivity bias.

    d. Discuss the issue of plausibility regarding this example. Do you think that perhaps the news moderators refrained from asking tough questions because they believed in the plausibility of the notion that studying the bible would prevent prisoners from committing future crimes? What do you think about that notion?

6.9   Additional Reading

*   Johnson, B. R. (2004). Religious programs and recidivism among former inmates in prison fellowship programs: A long-term follow-up study. *Justice Quarterly* 21(2), 329–354.

*   Rubin, A., & Babbie, E. R. (2017). *Research Methods for Social Work* (9th ed.). Boston, MA: Cengage Learning. Especially the chapters on evidence-based practice, causal inference and experimental and quasi-experimental designs, and program evaluation.

*   Thyer, B. A., & Pignotti, M. G. (2015). *Science and Pseudoscience in Social Work Practice*. New York, NY: Springer Publishing Co.

Chapter 7

Feasible Outcome Evaluation Designs

WHAT YOU'LL LEARN IN THIS CHAPTER

You'll learn about various outcome evaluation designs that are valuable despite not having the same degree of control as randomized clinical trials (RCTs) have for ruling out alternative explanations regarding causality. You'll learn how to strengthen the ability of these designs to reduce the plausibility of those alternative explanations. You'll learn how to choose the most appropriate design. You'll even learn a new, user-friendly statistical procedure that can add value to the most limited of these designs.

7.1   Introduction

Now that you have seen the logic of some designs that are more feasible than randomized clinical trials (RCTs), this chapter will examine how to choose the most appropriate design and how to improve the plausibility of any tentative causal inferences that can be drawn from them. You'll see how calculating a user-friendly statistic – the within-group effect size – can help improve the value of a basic one-group pretest–posttest design. The chapter then will move on to designs that offer more control for alternative explanations and thus more support for inferring causality. The chapter will conclude by discussing how to select the most appropriate design.

7.2   Descriptive Outcome Evaluations

Many human service agencies that conduct an outcome evaluation do so only because it was a funding requirement. For example, an agency that serves non-institutionalized older adults experiencing early stage dementia and their caregivers might receive funding for a new initiative in a rural area to provide outreach efforts to places of worship seeking to find people who need, but are not using, the kind of services it provides and engage them in the services they need.

The grant proposal might have estimated the number of people in the agency's geographical area of concern whose needs are being unmet, and then set increasing the number of such folks who utilize the relevant services as the goal of the initiative. The evaluation would simply show whether the promised number was reached (or at least nearly reached), show where the new cases were coming from, and perhaps identify some areas where outreach efforts need to be improved. As the evaluator, your task would probably be limited to devising a way to assess the number of previously unserved cases newly utilizing services and whether the new cases were more likely or less likely to have certain characteristics or come from some geographical areas or places of worship. You would not be able to claim that the new outreach effort *caused* the promised number to be reached, and therefore the evaluation might not be as exciting as an evaluation demonstrating the effectiveness of a new treatment for dementia, but the funding source would likely be satisfied knowing the promised goal was reached and thus be inclined to continue the funding. Therefore, your evaluation would help the agency in its efforts to serve more needy people, and your value to the agency would be enhanced.

7.3   One-Group Pretest–Posttest Designs

If you took a research methods course you probably learned about the *one-group pretest–posttest design*, which has the following notation:

$$O_1 \ X \ O_2$$

O_1 is the pretest administered before the onset of the program or intervention, X represents the program or intervention, and O_2 is the posttest that is administered after the conclusion of the program or intervention. Program success is indicated by improvement in scores from pretest to posttest: the more improvement, the better the outcome.

Research methods texts (like one that I co-wrote) describe this as "a pre-experimental design with low internal validity" (Rubin & Babbie, 2016, p. 236) that does not permit us to infer that the program or intervention *caused* any change from pretest to posttest. Thus, those texts tend to look down somewhat on this design. However, as implied earlier in this chapter, this design deserves a bit more respect in the field of program evaluation. It deserves more respect for four reasons, as follows.

1. Often it is the best design that is feasible in real-world agency practice settings because it does not burden the program with demands for a control group.
2. Evaluations in those settings typically do not aim to develop conclusive causal inferences, but instead simply need to show stakeholders (including funding sources) that progress has occurred.
3. If the degree of improvement is impressive and clinically (substantively) meaningful, then not only will stakeholders be especially impressed, but also the tentative notion that the program or intervention may have caused the improvement becomes more plausible.
4. The difference between the pretest and posttest can be expressed as an **effect size** statistic that can be compared with meta-analytic benchmarks.

7.4 Effect Sizes

The fourth reason needs some explanation, especially if you have not studied effect sizes before. Effect size statistics depict the strength of a relationship (such as between the treatment variable and the outcome variable), and they can be compared across evaluations that use different ways to measure outcome.

7.4.1 Between-Group Effect Sizes

One of the most commonly used effect size statistics divides the difference between two means by the standard deviation. In evaluations with a treatment group and a control group, the *between*-group effect size is called Cohen's *d*, which equals the difference between the treatment group mean outcome score and the control group mean outcome score divided by the pooled standard deviation of the outcome scores across both groups. Box 7.1 illustrates the meaning and calculation of the standard deviation statistic and the *pooled* standard deviation.

Box 7.1 The Meaning and Calculation of the Standard Deviation and Pooled Standard Deviation

The standard deviation statistic portrays how close (or far) on average the scores in a set of data are to the mean of that set of data. For example, if you enter the ten scores $1 + 1 + 1 + 1 + 1 + 10 + 10 + 10 + 10 + 10 = 55$ with a mean of 5.5 ($55/10 = 5.5$) in an online standard deviation calculator, you'll see that their standard deviation is 4.5. That standard deviation indicates that the ten scores on average are not clustering close to the mean of 5.5, but rather tend to be about 4.5 points away from it – closer to 1 or 10.

To understand the *pooled* standard deviation, imagine that the above ten scores were the posttest scores of a control group and that the following ten scores are the posttest scores of a treatment group: $10 + 10 + 10 + 10 + 10 + 8 + 8 + 8 + 8 + 8 = 90$. Without even calculating the standard deviation of the treatment group, you can visualize that it ought to be a lot lower than that of the control group because every one of the ten scores is within one point of the mean of 9 ($90/10 = 9$). (Its standard deviation is 1.) To calculate the pooled standard deviation across both groups, you would enter all twenty posttest scores in the calculation, including the ten control group scores and the ten treatment scores. You would then find that the *pooled* standard deviation is 3.7, which is lower than 4.5 because there is less variation in the ten treatment scores.

7.4.2 Within-Group Effect Sizes

In *one-group* pretest–posttest evaluations (i.e., there is no control group), an analogous *within*-group effect size statistic can be calculated – one that mirrors the calculation of Cohen's *d*, but with two differences: (1) The difference is between the pretest mean score and the posttest mean score; and (2) the standard deviation that gets divided into that difference is the pooled standard deviation across the pretest and posttest scores. Box 7.2 illustrates how to calculate the within-group effect size statistic.

Box 7.2   An Illustration of an Outcome Evaluation of the Implementation of a Research Supported Treatment (TFCBT) for Traumatized Children: The Use of within-Group Effect Sizes

Trauma-focused cognitive behavioral therapy (TFCBT) is considered to be an effective treatment for traumatized children and their parents. A full description of it can be found in Cohen *et al.* (2006). For this illustration, let's suppose you are evaluating the provision of TFCBT in a child guidance center with limited resources for training and supervision in TFCBT. Each of the center's five child therapists who have been trained in TFCBT (but did not receive the extent of training or supervision that was provided to the clinicians in the RCTs) provide it to six traumatized children (for a total sample size of thirty), and the (fictitious) pretest and posttest scores on a valid measure of trauma symptoms (the lower the score, the better) of the thirty children are displayed in Table 7.1. You can calculate the pretest and posttest means and standard deviations using Excel or other statistical software, or – if you have no such software – you can easily have an online standard deviation calculator do the computations. If you enter "standard deviation calculator," for example, Google will show you various options, such as the one at www.alcula.com/calculators/statistics/standard-deviation/.

You can begin entering the pretest scores and finding their mean and standard deviation, and then entering all the posttest scores and finding their mean and standard deviation. Your calculations will show that your pretest mean is 36.93, and your pretest standard deviation is 5.94. Your posttest mean is 28.86, and your posttest standard deviation is 6.45. Plugging those means and standard deviations into an online effect size calculator (such as the one at www.socscistatistics.com/effectsize/default3.aspx) yields a within-group effect size of 1.30, meaning that the posttest mean score is 1.30 standard deviations better than the pretest score mean.

Finding the Corresponding Benchmark

If you enter "within-group effect size TFCBT," your search engine will come up with the article Rubin *et al.* (2017) given in the References. The table of average (aggregated) within-group effect sizes displayed in that article shows that those averages are 1.48 for the TFCBT groups and 0.82 for the control groups. Comparison with your effect size of 1.30 indicates that your agency's providers are achieving an average outcome that is almost as good as the average of the TFCBT groups in the experimental outcome evaluations and that is much better than the average outcome of the control groups. Although your pretest–posttest evaluation lacked a control group, the comparison with the treatment group benchmark (1.30 versus 1.48) suggests that your agency's providers appear to be implementing TFCBT satisfactorily, especially in light of their limited training and supervision. The comparison with the control group benchmark (1.30 versus 0.82) supports the *plausibility* that *perhaps* your providers are implementing TFCBT effectively.

Table 7.1 *Pretest and posttest scores for illustration in Box 7.2*

Pretest scores
30, 40, 50, 35, 40, 35, 40, 35, 30, 40, 30, 35, 40, 35, 35, 50, 45, 25, 30, 40, 45, 35, 40, 30, 35, 40, 43, 37, 33, 30

Posttest scores
20, 30, 45, 30, 35, 25, 35, 30, 21, 32, 20, 30, 31, 25, 24, 40, 40, 17, 27, 33, 31, 26, 30, 20, 25, 30, 36, 29, 27, 22

The within-group effect size can be particularly useful in evaluations that assess how well an agency's treatment providers are implementing an intervention that is already known to have strong research supporting its effectiveness. That is, the agency would not be seeking to establish the effectiveness of an intervention already deemed "evidence-based." Instead, the agency would be asking whether its providers are implementing it properly. That assessment is needed because so many studies have found that, when interventions that have been found to be effective in research settings are implemented in everyday practice settings, the providers in the latter settings often implement the intervention improperly and are therefore less effective. Various reasons have been offered for this gap. For example, the providers in the everyday practice settings tend to have larger and more diverse caseloads than those in research settings. Likewise, they probably aren't trained and supervised as well. There are other reasons, too, including more caseload turnover and less practitioner commitment to the intervention in the everyday practice settings. You can compare the agency's within-group effect size with the average (aggregated) within-group effect sizes of the treatment and control groups in the various experimental studies that provided the strong research support for interventions deemed to be evidence-based.

If the agency's effect size compares favorably with the average effect sizes of the treatment and control groups in the experimental studies, that means that not only are the agency's providers reaching treatment goals, but also they are doing so about as well as those providing treatment under more favorable conditions in the experimental studies. And if the agency's effect size is much better than the average effect size of the control groups in the experimental studies, a reasonable argument can be made about the agency's plausible effectiveness with the intervention. After all, had a control group been feasible in your evaluation, it is reasonable to suppose that its within-group effect size would have not been much greater than the average within-group effect size of the control groups in the experimental outcome evaluations.

Box 7.2 illustrates this procedure in an example of a pretest–posttest evaluation of an agency's provision of trauma-focused cognitive behavioral therapy (TFCBT). My colleagues and I have published studies that provide benchmarks for within-group effect sizes across a variety of research-supported interventions. You can find them by searching the web with keywords like "within-group effect size benchmarks." With the accessibility of online calculators, the calculation of the within-group effect size can be done fairly easily, as illustrated in Box 7.2 and Table 7.1 as well as in Box 11.1 of Chapter 11.

7.5   Non-equivalent Comparison Groups Designs

The non-equivalent comparison groups design is notated as follows:

$$O_1 \ X \ O_2$$

$$O_1 \ TAU \ O_2$$

The first row above depicts the treatment group and contains a pretest before an intervention and a posttest after the intervention. The second row depicts the comparison group and contains a pretest and posttest with only treatment-as-usual (TAU) in between. (Treatment as usual is commonly offered to controls to avoid the ethical problem of denying or delaying treatment to control clients.) With this design, a successful outcome is indicated to the extent that the treatment group improves more than the comparison group. The latter (comparison)

Results supporting effectiveness of intervention	35 X 70
	35 TAU 35
Results *NOT* supporting effectiveness of intervention	35 X 45
	35 TAU 45

FIGURE 7.1 Alternative results of comparison groups designs (with higher scores indicating a better outcome).

group is like a control group, but it does not have the "control" label because the design, lacking random assignment, is quasi-experimental and not a true experiment with random assignment of participants to groups. A true experiment with random assignment would be notated as follows:

$$R \rightarrow \boxed{\begin{array}{c} O_1 \ X \ O_2 \\ O_1 \ TAU \ O_2 \end{array}}$$

The notation is the same as in the non-equivalent comparison groups design except for the $R \rightarrow$, which signifies that participants are being assigned randomly to the two treatment conditions. With a sufficiently large sample size (say, at least about fifteen participants per condition), it is reasonable to expect the random assignment to produce groups that share comparable non-treatment characteristics, including comparable pretest mean scores, and thus controls for a *selectivity bias*. Figure 7.1 displays results that support the effectiveness of an intervention with designs and results that would not support the effectiveness of the intervention.

7.6   Selectivity Biases

A *selectivity bias* exists to the extent that the two groups differ in characteristics that are likely to influence change from pretest to posttest. For example, if the treatment group consists of people who seek the treatment and the comparison group consists of people who do not seek it, then the people in the treatment group might be more motivated to change or perhaps experiencing a greater need for treatment. Likewise, those who are able to participate in treatment might have more socioeconomic resources, such as transportation, more flexible work hours, and so on.

In most agency-based outcome evaluations, obtaining an equivalent comparison group will be infeasible or at least very difficult. At best you might be able to find another program that – despite addressing the same target problem as does your program – differs from your program in some important ways. Its program participants might differ from yours in age, ethnicity, problem severity, or socioeconomic status. Practitioner caseloads might differ. The proportion of its clients participating involuntarily might be different. Maybe the costs, or difficulty, of attending the program will differ, resulting in differences between the two programs regarding participants' motivation to change. Especially with regard to the motivation factor, it is virtually impossible to be sure that two programs are truly equivalent regarding non-treatment factors that can explain away differences in outcome between the two programs. As noted earlier, the vulnerability of non-equivalent comparison groups designs to the impact of such factors is referred to by research methods texts as a *selectivity bias*.

Thus, if you use this design in your program evaluation you should be keenly aware of that possible bias and make sure you emphasize that limitation when discussing your results. However, if feasible, there is a way to extend this design so as to control for that bias and thus make this design almost as internally valid as a randomized experimental design. That extension involves providing the intervention to the comparison group after the posttest and then administering another posttest afterward. If you do that, you will have a *switching replication design*. (As discussed in research methods texts, the degree of internal validity reflects the degree to which it is logical to infer that the intervention, and not some alternative explanation, *caused* the desired outcome results.)

7.7   Switching Replication Design

The *switching replication design* is notated as follows:

$$O_1 \; X \; O_2$$

$$O_1 \; TAU \; O_2 \; X \; O_3$$

Suppose this design is feasible in an evaluation of a program to reduce binge drinking among college students, and the results are as follows for the average number of times the students in each program binge drank:

$$6 \; X \; 2$$

$$6 \; TAU \; 6 \; X \; 6$$

How would you interpret the above results? One hopes your answer would be that the evaluated intervention cannot be inferred to be effective because providing it to the comparison group led to no improvement. Thus, the difference at the first posttest looks like a function of a selectivity bias in which pre-existing differences between the two groups (perhaps in motivation to change or in the proportion of voluntary versus court-referred participants) explain the difference in outcome.

In contrast, suppose the results for that study are as follows:

$$6 \; X \; 2$$

$$6 \; TAU \; 6 \; X \; 2$$

How would you interpret the above results? One hopes you would interpret them as supporting a causal inference that the intervention – and *not* a selectivity bias – explains the improved outcomes. Your reasoning would be that if the intervention is ineffective, and the first posttest difference was due to a selectivity bias, then why would the comparison group improve in the same way as the treatment group after receiving the intervention? If the better improvement in the treatment group at O_2 was a function of the difference in group characteristics – which would imply that without those characteristics there would have been no – or much less – improvement, then the group without those characteristics would not have benefited from the intervention in the same way as the original treatment group. That logic is what gives the switching replication design virtually as much internal validity as the randomized experimental design.

7.8   Switching Replication Design Compared with Waitlist Quasi-experimental Design

Many outcome evaluations use a waitlist group design that compares the pretest and posttest scores of service recipients with the changes over the same time period of people while on a waiting list for treatment. Lacking random assignment to treatment and control groups, this design is vulnerable to a selectivity bias because the people who appear earlier for treatment might differ in important ways from those who appear later. This design can evolve into a switching replication design if the waitlist group receives the treatment after the posttest and then gets posttested again after receiving the treatment.

Some evaluators will provide the treatment to the waitlist group after the posttest only for ethical reasons – so as to avoid denying treatment to anyone. Consequently, this design can be confused with the switching replication design. Equating the two designs, however, is a mistake when the only reason for the eventual treatment for the waitlist controls is ethical. Of course, being ethical is a good thing, but without a second posttest and applying the logic of the switching replication data analysis to control for a selectivity bias, a waitlist control group design would not amount to a switching replication design. Moreover, the switching replication design handles the ethical issue by providing the treatment to the control group, regardless of whether the control group consists of people who arrive later for treatment and are put on a waitlist or of people who are already being served in a comparable setting that does not provide the tested intervention or program.

7.9   Time-Series Designs

If it is feasible in your outcome evaluation to administer multiple assessments of the outcome variable before the program or intervention begins as well as after it begins, you will have another way to strengthen inferences about causality. If you do that, you will be using a *time-series design*. Suppose, for example, you are the program evaluator for a city's police force, and the chief of police instituted an annual police training program in 2015 aimed at reducing the number of incidents of police shooting of innocent people. Examine the fictitious alternative time-series results A and B in Table 7.2, which shows the number of such incidents per year (as available in existing records in a fictitious city).

How would you interpret the A results in Table 7.2? To begin, notice that you can rule out the passage of time as an explanation for the A results because – unlike the B results – a declining trend in shootings did not predate the onset of the new program. Instead, the number of shootings remained pretty stable for five years. But what about history? You might wonder, "What else might have changed beginning in 2015 that might have caused the substantial decrease in the shootings?" Was there, for example, a huge increase in the media reportage and editorial outrage about such shootings? If you can find no such alternative explanations for the decrease, it would be reasonable for you to suppose that the new program is a *plausible* cause of the decrease. But you could not be sure. Maybe there really was some other cause of the change – one that you did not detect. So what! The mere *plausibility* that the new program caused the change can be grounds for continuing to fund and provide the training program. As

Table 7.2 *Alternative results of a fictitious time-series design to evaluate the effectiveness of an intervention to reduce incidents of police shooting of innocent people*

Results A											
2009	2010	2011	2012	2013	2014	2015	2016	2017	2018	2019	2020
6	7	7	6	7	7	Program start-up year	2	1	0	0	0
Results B											
2009	2010	2011	2012	2013	2014	2015	2016	2017	2018	2019	2020
7	6	5	4	3	2	Program start-up year	2	1	0	0	0

discussed in the previous chapter regarding finding a strong correlation, what possibly erroneous policy decision is the greater harm? Wasting some time and money on a training that does not reduce the shooting of innocent people? Or saving that time and money and thus having many more innocent people being shot? Therefore, as mentioned earlier in Chapter 6, sometimes the desire to infer causality in program evaluation can be too strong. That desire is nice as long as it does not lead to *the perfect becoming the enemy of the good*. We need to remember that with some kinds of program outcomes, important and appropriate program and policy decisions can be implied even when causality is uncertain. The next chapter will discuss another time-series design – one that can be used by direct service practitioners to evaluate their own practice – single-case designs.

7.10 Choosing the Most Appropriate Design

Despite the emphasis in Chapter 6 on feasibility and not letting the perfect become the enemy of the good, you should choose the most rigorous design whenever it is feasible to do so. Of the designs mentioned in this chapter, the RCT would offer the best evidence for inferring causality about the effectiveness of an intervention, program, or policy. But in order for it to be feasible, you would need an agency setting that is receptive to it. The setting would need to have a sufficient number of clients who could be randomly assigned to alternative treatment conditions. So as not to deny or delay services to the control group, the setting would need to have a routine treatment regimen in place so that the group receiving the new intervention being tested can be compared with controls who only receive treatment-as-usual (TAU). Thus, this design would fit best in an agency where the entire agency's program of services is not being evaluated and instead the agency just wants to evaluate the effectiveness of a new intervention that has been added to its existing services (perhaps supported by a funded grant proposal).

A pretest–posttest design would not be feasible if pretests are not feasible, such as when evaluating some crisis intervention for people who need immediate help or when the intervention aims to prevent future incidents of child maltreatment, police brutality, or criminal recidivism. In those situations you could compare the future incidents of the alternative treatment conditions, but lacking a pretest there would be less evidence as to whether the alternative groups were comparable to begin with. A time-series design might also be possible, but only if enough data were available to plot a graph showing the pre-intervention and post-intervention trends.

The switching replication design is almost as inferentially strong regarding causality as is the RCT design because of its control for a selectivity bias. You could choose it if you have all the prerequisites for an RCT except for random assignment. It would also require the use of pretests and posttests.

The weakest of the designs described in this chapter – the one-group pretest–posttest design – might be the most appropriate choice in one of the following three circumstances:

- The sole reason for doing the evaluation is because a funded grant (or other key stakeholders) required pretest–posttest data, only, and there are insufficient funds for conducting a more rigorous evaluation
- None of the other designs are feasible in or allowed by the agency
- The reason for the evaluation is *not* to generate compelling causal evidence, but rather to take a benchmark approach to assess how well an agency's treatment providers are implementing an intervention that is already known to have strong research supporting its effectiveness.

7.11   Chapter Main Points

- A limited – descriptive, only – evaluation might not be as exciting as an evaluation of the effectiveness of a program, but the funding source might be satisfied knowing if the promised goal was reached and might use that finding in considering whether to continue the funding.
- The *one-group pretest–posttest design* $(O_1 X O_2)$ does not permit causal inferences, but it might be the best *feasible* design in service-oriented agencies.
- If the degree of improvement is impressive and clinically (substantively) meaningful in a one-group pretest–posttest design, then the notion that the program or intervention had a causal impact becomes more plausible.
- Effect size statistics depict the strength of a relationship (such as between the treatment variable and the outcome variable), and they can be compared across evaluations that use different ways to measure outcome.
- The *between*-group effect size, called Cohen's d, equals the difference between the treatment group mean outcome score and the control group mean outcome score divided by the pooled standard deviation of the outcome scores across both groups.
- The within-group effect size equals the difference between the pretest and posttest means divided by the pooled standard deviation across the pretest and posttest scores.

- The within-group effect size can be particularly useful in evaluations that assess how well an agency's treatment providers are implementing an intervention known to have strong research supporting its effectiveness, and it can be compared with meta-analytic benchmarks.
- To facilitate the calculation of a within-group effect size, you can use Excel or other statistical software, or – if you have no such software – you can obtain the means and standard deviations, and then the effect size, using online calculators.
- You can strengthen the one-group pretest–posttest design by adding another (comparison) group, and thus have a non-equivalent comparison groups design.
- In most agency-based outcome evaluations, obtaining an equivalent comparison group will be infeasible or at least very difficult. Because there might be important differences in the characteristics of the participants between the two groups, the non-equivalent comparison groups design is vulnerable to a selectivity bias.
- You can control for a possible selectivity bias by using a switching replication design – if it is feasible.
- If it is feasible to administer multiple assessments of the outcome variable before the program or intervention begins as well as after it begins, another way to strengthen the plausibility of causality is to use a *time-series design*.
- The choice of a design will be influenced by factors such as feasibility, whether pretests are possible, the expectations of funders and other stakeholders, and whether the reason for the evaluation is *not* to generate *compelling* causal evidence, but rather to take a benchmark approach to assess how well an agency's treatment providers are implementing an intervention that is already known to have strong research supporting its effectiveness.

7.12   Exercises

1. Using a search term such as *within-group effect sizes* or *effect size benchmarks*, find at least one of the studies that have been done that offer benchmarks against which agencies can compare their within-group effect size. Discuss whether you believe such studies are potentially valuable to real-world practice agencies? Why or why not?
2. Read the article by Rubin & von Sternberg (2017) in the References. Do you agree with it? Do you think you will be able to follow its recommendations in your eventual practice? Why or why not?

3. Using the pretest and posttest data in Table 7.1 for Box 7.2, use the online standard deviation calculator www.alcula.com/calculators/statistics/standard-deviation/ to obtain the means and standard deviation in those data. Then calculate the within-group effect size using the online effect size calculator www.socscistatistics.com/effectsize/default3.aspx. If your effect size differs from the one in the box, discuss it with your peers and/or instructor.

7.13   Additional Reading

- Rubin, A., & Babbie, E. R. (2017). *Research Methods for Social Work* (9th ed.). Boston, MA: Cengage Learning.
- Thyer, B. A., & Pignotti, M. G. (2015). *Science and Pseudoscience in Social Work Practice*, New York, NY: Springer Publishing Co.

Chapter 8

Single-Case Designs for Evaluating Programs and Practice

> **WHAT YOU'LL LEARN IN THIS CHAPTER**
>
> You'll learn about a particular type of time-series design that can be used not only by a program to evaluate its outcome, but also by individual service providers to evaluate the outcome of their own practice with specific clients.

8.1   Introduction

Chapter 7 discussed the use and logic of time-series designs and how they can provide tentative causal inferences about the effectiveness of a program or policy. It also mentioned single-case designs, which are a type of time-series design that can be used not only to evaluate the outcomes of programs, but also by direct service practitioners to evaluate their own practice. This chapter will examine alternative single-case designs, their logic for making causal inferences, and how to use them to evaluate practice and programs.

8.2   What Is a Single Case?

The term single-case can refer to one person who receives an intervention, one family that receives an intervention, a group of recipients of a group intervention, or an entire community to which an intervention is provided. Because these designs can be applied to groups of people, some call them single-*system* designs.

The term single-*case* designs is commonly used when direct service practitioners use these designs to evaluate their own practice. Regardless of whether the service recipient is an individual, a family, or multiple participants in a group intervention, the first step is to select an outcome objective and define it operationally – that is, in measurable and quantifiable terms. The next step is to take repeated measurements of that objective before introducing the intervention being evaluated. The quantity observed at each measurement is called a *data point*. Each data point is plotted chronologically on a graph. The line of data points observed before the intervention is introduced is called the *baseline*. The data points continue to be plotted after the intervention is introduced. The baseline phase is represented by the letter **A**, and the intervention phase is represented by the letter **B**. Thus, the simplest type of single-case design is the **AB** design. When the B phase shows a sudden shift in the level or slope (trend) in data points, the effectiveness of the intervention is supported. Otherwise, the intervention's effectiveness is not supported.

8.3   Overview of Single-Case Design Logic for Making Causal Inferences

If you have been diagnosed as being allergic to something, you have a head start in understanding the logic of single-case designs. If it is an airborne pollen allergy, for example, you know that every time the pollen count rises, your symptoms worsen and every time the count falls your symptoms improve. Recognizing those repeated coincidences is enough for you to know what is causing the changes in your symptoms. The same logic applies if you eat or drink something that has an ingredient that your body cannot tolerate. That is, if a particular observed phenomenon consistently goes up or down each time a possible cause of that phenomenon is introduced or withdrawn, that possible cause becomes the more plausible cause of the changes than alternative explanations like history, passage of time, or regression to the mean.

The main way to interpret outcomes involves eyeballing the chronologically graphed outcome measures. If the level and/or trend in the measurement points changes dramatically in a way that coincides with the change from the baseline phase to the intervention phase, then the graph is deemed to be visually significant and indicative of treatment success (and perhaps effectiveness). Three visually significant graphs are illustrated in Figure 8.1. Each graph plots a positive behavior for which an increase in the level or slope of the graph would be desirable and indicative of a positive outcome. Graph A is visually significant – and thus supports the effectiveness of the intervention – because of the dramatic coincidence in which the *slope* of the target behavior improves only at the end of the baseline period and the onset of the intervention period, rendering implausible alternative explanations such as history or passage of time. Graph B is visually significant because of the dramatic coincidence in which the *level* of the target behavior improves only at the end of the baseline period and the onset of the intervention period. Graph C is visually significant in light of the improvement in both slope and level.

In contrast, the two graphs in Figure 8.2 are not visually significant. They clearly show no basis for inferring intervention effectiveness. In Graph A, for example, the improvement during the intervention phase appears to be merely a continuation of an improving trend during the baseline phase, suggesting that a pre-existing, ongoing change process was unaffected by the intervention. Likewise, Graph B shows no improvement in either slope or level.

Clinical Significance. Visual significance pertains to inferring whether an intervention appears to be effective, but does not necessarily imply that the impact

Graph A (Improvement in Slope)

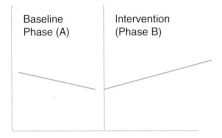

Graph B (Improvement in Level)

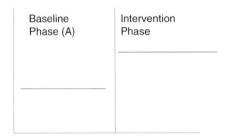

Graph C (Improvement in Slope and Level)

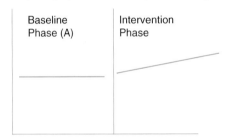

FIGURE 8.1 Three visually significant single-case design graphs for desirable behaviors.

on the target problem is strong enough. Suppose there is a visually significant graph showing that when intervention is introduced the number of times a child physically assaults a classmate drops from twice per week to once per week or the number of hours a depressed client sleeps per night increases from one hour to two hours. Even if the intervention is responsible for the improvement, it might be replaced with another intervention in the hope of attaining an improvement that is more clinically significant. Visual significance, like statistical significance (as will be discussed in Chapter 12), does not ensure that the degree of change is enough to be meaningful or sufficient. Reducing physical assaults on classmates from twice each week to once, or increasing sleep time from one hour to two, is no basis for feeling that the problem has been alleviated adequately.

Graph A (No Improvement in Slope)

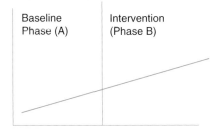

Baseline
Phase (A)

Intervention
(Phase B)

Graph B (No Improvement in Slope or Level)

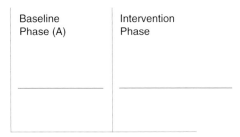

Baseline
Phase (A)

Intervention
Phase

FIGURE 8.2 Two single-case design graphs for desirable behaviors that do not support the effectiveness of the intervention.

8.4 What to Measure and by Whom?

Because single-case designs require the chronological plotting of many repeated measures in a way that can show a sudden shift that coincides with the start of the intervention (B) phase, the outcome indicator being measured must be something that can vary from day to day (if each data point is a day) or week to week (if each data point is a week). Measuring something like suicide attempts by a depressed client, therefore, won't work. Better options would be hours slept each night or self-reports of level of sadness each day. For a family referred for child abuse or neglect, incidents of serious physical abuse won't work, but what might work would be the amount of time a parent played with their child each day or whether a parent yelled angrily at the child each day.

Measurement in single-case designs is usually done either by means of direct behavioral observation or by self-report. In rare instances existing records might be available that show how the target behavior fluctuates in a way that corresponds to the time intervals on the graph, such as when a residential treatment center's records show the daily or weekly instances when a child did or did not do their homework or get reported for a problem behavior. Self-report data can be collected via interviews or written self-report scales. Self-report can be the most convenient option for practitioners who are evaluating their own practice because the clients report on their own behavior or moods, such as by ongoing self-monitoring of each behavioral incident or by completing a brief self-report scale, such as on their average mood level each day or week or the estimated frequency of the target behavior for the time period. Each of these measurement options has the advantages and disadvantages that were discussed in Chapter 5, and consequently triangulating them is recommended when feasible. Although it is convenient, the self-report option can be particularly vulnerable to a social desirability bias when clients are reporting – either through an interview or on a scale – the frequency or magnitude of their desirable or undesirable behaviors or moods. And when self-report includes self-monitoring (that is, recording each instance when it occurs), it can be vulnerable to the possibility that any improvements are being caused by the act of self-monitoring and not the intervention.

As an alternative to having clients self-monitor their own behavior, the monitoring can be done by a significant other, such as a parent regarding behavior at home, a teacher regarding classroom behavior, or a cottage parent regarding behavior in a residential treatment center.

8.4.1 Obtrusive and Unobtrusive Observation

Each of the monitoring options has some possible vulnerability to observer bias, but if the client is not aware that the significant other is monitoring and recording certain target behaviors, the measurement is considered to be *unobtrusive*, and therefore less vulnerable to a client's social desirability bias. The opposite of unobtrusive observation is *obtrusive* observation. The more aware the client is of being observed, the more obtrusive it is. For example, a child knows that a cottage parent or teacher *routinely* observes their behavior, but the observation is relatively unobtrusive if the child does not know that the parent or teacher is jotting down a mark for every time the child does something desirable or undesirable regarding the target behavior. Conversely, if a child welfare practitioner on a home visit is observing parent–child interactions, the parent would be keenly aware of the observation, the reasons for it, and the implications of the targeted behaviors. Therefore, the observation would be quite obtrusive and vulnerable to a social desirability bias. To enhance feasibility and unobtrusiveness when a significant other is monitoring, the monitoring can be done via *spot-check recording*, which involves briefly observing the target behavior at specified times when the target behavior is expected to occur. For example, a cottage parent in a residential treatment facility could briefly look in on the study area each evening and jot down whether a particular child is studying (yes or no) or the number of children who are studying at that moment. To minimize obtrusiveness, the exact time of the spot-check can be varied from day to day (Rubin & Babbie, 2017).

8.4.2 Quantification Options

Measurements can be recorded and graphed according to their *frequency* (e.g., number of angry outbursts), *duration* (e.g., how long each temper tantrum lasted), or *severity* (e.g., did the outburst involve violence to person or property). These options are not mutually exclusive; more than one of them can be recorded and graphed. For example, a cottage parent could casually drop by the recreation area for a few minutes at different times each day and record whether a child is having an angry outburst, the duration of the outburst, and whether physical aggression is involved.

8.5 Baselines

Baselines should include enough data points (repeated measurements) to make history, the passage of time, and regression to the mean implausible explanations for any change in the graph that coincides with the onset of the intervention. That is, intervention effects should be the most plausible explanation. For example, if only two or three days of observation comprise the baseline phase, and a child's behavior or trauma symptoms improve steadily beginning on the first or second day of the intervention (B) phase, it would not be implausible to suppose that perhaps an improving trend predated the intervention phase and that the couple of days of baseline merely represented a temporary blip in the ongoing trend. The longer the lack of improvement was observed during baseline, the less plausible that alternative explanation would become. In addition to having an ample number of data points, causal inference is enhanced if the baseline trend is *stable*. If the baseline graph is fluctuating wildly in no discernable direction, it is harder to visually perceive a change in level or slope that commences with the intervention (B) phase. Consequently, when a baseline graph is unstable, it is desirable – if feasible – to prolong baseline until a stable trend emerges. Prolonging baseline might also be desirable if the baseline shows that an improving trend is already in process – to see if the trend levels off – because the greater the slope is of the improving trend during baseline, the more difficult it is to find a visually significant spike in the desired direction when intervention commences.

Are Baselines Ethical? The idea of delaying the onset of an intervention for the sake of establishing a baseline ethically jars some practitioners (and students). And well it should, if we are talking about delaying service provision when a client is not already receiving some sort of intervention or is experiencing a dangerous crisis. However, delaying an intervention does not necessarily mean delaying treatment or service provision. A client might already be receiving routine services or an intervention without showing a satisfactory level of improvement. If so, the baseline phase can take place while they are receiving services and before introducing an intervention that is hoped to be more effective. In fact, introducing that intervention without a baseline can be *less ethical* than establishing a baseline first. That is because evaluating whether specific interventions are actually helping (and not harming) people is more ethical than not evaluating and thus not trying to ensure that clients are receiving the best service possible.

8.6   Alternative Single-Case Designs

Alternative single-case designs range from the simple AB design containing one baseline (A) phase and one intervention (B) phase to more complex designs containing more than one A phase and more than one B phase. The purpose of adding more phases to the more complex designs is to decrease the plausibility of history as an alternative explanation for a graph's visual significance. For example, I once provided eye movement desensitization and reprocessing (EMDR) therapy to a lad who had trouble controlling his temper. One week after the EMDR began, his mother called to thank me for his miraculous improvement. However, I later learned that the boy's psychiatrist began prescribing a relevant medication at the same time that the EMDR treatment began. Despite my desire to be an effective therapist, I couldn't help but suppose that his improvement had more to do with the medication than it did with my EMDR therapy. Had I conducted a study using a single-case design with more than one baseline phase and more than one intervention phase, I would have noticed that the boy's improved behavior did not worsen when I interrupted the EMDR treatment or resume after I reintroduced the EMDR. That would have lessened the plausibility of EMDR as the cause of the change in his behavior. Alternatively, if his behavior worsened (or stopped improving) when EMDR was interrupted and started to improve again when EMDR was reintroduced, the plausibility of EMDR as the cause of the changes would be strengthened substantially.

8.6.1   The AB Design

The AB design is the simplest single-case design in that it has only one A phase and one B phase. It was illustrated in Figures 8.1 and 8.2, and its interpretation regarding visual significance was discussed in relation to those two figures.

8.6.2   The ABAB Design

The ABAB design adds another A phase and another B phase to the AB design to improve the ability to rule out the plausibility of history as an explanation for visually significant results. Figure 8.3 illustrates one ABAB graph with visually significant results and one without visual significance. Each graph plots a positive behavior for which an increase in the level or slope of the graph would be desirable and indicative of a positive outcome. Graph A is visually significant because the level or slope improves with the start of each B phase. It would be far-fetched to suppose that some extraneous event that positively affects outcome occurs only at the time that intervention is introduced. Graph B is not visually significant despite the improvement with the first B phase because no subsequent changes in level or slope occur when withdrawing and then re-introducing the intervention. However, it is conceivable that the intervention was effective with *irreversible effects*. Perhaps, for example, the client learned during the first B phase to use a cognitive technique to alleviate their anxiety and they learned it so well that withdrawing the intervention or reintroducing it had no bearing on their propensity and ability to use the technique effectively. To ascertain if the intervention had irreversible effects, the practitioner could evaluate it in ABAB designs with future clients with the same problem and outcome target. If those evaluations yield similar results, then the series of consistently replicated results would achieve visual significance and support the effectiveness of the intervention.

Graph A (Visually Significant)

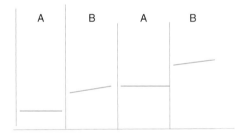

Graph B (Not Visually Significant)

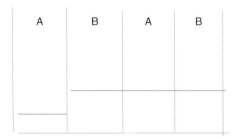

FIGURE 8.3 Two ABAB design graphs for desirable behaviors: one that has visual significance and one that does not.

8.6.3   The Multiple-Baseline Design

Another approach to using replication to improve the ability to rule out the plausibility of history as an explanation for visually significant results is to use a multiple-baseline design. This approach involves graphing using more than one graph to evaluate one particular intervention and starting of the B phase at different times in each graph. For example, perhaps a cognitive-behavioral intervention could target different targets at different times.

As illustrated in Figure 8.4, the intervention could target feelings of anxiety first and incidents of angry outbursts later. Figure 8.4 illustrates visual significance because improvement in the target problem is replicated to commence only when the intervention targets that problem. Notice, for example, that the angry outbursts baseline extends beyond the point in time when the intervention targeting anxiety is introduced. If some extraneous event were causing the client to improve, the angry outbursts graph probably would have commenced its improvement around the time the anxiety graph improved and while the angry outbursts graph was still in the baseline phase.

In contrast, Figure 8.5 illustrates a multiple-baseline pattern that is not visually significant because both targets improve at the same time and while one is still in the baseline phase. Therefore the plausibility of an extraneous event (history) causing the client's improvement with regard to both target problems does not seem to be far-fetched. However, it is conceivable that the intervention

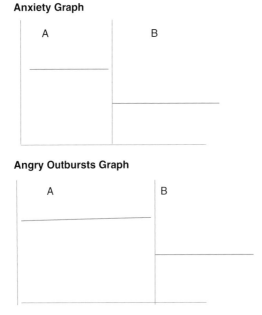

FIGURE 8.4 A visually significant set of multiple-baseline graphs for an intervention that targets feelings of anxiety first and incidents of angry outbursts later.

Anxiety Graph

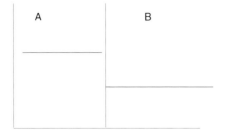

Angry Outbursts Graph

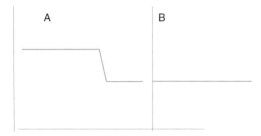

FIGURE 8.5 A set of multiple-baseline graphs that lacks visual significance regarding an intervention that targets feelings of anxiety first and incidents of angry outbursts later.

was effective with **generalizable effects**. Perhaps, for example, the intervention affected both target problems at the same time when it was introduced in the top graph with the intent to have it target anxiety, only. To ascertain if the intervention had generalizable effects, the practitioner could evaluate it in a future multiple-baseline design with a future client with the same target problems. If that evaluation yields similar results, then the series of consistently replicated results would achieve visual significance and support the interpretation that the intervention is effective with irreversible effects. Using the same logic, multiple-baseline designs can be used with more than one client with the same target problem. The baseline for one (or more) client(s) would be extended beyond the point when the intervention is introduced to one client to see if each client improves while only one client is receiving the intervention. If they do, then it is plausible to suppose that some extraneous event is causing the improvement. But if the clients know and come into contact with each other, then generalization of effects is an equally plausible explanation. Again, replication could be used to resolve the conundrum, and if the same results are replicated, then the notion that the intervention is effective with generalizable effects becomes the more plausible explanation.

8.6.4   Multiple-Component Designs

If no improvement in outcome is observed during the intervention phase of an AB design, the practitioner might decide to try a different intervention and to add a phase C to use the previous phases as the baseline for C. If they do, the design then becomes an ABC *multiple-component design*, with B and C comprising the multiple components. If phase C shows no improvement, the practitioner might change to a third intervention which gets evaluated in a D phase, thus evolving the evaluation to an ABCD design. Another possibility is to intensify the original intervention in C instead of replacing it. Multiple-component designs make more sense than refusing to replace an intervention that isn't working with a new one. However, these designs come with an important caveat. If improvement is not observed until the C or D phase, there is the possibility that it would not have happened had the previous intervention(s) not preceded it. Therefore, if no improvement is observed until a C or a D phase, it would be a mistake to con-clude that the C or D intervention is all that is needed. It might be, but replication with different sequencing of the interventions is needed to sort out which inter-vention or combination of interventions is needed and in what order to attain the desired treatment outcome.

8.7   B Designs to Evaluate the Implementation of Evidence-Supported Interventions

As was mentioned in Chapter 7, many studies have found that, when inter-ventions that have been found to be effective in research settings are imple-mented in everyday practice settings, the providers in the latter settings often implement the intervention improperly and therefore the intervention can be less effective than it was in the research studies. Consequently, it is wrong to assume that an intervention known to be effective in the research litera-ture will be effective when it is adopted in a service agency. Chapter 7 (and later Chapter 12) address how within-group effect size benchmarks can be used to assess whether a research-supported intervention appears to be being implemented adequately in a service agency setting. Single-case designs pro-vide another option for assessing the adequacy of the implementation. In fact, when the aim is limited to assessing the adequacy of the implementation of interventions that already have ample research support for their effectiveness, a baseline phase is not necessary, because instead of seeking to make causal inferences the aim is simply to see if clients make a desired degree of progress. If they do, it is reasonable for the practitioner to suppose that they might be implementing the intervention adequately. Conversely, if inadequate progress is observed in the B graph, that would create doubt about how appropriately the practitioner was implementing an intervention that is supposed to be effect-ive and that should be accompanied by progress if it is being implemented properly.

8.8   Using Single-Case Designs as Part of the Evidence-Informed Practice Process

As mentioned in Chapter 1, the final stage of the evidence-informed practice process is to evaluate the intervention that was implemented in light of the best evidence. That step is important not only because of possible flaws in the way the practitioner might be implementing the intervention, but also because, even when implemented properly, interventions with strong research support might not be the best fit for some clients. By conducting a single-case evaluation, practitioners can evaluate whether the chosen intervention appears to be a good fit for a client. They can use any single-case design to do that – even a design with no baseline and just a B phase. If during the intervention the plotted data points are showing no improvement, the practitioner can try a different intervention – perhaps one with research support that is not quite as strong as the first intervention had.

Moreover, the evidence-informed practice process allows practitioners to tweak interventions to adapt them to the client's idiosyncratic characteristics and circumstances. Perhaps the tweaks – no matter how minor – made the intervention less effective than it was in the research studies that supported it. That is another reason why practitioners should employ single-case designs as part of evidence-informed practice. Doing it with a baseline phase would be preferable, but if they cannot include a baseline phase, just using a B design can provide evidence to monitor whether the intervention appears to be a good fit for the client. When a B design is used for this purpose, the practitioner need not feel obliged to continue the intervention until all the intervention data points are plotted. Instead, if the data points are not reflecting adequate progress, she can abort the intervention at any time that seems to be clinically warranted in light of the data points already plotted and then start a new intervention – with new data points – to monitor whether the client appears to be making better progress with the replacement intervention.

8.9   Aggregating Single-Case Design Outcomes to Evaluate an Agency

If all or most of the service providers in an agency employ a single-case design to evaluate outcome with each of their clients – either in the context of an on-going required agency procedure, or as a time-limited program evaluation – the proportion of visually significant outcomes can be reported as a sort of agency batting average. The higher the proportion, the better the agency looks in terms of service effectiveness.

8.10   Chapter Main Points

- The term *single-case* can refer to one person who receives an intervention, one family that receives an intervention, a group of recipients of a group intervention, or an entire community to which an intervention is provided.

- The first step in a single-case design evaluation is to select an outcome objective and define it in measurable and quantifiable terms. The next step is to take repeated measurements of that objective before introducing the intervention being evaluated.

- The logic of single-case designs is based on reasoning that if a particular observed phenomenon consistently goes up or down each time a possible cause of that phenomenon is introduced or withdrawn, that possible cause becomes the more plausible cause of the changes than alternative explanations like history, passage of time, or regression to the mean.

- The main way to interpret the outcomes of single-case designs is by eyeballing the chronologically graphed outcome measures. If the level and/ or trend in the measurement points changes dramatically in a way that coincides with the change from the baseline phase to the intervention phase, then the graph is deemed to be visually significant and indicative of treatment success.

- Visual significance does not imply clinical significance; an intervention might cause improvement, but the degree of improvement might not be clinically meaningful.

- Because single-case designs require the chronological plotting of many repeated measures in a way that can show a sudden shift that coincides with the start of the intervention (B) phase, the outcome indicator being measured must be something that can vary from day to day (if each data point is a day) or week to week (if each data point is a week).

- Measurement in single-case designs is usually done either by means of direct behavioral observation or by self-report.

- Self-report data can be collected via interviews or written self-report scales. Clients can self-report on their own behavior or moods, such as by ongoing self-monitoring of each behavioral incident or by completing a brief self-report scale.

- Self-report can be particularly vulnerable to a social desirability bias.

- Unobtrusive observation is less vulnerable to a social desirability bias than is obtrusive observation.

- As an alternative to having clients self-monitor their own behavior, the monitoring can be done by a significant other.

- Measurements can be recorded and graphed according to their *frequency*, *duration*, and/or *severity*.
- Baselines should include enough data points (repeated measurements) to make history, the passage of time, and regression to the mean implausible explanations for any change in the graph that coincides with the onset of the intervention. In addition to having an ample number of data points, causal inference is enhanced if the baseline trend is stable.
- Alternative single-case designs range from the simple AB design containing one baseline (A) phase and one intervention (B) phase to more complex designs containing more than one A phase and more than one B phase. The purpose of adding more phases to the more complex designs is to decrease the plausibility of history as an alternative explanation for a graph's visual significance.
- If no improvement in outcome is observed during the intervention phase of an AB design, the practitioner might decide to try a different intervention and to add a phase C (and maybe a D phase) while using the previous phases as the baseline for C or D. If they do, the design then becomes an ABC or ABCD *multiple-component design*. If improvement is not observed until the C or D phase, there is the possibility that it would not have happened had the previous intervention(s) not preceded it. Therefore, if no improvement is observed until a C or a D phase, it would be a mistake to conclude that the C or D intervention is all that is needed

8.11 Exercises

1. A practitioner obtains the following data in an AB single-case evaluation of her effectiveness in using play therapy to reduce a child's nightmares:
   A: 3 3 4 2 3 4 3 4 4   B: 1 1 0 1 0 0 0 0 0
   What should the practitioner conclude from these data?
2. A practitioner obtains the following data in an AB single-case evaluation of her effectiveness in using play therapy to reduce a child's nightmares:
   A: 3 3   B: 1 1
   What should the practitioner conclude from these data?
3. A practitioner obtains the following data in an AB single-case evaluation of her effectiveness in using play therapy to reduce a child's nightmares:
   A: 5 5 4 4 3 3 2 2   B: 1 1 1 0 0 0 0 0 0
   What should the practitioner conclude from these data?
4. Suppose you use an ABAB design to evaluate the effectiveness of a group intervention aimed at helping a particular child improve her social skills. Your outcome indicator is the number of friends she plays with after school each day, and you obtain the following results:

A_1: 0 0 0 0 0 B_1: 1 1 2 3 3 A_2: 2 1 0 0 0 B_2: 1 2 2 3 3
What should you conclude from these data?

5. Suppose you conducted a multiple-baseline study to evaluate a group intervention to help three girls who attend the same school improve their social skills. In this study, you introduce the three girls to the group at different points, and you obtain the following results regarding the number of friends each plays with after school each day (backslash "/" signifies start of intervention phase):

Jan: 0 0 0 /1 1 1 2 2 2 2

Nan: 0 0 0 1 1 /1 2 2 2 2

Fran: 0 0 0 1 1 1 1 /2 2 2

What should you conclude from these results?

6. Suppose you evaluated the same intervention with one girl, but, before starting the group intervention, you tried a social skills intervention with the client in an individual context. Suppose your ABC design yielded the following results regarding the number of friends she plays with after school each day:

A: 0 0 0 0 0 0   B: 0 0 0 0 0 0   C: 1 1 1 2 2 2

What should you conclude from these results?

7. Choose a self-change goal that you are willing to share with your classmates. Possible examples include smoking cessation, increased exercise, better study habits, improved diet, improved sleeping, etc. Select a self-change intervention to help you attain that goal. (If you are trying to lose weight, you might want to Google "MyFitnessPal" to use in your intervention.) Self-monitor your progress (or lack of progress) toward reaching your goal in an AB design. Self-monitor and enter seven days of data points in the baseline phase and in a seven-day intervention phase. Share your graph and interpretation of it with your classmates and instructor. Include comments on what you experienced regarding the self-monitoring process. For example, did you experience any social desirability bias or any impact of the self-monitoring process itself on your efforts to change?

8.12   Additional Reading

- Bloom, M., Fischer, J., & Orme, J. G. (2009). *Evaluating Practice: Guidelines for the Accountable Professional* (6th ed.). Boston, MA: Allyn & Bacon.
- Rubin, A., & Bellamy, J. (2012). *Practitioner's Guide to Using Research for Evidence-Based Practice* (2nd ed.). Hoboken, NJ: John Wiley & Sons, Inc.

Chapter 9

Practical and Political Pitfalls in Outcome Evaluations

> **WHAT YOU'LL LEARN IN THIS CHAPTER**
>
> In this chapter we move from the technical aspects of outcome evaluations to the practical and political pitfalls that will bear on your ability to carry out an evaluation as intended. You'll also learn about anticipating and dealing with those pitfalls.

9.1   Introduction

No matter how rigorous and sophisticated an outcome evaluation design might be, various political and practical agency factors can interfere with its successful completion. This chapter will discuss those factors and what can be done to try to enhance the likelihood of successful completion of an evaluation and utilization of its findings and recommendations. To be a successful evaluator, you will need to be able to anticipate how practical realities in service-oriented settings can pose barriers to particular evaluation designs and data collection methods and how vested interests in the results of an outcome evaluation can affect compliance with an evaluation protocol and utilization of the report and recommendations of an evaluation.

9.2   Practical Pitfalls

Program evaluation usually is – at best – a minor concern of agency personnel in their day-to-day routines. These personnel may not understand the logic of outcome designs or the requisites of valid and unbiased measurement procedures. Moreover, they have enough other priorities to be concerned about in their jobs – priorities that may have dominated their attention for years before some evaluation came along to bother them.

Consequently, seasoned and novice evaluators alike can recount various ways in which an evaluation that they designed well nevertheless went awry due to its low priority among agency clinical or administrative personnel. For example, when a promising new treatment is being evaluated, it sometimes happens that clinical practitioners can finagle a way to get that treatment to those among their clients whom they think really need it, even if the evaluation had those clients assigned to a treatment-as-usual control group. Sometimes intake workers who are asked to have clients complete a particular pretest in addition to the agency's routine intake procedure might forget to do it. Some might even have resented having to perform the extra work, which might have made it easier for them to forget to do it. Sometimes an agency or governmental policy change affects the agency's procedures and consequently affects the evaluation, and the administrator might not realize that the evaluation team needs to be informed of the change without delay. Those are just a few examples of the ways that a well-designed evaluation can be impeded in an agency setting. Here are some more.

9.2.1   Intervention Fidelity

When a particular intervention's effectiveness is being evaluated, it is crucial that practitioners provide it with fidelity. An intervention has fidelity when it is provided as intended. Various factors can hamper fidelity. The practitioners providing it might not have learned it adequately. Perhaps the agency could not afford to provide sufficiently high-quality training, or, if they could afford it, maybe some practitioners were not adequately enthused about the intervention or the training, or perhaps they just weren't good learners. Perhaps the agency could not afford to purchase adequate supervision for the practitioners who are new to the intervention. Clinical interventions – even those with the strongest research support – need to be provided in the context of a good therapeutic alliance in order to be effective. In fact, some research has suggested that the quality of the client–therapist relationship has a stronger impact on treatment outcome than the particular intervention chosen (Wampold, 2015). Some clinicians providing the new intervention might be inexperienced recent graduates who lack clinical confidence and might need to improve their relationship skills. The therapeutic alliance also can suffer due to clinician turnover – especially in agencies that cannot afford to pay their clinicians competitive salaries. Some agencies might use field practicum students to intervene with some clients. Students can be particularly vulnerable to lacking clinical expertise and confidence. Consequently, if those students are providing the intervention to some clients participating in the evaluation, that won't help the chances of obtaining results that will support the effectiveness of the intervention.

Even experienced clinicians can impede intervention fidelity, especially if they are wedded to some other intervention approach and have some doubts about the new intervention. Some research has suggested that therapists' expectations about treatment outcome can influence the outcome (Wampold, 2015). Moreover, even with the best intentions to adhere to intervention fidelity, the intervention with which clinicians are more familiar might occasionally slip in. For example, some cognitive-behavioral therapies discourage therapists from engaging in psychodynamic interpretations, but a psychodynamically oriented therapist attempting to provide a cognitive-behavioral therapy with fidelity might not be able to resist such interpretations when they think they will help the client.

There is a flip side to intervention fidelity. Just as it is possible for providers of the tested intervention to let aspects of a different intervention with which they are more familiar slip in, some providers of treatment-as-usual (TAU) might have previously read about the tested intervention and incorporated some of its techniques into their routine treatment approach. The practitioners providing TAU might unintentionally include some of these techniques or feel that their clients are receiving inferior treatment and might therefore intentionally provide some aspects of the tested intervention.

It is important, therefore, to assess intervention fidelity of both the tested intervention and TAU early and throughout an outcome evaluation. If problems are detected early, perhaps they can be corrected. Ideally, a representative sample of treatment sessions should be recorded that can be viewed (or listened to) to check on the fidelity of each treatment condition. The fidelity of the tested intervention can be rated by an expert in the intervention, perhaps on a scale from unacceptable fidelity or minimal fidelity to acceptable or excellent fidelity. If the outcome results do not support the effectiveness of the intervention, and the fidelity ratings are low, the appropriate implication might be that the intervention might be more effective than indicated in the outcome results because it was not implemented adequately. Likewise, if the TAU fidelity checks find that TAU contained many aspects of the tested intervention, that could indicate that the results underestimated the effectiveness of the tested intervention. Therefore, obtaining fidelity ratings before the evaluation begins – perhaps in a brief pilot study – would be better than getting the ratings after the evaluation begins. That way, the start of the evaluation can be delayed until the fidelity problem is corrected.

9.2.2 Contamination of the Case Assignment Protocol

If the outcome evaluation involves comparing groups that receive different treatment conditions, it is crucial that the clients in each group receive the treatment to which they were assigned. If practitioners are supposed to provide the tested intervention to some of their clients and only TAU to others, it can be challenging to make sure that they are following the design protocol. They might need to be reminded continually in case they forget which clients get what. They might not understand or appreciate the logic of experimental or quasi-experimental designs and consequently see no harm in providing the tested intervention to a TAU client whom they think really needs it. I encountered this problem a few decades ago when I was evaluating the effectiveness of an after-school group intervention for middle-school students. In order to be able to describe the group intervention, one day I showed up to observe the group activity and noticed that one of the students who had been assigned to the control condition was participating in the group activity. When I asked the teacher leading the activity – who had been informed of students assigned to each condition – why a control group student was participating in the tested intervention, she replied that he was a friend of one of the boys in the group, who had brought him along, and that she did not want to refuse the boy's request to let his friend participate.

That experience is but one example of how easily group assignment can be contaminated. Suppose the intervention being evaluated is a special class on the dangers of unsafe sex, substance abuse, or bullying. Some students in the same school who do not participate in the class can be influenced by their friends who do participate. Consequently, the intervention might influence the behavior of the non-participants and thus dilute group differences in the outcome behaviors being assessed.

The risk of that sort of contamination can be reduced by having the evaluation take place in different schools so that the control group students do not interact with the experimental group students. Likewise, when evaluating an intervention that aims to enhance the mood and morale of nursing home residents, it is advisable to provide the intervention in one home and not another, instead of providing it to some residents and not to others in the same home. But if it is not possible to have two separate sites for the evaluation, and you are stuck with only one site, you need to be vigilant in your efforts to help service providers adhere to the case assignment protocol. Minimally, ongoing reminders should be sent to the providers regarding what intervention should be provided to what participants.

9.2.3 Recruiting Participants

Recruiting enough people to participate in an experimental or quasi-experimental outcome evaluation is important. As will be discussed in Chapter 11, the chances that the differences in outcome between different groups in an experimental design or quasi-experimental design will be statistically significant can be slim with a small sample size of fewer than about forty participants per group. Recruiting that many people to participate in an outcome evaluation can be challenging, especially if it involves them agreeing to the chance that they might be in the control condition and thus not receive the promising new intervention being evaluated. That aspect of refusal to participate can be alleviated by using a switching replication design. As you may recall from Chapter 7, with that design the control participants receive the tested intervention after the first round of posttests. Rewarding clients for the pretests and posttests – perhaps with a reasonably priced gift card – also can help encourage participation.

The problem of inducing people to agree to participate is compounded by the difficulty of finding enough potential participants to begin with. For example, suppose you work in a community-based, non-institutional agency serving older adults living with dementia and their caregivers, and you want to evaluate a promising new intervention to alleviate caregiver burden among older adults who serve as caregivers for a loved one living with early stage dementia. If you do not want to have to recruit participants from other agencies or the community at large, you'll need to ascertain the current size of the agency's caseload, the number of cases with dementia still in an early stage, the number of those cases in which the caregiver is able to participate in light of their limited time and perhaps their own cognitive impairments, and the projected number of new cases that will enter the agency during your evaluation's timeline that meet the eligibility requirements of the evaluation. Relying on staff estimates of the number of cases that will be eligible for your evaluation within a certain time period can be hazardous, especially in an agency with no prior experience with an outcome evaluation like yours.

Staff members might not be sufficiently cautious with their projections regarding the number of current clients who meet your eligibility requirements or the number of new cases that will do so within your timeline. They might overestimate the number of new cases that will enter the agency or the number of caregivers who would be able and willing to participate.

They might overestimate the number of current cases with early stage dementia, overlooking how many of them there are in which the early stage is on the cusp of moving to a later stage in which the degree of cognitive impairment will be too advanced for your intervention to be applicable. Instead of just relying on seat-of-the-pants rough estimates by staff members, you should conduct a careful investigation regarding the accuracy of those estimates by examining case records regarding client characteristics and trends regarding the arrival of new cases. You should also interview service providers about the specifics of their caseloads. You might even conduct a brief pilot test of your planned evaluation to see if recruiting and retaining participants is more problematic than anticipated.

9.2.4   Retaining Participants

Some people who agree to participate in your evaluation might not complete it, which can reduce your sample size. Some who are assigned to the intervention condition might not complete the intervention because attending all the sessions becomes too burdensome due to the demands of caregiving on their time, transportation difficulties, their own deteriorating physical or cognitive well-being, and so on. In addition, they might feel that the intervention is not the panacea they expected it to be. Those who are assigned to the control (or TAU) condition might stop participating because they are disappointed about not receiving the special intervention, especially if TAU doesn't seem to be very helpful. Sometimes the TAU protocol seems more boring or arduous to participants than the intervention being tested. For example, Shadish *et al.* (2001) found that, when evaluating family therapy for drug addiction and using discussion groups as the TAU control condition, the least motivated and most dysfunctional participants might be more likely to drop out of TAU than to drop out of family therapy.

The term for prematurely dropping out of an evaluation is *attrition*. When the rate of attrition is high, it can distort the meaning of evaluation results. For example, if the least motivated and most dysfunctional participants are more likely to drop out of the treatment condition, that will create a selectivity bias in which the treatment group participants on average are more likely to have better outcomes than the control participants. The reverse would be true if the least motivated and most dysfunctional participants are more likely to drop out of the control condition. When the attrition rate is higher for one treatment condition than the other, you should consider using an intent-to-treat (ITT) analysis when you analyze your results. ITT analyses use complicated statistical procedures for imputing posttest scores for participants who did not complete posttests. ITT analyses are controversial; you can learn about the controversy and alternate ITT data analysis approaches by reading Armijo-Olivo *et al.* (2009).

Many techniques have been suggested to try to minimize attrition (Rubin & Babbie, 2017; Shadish *et al.*, 2001). During recruitment and orientation, you can try to make sure that participants have reasonable expectations about how long it will take before they start noticing treatment effects. You can minimize the amount of time that elapses between recruitment and treatment onset. You can use measurement procedures that do not exceed the attention span, stamina, or resources of participants, and make sure they have accurate expectations of, and are not surprised (and thus alienated) by, their difficulty. When obtaining their consent to participate, you can make sure that you do not mislead participants by underestimating the demands of the measurement procedures, including possible difficulties regarding childcare, transportation, and scheduling. You can administer measures at the participants' residences if needed. Alternatively, you can reimburse them for transportation and childcare costs, and perhaps provide a childcare service for looking after small children at the measurement site. In addition to reimbursing participants for the time and costs of completing the measurements, you can offer a bonus reimbursement for completing the posttests and for not dropping out of the evaluation.

Some who drop out of the evaluation might have changed their residence and be hard to locate. Being older adults, some might have passed away before the time of the posttests. There's not much you can do about that, but at least you should anticipate it when estimating your sample size. To enhance retention of low-income or residentially transient participants, you can use some of the tracking techniques for finding them and trying to maintain their participation suggested by Rubin & Babbie (2017) and Shadish *et al.* (2001). One recommendation is to obtain ample information about how to find them. You should try to obtain the location information at the start of their participation, and you can seek it from them, from their friends, and from their relatives. You can also seek the information from agencies with which they are involved. You can develop relationships with staff members at those agencies who might be able to help you find them later. You can also give participants a card with information about how to contact you, the times of their treatment and measurement appointments, and a toll-free telephone number for leaving messages about changes in how to locate them or changes in appointment times.

9.3   Engage Agency Staff Meaningfully in Planning the Evaluation

As a first step in attempting to anticipate and avoid all of the above pitfalls (and perhaps some others), you should involve service providers and other relevant staff members in planning the evaluation. And they should be involved in all phases of the planning, including from the outset. Don't just explain to them what you want to do and why; listen to them! They probably know the day-to-day workings of the agency better than you do, and you can learn from their input about potential practical pitfalls and perhaps how to avoid them. For example, you might learn from them about difficulties that many clients might have in understanding or completing the measurement instruments you were considering. Or you might learn that the data collection procedures you were considering might be too burdensome for agency staff or clients. Perhaps you'll learn of resistances to your case assignment protocol ideas or of clinician resistances to withholding elements of the tested intervention from TAU clients. Although you can try to explain the importance of that withholding, your explanations might go in one ear and out the other among practitioners whose priorities are not your evaluation. It's worth repeating that you should consider their input seriously and try to come up with an approach that they will find acceptable.

9.4   Fostering Staff Compliance with the Evaluation Protocol Goes On and On

Engaging staff meaningfully in planning the evaluation is vital, but it is just the first step in fostering their compliance. As I have repeatedly mentioned, they have other priorities that can make it easy for them to forget about your evaluation protocol. For example, later in this chapter I will present a case study of an evaluation in which a new treatment program unexpectedly emerged in another agency – a program that provided the same intervention as the one being evaluated – and the director of the program being evaluated referred TAU clients to that program, thus fatally contaminating the evaluation's quasi-experimental design. She did that despite my spending countless hours brainstorming with her about the evaluation protocol and its design logic. But in the weeks that elapsed after the planning, either she forgot about the protocol or her concern for providing clients with the best treatment possible trumped her commitment to the protocol. I would not have learned that she had done that had I not had evaluation staff members on site at the agency every day monitoring the implementation of the evaluation protocol. They learned of what she had done too late to prevent it, but at least I learned about it. Had I not, I would not have been able to incorporate the problem in my interpretation of the evaluation results, which showed little difference in outcome between the intervention group and the (intended) TAU group.

Of course, it would have been better if my staff had learned of her intentions earlier, in time to prevent the referrals. Consequently, I regretted not having arrangements in place where my staff could meet weekly with the director and her staff to discuss how the evaluation was going and any changes they were considering that could impact the protocol.

One way to try to prevent or minimize problems in intervention fidelity is to give service providers a detailed treatment manual and train them in the intervention, including role-playing with simulated clients as well as booster sessions. Although that certainly might help, it might not be sufficient. Given the various factors that can lead to slippage from what they were trained to do, there should be ongoing meetings with service providers to discuss how they are implementing the intervention and any problems that come up (Royse *et al.*, 2016). Table 9.1 lists all the practical pitfalls discussed in this chapter and suggestions for offsetting them.

Table 9.1 *Practical pitfalls and suggestions for offsetting them*

Pitfalls	Suggestions
Miscellaneous pitfalls	• Involve all practitioners (along with other stakeholders) in planning the evaluation. • Don't just explain to them; incorporate their input! • Have evaluation staff on site day-to-day to meet with agency staff and monitor compliance with the evaluation protocol.
Overestimates of the expected number of participants	• Examine case records regarding client characteristics and trends regarding the arrival of new cases. • Interview service providers about the specifics of their caseloads. • Conduct a brief pilot test of your evaluation protocol to see if recruiting and retaining participants is more problematic than anticipated.
Problems in the fidelity of the tested intervention and of TAU	• Give service providers a detailed treatment manual and train them in the intervention, including role-playing with simulated clients as well as booster sessions. • Ongoing meetings with service providers to discuss how they are implementing the intervention and any problems that come up. • Record a representative sample of treatment sessions that can be viewed (or listened to) to check on the fidelity of each treatment condition.

Table 9.1 (*Cont.*)

Pitfalls	Suggestions
	• Have an expert in the tested intervention rate the fidelity of the recorded sessions. • Obtain fidelity ratings before the evaluation begins – perhaps in a brief pilot study.
Contamination of the case assignment protocol	• Locate the different treatment conditions at separate sites. • Send ongoing reminders to providers regarding what intervention should be provided to what participants.
Retention problems (minimizing attrition)	• Make reminder calls before treatment and measurement sessions. • Provide coffee, cold drinks, and snacks at the assessment sessions. • Use anchor points and tracking methods to locate residentially transient participants. • Use measurement procedures that are not too complicated or burdensome for participants. • Make sure that participants have reasonable expectations about how long it will take before they start noticing treatment effects. • Minimize the amount of time that elapses between recruitment and treatment onset. • Use measurement procedures that do not exceed the attention span, stamina, or resources of participants. • When obtaining their consent to participate, do not mislead participants by underestimating the demands of the measurement procedures, including possible difficulties regarding childcare, transportation, and scheduling. • Administer measures at the participants' residences if needed. • Use tracking methods to find, and try to retain participation by, low-income or residentially transient participants. • Reimburse participants for the time it takes to complete the pretests and posttests and any transportation and childcare costs they will encounter.

Table 9.1 (*Cont.*)

Pitfalls	Suggestions
	• Provide a childcare service for looking after small children at the measurement site.
	• Provide a bonus reimbursement for completing the posttests and for not dropping out of the evaluation.
All of the above and more	• Conduct a *pilot study* to
	° check the estimated rate of new referrals and agency estimates of sample size;
	° check and correct intervention fidelity;
	° check and correct problems in case assignment;
	° check and correct problems in data collection;
	° show the funding source that you have detected and resolved pitfalls.

9.5   Political Pitfalls

The findings of outcome evaluations can affect the vested interests of some stakeholders. Administrators are likely to hope for positive findings to bolster efforts to procure more funding, and they may fear negative findings that might impede those efforts. Service providers, too, can have vested interests in the findings because procuring more funding might help their sense of job security. Moreover, negative findings might reflect poorly on their professional competence. Nobody likes to hear that they are doing their job poorly. On the other hand, some stakeholders might hope for negative findings. They might include board members hoping to get rid of an administrator or a program that conflicts with their own values and beliefs. Perhaps some religiously conservative members would like to see a safe-sex education program fail and be replaced with an abstinence-only approach. Perhaps some less religious members would like to see a sex abstinence program fail and get replaced with a safe-sex approach. Some staff members might attempt to undermine the evaluation because they fear the prospect of negative findings or resent outsiders scrutinizing them. Some staff members might resent and undermine an evaluation because they view it as another way in which the agency administrator – whom they might dislike – is giving them more work to do just for the sake of administrative priorities.

It is important that you anticipate and be prepared to deal with these political pitfalls, because they can wreck a well-designed evaluation and turn it into a nightmare for the evaluator. And, if you are employed by the agency providing the program being evaluated, you might fear for your job security if certain stakeholders are displeased with the way the evaluation is being conducted or with its results.

9.5.1   In-House versus External Evaluators

If you are employed by the agency providing the program being evaluated, you are considered to be an *in-house evaluator*. If you are not employed by the agency but instead have a contract solely to carry out the evaluation, you are called an *external evaluator*. Being an in-house evaluator offers several advantages. Unlike an external evaluator, you are likely at the outset to know the ins and outs of the program, have relationships (ideally, good ones) with agency personnel, and be sensitive to the ways in which certain evaluation methods or designs might clash with existing agency procedures or staff sensitivities. As a staff member yourself, you might pose less of a threat than some outsider.

But being an insider offers several disadvantages, as well. Some coworkers might dislike you or envy you and consequently be less cooperative with the evaluation. Your own objectivity could be imperiled by your hope to obtain findings that won't displease your coworkers or threaten your own job security. Your coworkers, whose cooperation you need for the evaluation to be implemented properly, might be aware of your imperfections and may be less motivated to comply with the evaluation procedures than they would be if the evaluator was an outside "expert." Table 9.2 lists the various advantages and disadvantages of in-house versus external evaluators.

Table 9.2 *Advantages and disadvantages of in-house versus external evaluators*

		In-house evaluators	External evaluators
Advantages	Have good relationships (with agency personnel)	More likely	Less likely
	Sensitivity to the ways in which certain evaluation methods or designs might clash with existing agency procedures or staff sensitivities	More likely	Less likely
	Pose less of a threat to staff	More likely	Less likely

Table 9.2 (*Cont.*)

		In-house evaluators	External evaluators
	Regularly on site to monitor compliance with evaluation protocol	More likely	Less likely
	Esteemed by staff as an expert	Less likely	More likely
Disadvantages	Dislike or envy by coworkers	More likely	Less likely
	Pressure for positive outcome findings	More pressure	Less (but still some) pressure

Perhaps the most problematic aspect of being an in-house evaluator is the pressure you might feel to come up with positive outcome findings that support the effectiveness of the program being evaluated. But it would be a mistake to assume that external evaluators are immune from that pressure. They might hope to be rewarded with future evaluation contracts from the agency and know that those contracts might not be forthcoming unless they produce findings and recommendations that the agency's administrators desire. They might have had longtime friendly relationships with administrators and therefore not want to alienate them. Early in my career as an external evaluator for a support group for battered women that had the aim of motivating the women to leave the batterer, I was disappointed that my findings did not support the program's effectiveness. I believed that it was my ethical obligation to publish my findings so that better ways could be tried to achieve the aims of such support groups. But one of the program's staff members tried to pressure me to not publish my study by saying that it would threaten the future funding of the program and thus hurt the women it was [ineffectively] trying to help. Consequently, she said that if I published my report I was no better than the men who were batterers. As a guy who likes to think of himself as an enlightened feminist, that really hurt!

Another mistake is to assume that those who fund the program themselves lack vested interests in your outcome findings and are open to learning that the program being funded is ineffective. Another incident early in my career robbed me of that naïve assumption. I was an external evaluator for a grant funded by the National Institute of Mental Health (NIMH) with the aim of assessing how graduate schools of social work were using their NIMH training grants to prepare their master's students for eventual work in the field of community mental health. The evaluation findings indicated that, instead of using the funds to develop innovative community mental health curricula, they were using the funds on their traditional curricula. I naïvely expected the funders, who were the staff of the social work training branch of the NIMH, to appreciate that finding, but they did not. They had a vested interest in getting findings that cast a more favorable light on the programs that they were funding, and feared that my evaluation findings could be used by bureaucrats in other NIMH units to secure more funds for their units at the expense of the social work training unit. Consequently, they urged me to tone down my conclusions. Box 9.1 provides another experience earlier in my career that illustrates the vested interests of funders. It also illustrates most of the pitfalls covered throughout this chapter.

Box 9.1   The Evaluation from Hell

During the early 1990s I received a contract to be the external evaluator for an outcome evaluation of a federally funded child welfare demonstration project that served families in which substance-abusing parents were referred to the Child Protective Services (CPS) agency for child maltreatment. The project was provided by a special CPS unit that aimed to prevent out-of-home placements of children and improve parental functioning. Unlike other CPS units, the project's emphasis was on family preservation. In keeping with that aim, project staff were expected to conduct home visits much more frequently than in the other CPS units. The duration of treatment for each family was to be ninety days.

The evaluation was to include a quasi-experimental design that attempted to minimize a selectivity bias by having families served in the demonstration project be those who were referred when the project had an opening in their caseload that could handle 42 families at any given time. Families referred when the project's caseload was full received TAU in the other units of the agency. The outcome measures were to be administered in pretests and posttests before and after treatment for each of four cohorts that would receive ninety days of treatment per cohort during a one-year period. The pretests and posttests consisted of a standardized self-report scale that assessed parental risk of maltreatment and the need for out-of-home placement. Data regarding out-of-home placements were to be gathered from the CPS case records by evaluation research assistants. The project director assured me that the case records would be easily retrieved from the agency's computerized files. The entire evaluation design had been planned in close collaboration with the demonstration project's director, whom I met with in lengthy, repeated brainstorming meetings from the very start of the planning.

Uh Oh!

Early in the evaluation, my assistants found that none of the case record data had been entered into a computerized database. Consequently, they had to spend several hours per case trying to find and retrieve data from voluminous hard copies of case record files that were scattered in a disorganized way in various offices of the agency. Because of the unanticipated amount of time this required, I had to halve the evaluation's sample size. The sample size had to be further reduced when I learned from an on-site research assistant that she had accidentally overheard the project director talking about how she had decided to extend the ninety-day treatment period per case to one year. Therefore, instead of having results on four cohorts of 42 cases each during the year – for a sample size of 168 – I would have data on only one cohort of 42 cases, which reduced my probability of obtaining statistically significant results (see Chapter 11 regarding statistical power) from over 0.90 to less than a 50/50 chance. The smaller sample size also prevented the possibility of a planned multivariate analysis that would examine outcomes by different client characteristics.

Omigod!

About six months into the evaluation, one of my on-site research assistants found out that the project director had been referring many TAU cases to another agency that was providing a family preservation intervention similar to the one that her project was providing. She did this without the evaluation staff knowing, and it destroyed the logic of the pretest–posttest part of the outcome study. To make matters worse (was worse even possible?!), I learned that the project director never conformed to the case assignment protocol that she helped design when collaborating with me in the evaluation planning. Instead, she had been assigning the cases with the poorest prognoses to her unit on the rationale that they were the ones who most needed her unit's intensive services. By doing that, she did not just undermine the evaluation that she helped plan; she was demolishing its logic from the very start.

My final report had to be limited to an analysis of the out-of-home placement data found in the case records. My findings were inconclusive. The CPS executive director (to whom the project director reported) was unhappy with my inconclusive findings. She harshly criticized my methodology and demanded that I rewrite the report in a way that portrayed the project as effective. When I refused to do that, she said

Box 9.1   (Cont.)

that she would write her own evaluation report and base it on what the project service providers told her about their effectiveness. She said that she would submit her report to the funders and bury my report someplace where it would never be seen. I never saw or heard from her or the project director again. A few decades have elapsed, and I have never heard from the federal funders to inquire about not receiving my report as the external evaluator. I guess they weren't interested in my report and were satisfied with the executive director's "evaluation."

Lessons Learned

I learned some important lessons from this living nightmare, as follows.

- Don't rely too much on the recommendations in program evaluation textbooks that suggest that, if you involve stakeholders from the outset in planning an evaluation, you can promote compliance with the evaluation protocol. Such planning is necessary, but far from sufficient.
- Don't assume that administrator familiarity with some research methods will significantly improve the chances of compliance with the evaluation protocol. This project's director had a master's degree from a program that required two research methods courses.
- Promoting staff compliance with an evaluation's protocol requires close day-to-day on-site monitoring of compliance and regular meetings between program evaluation staff and agency staff to keep reminding staff of the protocol and to learn from them about any agency decisions that could affect the protocol.
- Don't assume that the funding source for a project being evaluated wants the evaluation to use a rigorous design and produce unbiased results. I learned this at a meeting in Washington, DC between staff of the federal bureaucracy that was funding the various demonstration projects around the country and administrators of those projects. The funding staff urged the project managers to eschew well-controlled outcome designs and instead use ones that were predetermined to produce results favoring program effectiveness. Why did they do that? My best guess is that they had vested interests in wanting to protect future Congressional funding to their bureau by telling Congress that the programs that they funded were successful. I guess that's also why they never contacted me wondering what had happened to the external evaluator's report.

9.6   Conclusion

A key tenet of organizational theory is the concept of *goal displacement*, which pertains to the tendency of organizations to neglect the formal goals in an organization's mission, and which an organization was established to pursue, in favor of goals associated with maintaining and growing the organization and the career interests of its personnel (Merton, 1957). Savvy program evaluators need to keep that concept in mind because, if program personnel care more about maintaining and growing their program and promoting their own careers than about attaining formal program goals, it would be naïve to suppose that compliance with a protocol designed to assess objectively the attainment of those formal program goals will remain high on their list of priorities.

But being savvy does not require being cynical. Not all program evaluations are wrecked by the pitfalls described in this chapter. Some of the evaluations that I have conducted were done in agencies where the idealistic administrators sincerely cared about program effectiveness and wanted and supported a rigorous, unbiased evaluation. When you have the good fortune to conduct evaluations in settings with administrators like them, you will likely have a successful and gratifying evaluation experience. Nevertheless, you should not naïvely assume that all of your evaluations will be conducted on smooth seas with the wind at your back. Some can be very challenging, and you should be prepared to anticipate the pitfalls discussed in this chapter and take the recommended actions to prevent those pitfalls from fatally harming your evaluation. If you do so, you will improve your chances of producing a successful evaluation despite the rough waters and the wind in your face.

9.7   Chapter Main Points

- It is important to assess intervention fidelity of both the tested intervention and TAU early and throughout an outcome evaluation (perhaps in a brief pilot study).
- If the outcome evaluation involves comparing groups that receive different treatment conditions, it is crucial that the clients in each group receive the treatment to which they were assigned. Minimally, ongoing reminders should be sent to the providers regarding what intervention should be provided to what participants.
- Recruiting enough people to participate in an experimental or quasi-experimental outcome evaluation is important. It will improve the chances that the differences in outcome between different groups in an experimental or quasi-experimental evaluation will be statistically significant. Refusal to

participate in a quasi-experimental evaluation can be alleviated by using a switching replication design. Rewarding clients for the pretests and posttests – perhaps with a reasonably priced gift card – also can help encourage participation.

- Relying on staff estimates of the number of cases that will be eligible for an evaluation within a certain time period can be hazardous.

- Participant retention efforts can include making reminder calls before treatment and measurement sessions, providing transportation to and from each assessment session, providing coffee, cold drinks, and snacks at the assessment sessions, using anchor points to locate residentially transient participants, using measurement procedures that are not too complicated or burdensome for participants, and providing rewards for completing the measurements – perhaps with a reasonably priced gift card.

- Conducting a pilot study can help check the estimated rate of new referrals and agency estimates of sample size, check for and correct any intervention fidelity problems, check and correct problems in case assignment, check and correct problems in data collection, and show the funding source that you have detected and resolved pitfalls.

- The findings of outcome evaluations can affect the vested interests of some stakeholders. Therefore, it is important to anticipate and be prepared to deal with political pitfalls that can wreck a well-designed evaluation.

- If you are employed by the agency providing the program being evaluated, you are considered to be an *in-house evaluator*. If you are not employed by the agency but instead have a contract solely to carry out the evaluation, you are called an *external evaluator*. Both types of evaluator have advantages and disadvantages.

- Program funders might have vested interests in outcome findings and want to see that the programs they are funding are being effective.

- Involving stakeholders from the outset in planning an evaluation is necessary, but not sufficient to assure compliance with the evaluation protocol.

- Promoting staff compliance with an evaluation's protocol requires close day-to-day on-site monitoring of compliance and regular meetings between program evaluation staff and agency staff to keep reminding staff of the protocol and to learn from them about any agency decisions that could affect the protocol.

- A key tenet of organizational theory is the concept of *goal displacement*, which pertains to the tendency of organizations to neglect the formal goals in an organization's mission, and which an organization was established to pursue, in favor of goals associated with maintaining and growing the organization and the career interests of its personnel. Savvy program evaluators will keep that concept in mind and realize that, if program personnel care more about maintaining and growing their program and promoting their own careers than about attaining formal program goals, then they might not care about complying with a protocol designed to assess objectively the attainment of those formal program goals.

- Being savvy about political pitfalls does not require being cynical. Some evaluations take place in agencies where administrators sincerely care about program effectiveness and will support a rigorous, unbiased evaluation. Nevertheless, you should not naïvely assume that all of your evaluations will be conducted in such settings. Some can be very challenging, and you should be prepared to anticipate the pitfalls discussed in this chapter and take the recommended actions to prevent those pitfalls from fatally harming your evaluation. If you do so you will improve your chances of producing a successful evaluation.

9.8   Exercises

1. In your first job after graduating, you have been assigned to design and conduct an outcome evaluation of a new, federally funded demonstration project in your agency. Describe the following.
    a. How you would feel about having this responsibility? Would you welcome it? Fear it? Why?
    b. What steps would you include in the evaluation to reduce the chances that the pitfalls discussed in this chapter will ruin your evaluation?
2. Get together with some of your classmates to see if any of you know of or can find an agency that has recently experienced an outcome evaluation. Interview at least one administrative staff member and at least one service provider at that agency regarding how they experienced the evaluation and how they feel about its protocol and findings. Also interview the evaluator who conducted the evaluation. On the basis of those interviews, write a report identifying the practical and political pitfalls discussed in this chapter that were evident in the evaluation, whether and how they were dealt with, and the impact they had on the evaluation protocol and its findings.

9.9   Additional Reading

- Lipsky, D. B., Seeber, R. L., Avgar, A. C., & Scanza, R. M. (2007). *Managing the Politics of Evaluation: Lessons from the Evaluation of ADR Programs*. Cornell University, https://pdfs.semanticscholar.org/2c52/27799121 ad162226d46d7580fd8090e026d9.pdf.
- Shadish, W. R., Cook, T. D., & Campbell, D. T. (2001). *Experimental and Quasi-experimental Designs for Generalized Causal Inference*. Boston, MA: Houghton Mifflin.
- Song, M., & Herman, R. (2010). Critical issues and common pitfalls in designing and conducting impact studies in education: Lessons learned from the What Works Clearinghouse (Phase I). *Educational Evaluation and Policy Analysis*, 32(3), 351–371.

PART IV

ANALYZING AND PRESENTING DATA

The chapters in this section will address how to analyze and present the data produced by formative, process, and summative evaluations. Most of those data will be quantitative in nature – that is, they are in the form of numbers and statistics. Some of the data will be qualitative – that is, they are in the form of words, not numbers. Chapter 10 will focus on analyzing and presenting both forms of data in connection to formative and process evaluations. Chapter 11 will cover analyzing data from outcome evaluations. After that, Chapter 12 will discuss how to present findings when writing evaluation reports. Finally, an Epilogue will examine the steps you can take throughout the evaluation to increase the chances that your report will be utilized and have an impact.

Chapter 10

Analyzing and Presenting Data from Formative and Process Evaluations

---

WHAT YOU'LL LEARN IN THIS CHAPTER

You'll learn how to use various data analysis techniques to analyze and present the results of evaluations of the kinds discussed in Chapters 3 and 4 – evaluations that do not seek to make causal inferences about program effects but instead aim to describe client needs and satisfaction and issues in program implementation. After learning about data analysis techniques for the quantitative methods used in formative and process evaluations, you'll learn about ways to analyze the data that emerge from the qualitative methods.

10.1   Introduction

The data collected in formative and process evaluations can come in either or both of two overarching types: quantitative data and qualitative data. This chapter will begin with a brief discussion of those two types of data. Because quantitative data are more likely to comprise the bulk of most evaluation reports, and because the methods for analyzing and reporting them are more systematic, the chapter will start with a focus on quantitative data analysis methods and will follow with a focus on qualitative data analysis methods.

10.2   Quantitative and Qualitative Data Analyses: Distinctions and Compatibility

Quantitative data are in the form of numbers, and pertain to things like age, percentages, and income. Qualitative data are in the form of words, and pertain to things like quotations, explanations, and lengthy statements that give more meaning to people's views and experiences. For example, a quantitative analysis in an assessment of needs for a homeless shelter might be in the form of the number of homeless people who say they would or would not use the shelter, their ages, how long they have been homeless, the proportions of them who are men and women, how strongly they agree or disagree with statements about views of the advantages and disadvantages of shelters, and so on. In contrast, a qualitative analysis in an assessment of needs for a homeless shelter might look for quotes or paragraphs that illustrate what using a shelter means to them or how strongly they feel about using or not using the shelter. For example, the quantitative analysis in a needs assessment or client satisfaction study regarding a shelter might find a surprisingly high proportion of those surveyed who say they would not even consider using the shelter. To give more meaning to that quantitative finding, an analysis of the qualitative data might yield quotations like the following (fictitious) statement from a homeless woman: "When I enter a shelter I lose my dignity. How can anyone have dignity in a crowded hovel where they have to wait in line to use filthy and often out of order toilets and showers, sleep on louse-infested bedding, and fend off those who try to rob or attack them. When I am on the streets I might often be physically uncomfortable, but I still have my dignity and can enjoy being near my buddies who will look after me."

Quantitative analysis and qualitative analysis differ, but are not incompatible. For example, if the quantitative survey had already been completed and analyzed, the foregoing quote can provide report readers with a deeper, more empathic understanding of the quantitative findings. If the survey were still being planned, seeing the foregoing quote from one person in a qualitative analysis might imply the need to conduct a survey to quantify the proportion of the target population that shares that woman's view or experience of shelters. The woman's statement might indicate the need to add items to a survey questionnaire – items that reflect the woman's reasons for not using a shelter or being dissatisfied with it. For example, an item about the likelihood of using a shelter might be followed by a checklist of reasons for not using a shelter that might include the following response categories:

unsuitable bathroom or shower conditions
unsuitable bedding
physically unsafe
being robbed

10.3 Descriptive Statistics

Suppose there are many respondents to your client satisfaction survey, say as many as 100 or more. Imagine what a nightmare it would be to read your report if you just listed each person's response to every survey item. Suppose one item asked clients to indicate on a seven-point scale how satisfied or dissatisfied they were with your agency: as follows:

1. Very dissatisfied
2. Moderately dissatisfied
3. Slightly dissatisfied
4. Neither satisfied nor dissatisfied
5. Slightly satisfied
6. Moderately satisfied
7. Very satisfied

Imagine stakeholders reading a list of 100 or more responses that looked like this:

2

3

7

5

4

1

6

3

7

2

5

1

6

4

etc.

They'd stop reading and perhaps complain about your competence. To make your findings readable and comprehensible, you'll need to use descriptive statistics that present your data in a manageable format. If the purpose is to show how many people had a particular response you'll need to use tables and graphs that display *frequencies*. If the purpose is to show the average degree of satisfaction or dissatisfaction you'll need to display measures of **central tendency** (i.e., mean, median, mode) and **dispersion** (i.e., standard deviation, etc.). Let's look first at how to display frequencies.

10.3.1 Frequency Distribution Tables and Charts

A frequency distribution lists each response category and the number (frequency) and proportion of respondents in each category. So, if most of the 200 respondents to your survey are satisfied, your frequency distribution table might look like the one in Table 10.1.

Many stakeholders prefer to see pictorial representations of frequencies – visual charts or graphs that display statistical results – and might become alienated if they are forced to grapple solely with tables with lots of numbers. One pictorial option that is commonly used is a pie chart that displays percentages as slices of a pie. You can create pie charts using statistical software packages or by searching online for a site that will enable you to choose the chart format you want, and create that chart after you enter your frequencies. One useful free site is that at https://bigcrunch.io/v/qdLz6FVFAhDU3pAcqLDmrt. Figure 10.1 displays a pie chart for the frequencies that were displayed in Table 10.1. Another oft-used pictorial option is a bar graph, which also can be created online or in statistical software, such as the one displayed in Figure 10.2.

Sometimes the categories of the data you want to display are so numerous that you need to collapse them into broader categories to make the frequency

Table 10.1 *Number and proportion of clients by level of satisfaction or dissatisfaction*

Level of satisfaction/ dissatisfaction	Frequency	Percentage	Cumulative percentage
Very satisfied	40	20	20
Moderately satisfied	60	30	50
Slightly satisfied	40	20	70
Neither satisfied nor dissatisfied	20	10	80
Slightly dissatisfied	16	8	88
Moderately dissatisfied	14	7	95
Very dissatisfied	10	5	100

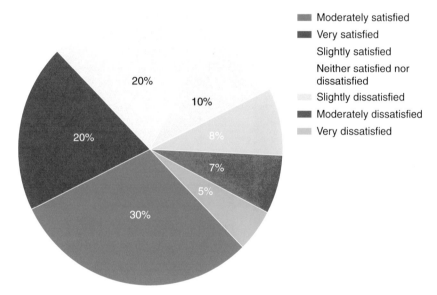

FIGURE 10.1 Pie chart of proportion of clients at different levels of satisfaction or dissatisfaction.

table manageable. For example, suppose you are reporting the ages of your 200 clients, and there is at least one person for every age between 14 and 88. It wouldn't make sense to have a separate frequency category for categories 18, 19, and everything in between up to 88. Instead, you should create a grouped frequency distribution table such as the one in Table 10.2. When your analysis is dealing with particular variables expressed as numerical quantities exhibited by each person in your survey, such as age, level of satisfaction score, number of years homeless, and the like, you can augment your frequency tables, charts, and graphs with measures of *central tendency* and *dispersion*.

Table 10.2 *Grouped frequency distribution of client ages*

Age	Frequency	Percentage	Cumulative percentage
70 and older	20	10	10
60 to 69	30	15	25
50 to 59	40	20	45
40 to 49	50	25	70
30 to 39	30	15	85
20 to 29	20	10	95
19 and younger	10	5	100

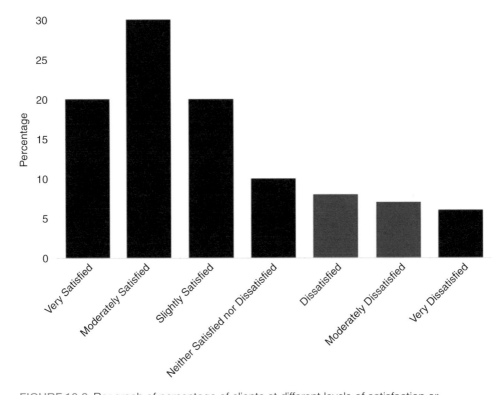

FIGURE 10.2 Bar graph of percentage of clients at different levels of satisfaction or dissatisfaction.

10.3.2 Central Tendency

Measures of central tendency include the *mean, median, and mode*. I am going to assume that you know the definitions of these terms from your prior education, but if you do not, you can google each one to find the definition. Instead of defining them, I want to call your attention to potential pitfalls in interpreting them and reporting them. For example, many people mistakenly interpret the mean as indicative of the typical value or the value closest to the middle of the range of values. To illustrate how that can be misleading, let's return to the example of client satisfaction scores that can range from 1 (very dissatisfied) to 7 (very satisfied). Suppose half of your 200 clients check 1. Very dissatisfied, and the other half check 7. Very satisfied. The mean would equal [100 × 1] plus [100 × 7] divided by 200. That would come to 800/200 = 4. But 4 on your scale would mean "Neither satisfied nor dissatisfied." If you were to report that on average your clients were neither satisfied nor dissatisfied, that would be very misleading because in fact half of your clients seem to love your program and half seem to hate it.

10.3.3 Dispersion

To avoid misinterpreting the mean, you can use measures of dispersion. One way to display dispersion would be in a frequency distribution. But when the number of possible values is more extensive – say as with age, income, and so on – frequency tables are less efficient ways to convey dispersion and are harder on the eyes than using a dispersion statistic. The most commonly used measure of dispersion is the *standard deviation*. The standard deviation depicts how far away – on average – most of the values are from the mean. For example, in the above bifurcated (love/hate) distribution of client satisfaction scores the mean would be 4, and the standard deviation would be 3. If you reported those two statistics, it would show that on average clients are scoring 3 points away from the mean of 4; that is, at 1 or 7. You could easily interpret that to your readers as indicating that about half of your clients appear to be very satisfied with your program and about half seem very dissatisfied with it. (Ideally, you would also have asked about their reasons for satisfaction or dissatisfaction – either via quantitative survey items or via in-depth probing qualitative interviews.)

10.3.4 The Influence of Outliers

Another way in which the mean can be misleading due to dispersion is when it is skewed by a small number of extreme values that are far away from most of the other values. Those far-away values are called *outliers*. Suppose, for example, that 90 percent (180) of your 200 clients score 7 (very satisfied) on your scale and 10 percent (20) score 1 (very dissatisfied). Your mean would be [20 × 1] plus [180 × 7] divided by 200, which would come to 1280/200 = 6.4. Not taking dispersion into account – in this case outliers – could result in the misleading interpretation that your clients are on average moderately satisfied. That's not too bad, but it ignores the fact that 90 percent of your clients are very satisfied. Again, a frequency distribution would help avoid this misinterpretation, but so would two additional central tendency statistics: the *median* and the *mode*. The median is the value in between the highest half of scores and the lowest half. In this example, the median would be about 7, because less than 50 percent of the scores are below 7. The mode, which is the most frequently occurring value, also would be 7. So, if you reported a mean of 4, a mode of 7, and a median of about 7, it would be apparent that the distribution of values was skewed, with the bulk of values at or near 7 and some outliers yanking the mean away from those values.

10.4   Analyzing Qualitative Data

Given the wide-open nature of qualitative evaluation methods, combined with the seemingly endless forms in which the words and paragraphs of qualitative data can appear, there are no simple steps for analyzing qualitative data. Consequently, students with math anxiety who expect qualitative evaluations to be a lot simpler than quantitative ones are often surprised at how much more challenging and labor intensive is the less structured process of analyzing reams of qualitative data.

10.4.1   Coding

Although there is no universal set of procedures for analyzing qualitative data, the typical way to begin is by *coding*, which involves classifying, or labeling pieces of data according to a concept they represent or depict. For example, suppose a homeless woman says "When I enter a shelter I lose my dignity. How can anyone have dignity in a crowded hovel where they have to wait in line to use filthy and often out of order toilets and showers, sleep on louse-infested bedding, and fend off those who try to rob or attack them. When I am on the streets I might often be physically uncomfortable, but I still have my dignity and can enjoy being near my buddies who will look after me." That quote might receive several codes. Those codes might read something like the following: "woman," "dignity," "emotion," "bathrooms," "sleep," "bedding," "fear," "safety," "friends," etc. Unlike quantitative analysis, it is not necessary to establish the code categories in advance, although you could do so. Instead, the code categories can emerge as you read the data. Notice in the above example that any piece of data can be given multiple codes, representing more than one concept. As you code your data, you should jot down *memos* to yourself about ideas that occur to you during the coding – ideas that might help you think about ways to synthesize the myriad data. For example, if the interview with the homeless woman contains a passage where she says "Heck, even the bathrooms at the state hospital weren't *that* bad," your memo might remind you to consider mental illness or deinstitutionalization as part of your analysis.

Box 10.1   Qualitative Data Analysis Resources and Software

- Analytic Software for Word Based Records: AnSWR
- Atlas.ti
- MAXQDA
- N-Vivo
- QDA Miner
- Qualrus
- Text Analysis Markup System (TAMS)
- T-LAB (www.tlab.it)
- Weft QDA

After all your chunks of data that vary in length (words, quotes, paragraphs, etc.) have been entered along with their codes into your word processor, you could search for certain words or codes to examine chunks of qualitative data that have commonalities or that form patterns. Alternatively, you can enter all of your data into a qualitative data analysis program, such as one of those listed in Box 10.1, and have it run the analysis.

Just as there is no set of simple rules or simple formula for collecting or analyzing qualitative data, there is no simple set of rules or formula for reporting the results of your analysis. You might use quotes to illustrate the deeper meanings of how people experience the phenomena in question. For the same purpose, you might present longer case vignettes. You might even blend in quantitative aspects, such as noting how many people complained about feeling unsafe in a shelter, what proportion of them were women, and so on.

10.5   Chapter Main Points

- Quantitative data are in the form of numbers, and pertain to things like age, percentages, and income.
- Qualitative data are in the form of words, and pertain to things like quotations, explanations, and lengthy statements that give more meaning to people's views and experiences.
- Quantitative analysis and qualitative analysis differ, but are not incompatible.
- To make your findings readable and comprehensible, you'll need to use descriptive statistics that present your data in a manageable format.
- If the purpose is to show how many people had a particular response, you'll need to use tables and graphs that display *frequencies*.

- If the purpose is to show the average of some numerical value, you'll need to display measures of *central tendency* (i.e., mean, median, mode) and *dispersion* (i.e., standard deviation, etc.).
- A frequency distribution table lists each response category and the number (frequency) and proportion of respondents in each category.
- Many stakeholders prefer to see pictorial representations of frequencies – visual charts or graphs that display statistical results.
- Pie charts display percentages as slices of a pie; bar graphs depict them as vertical bars that vary in height.
- If the categories of the data you want to display are very numerous, you'll need to collapse the categories into a grouped frequency distribution table.
- The mean should *not* be interpreted as indicative of the typical value or the value closest to the middle of the range of values.
- To avoid misinterpreting the mean, you can use measures of dispersion.
- The most commonly used measure of dispersion is the *standard deviation*. The standard deviation depicts how far away – on average – most of the values are from the mean.
- Another way in which the mean can be misleading due to dispersion is when it is skewed by a small number of extreme values that are far away from most of the other values. Those far-away values are called *outliers*.
- Given the wide-open nature of qualitative evaluation methods, combined with the seemingly endless forms in which the words and paragraphs of qualitative data can appear, there are no simple steps for analyzing qualitative data.
- Although there is no universal set of procedures for analyzing qualitative data, a commonly used way to begin is by *coding*, which involves classifying, or labeling, pieces of data according to a concept they represent or depict.
- Code categories can be determined in advance or they can emerge as you examine the data.
- Any piece of qualitative data can be given multiple codes, representing more than one concept.
- If your codes are emerging as you examine the data, you should jot down memos to yourself about ideas that occur to you during the coding – ideas that might help you think about ways to synthesize the myriad data.
- After all the chunks of qualitative data have been entered along with their codes into your word processor, you could search for certain words or codes to examine chunks of qualitative data that have commonalities or that form patterns. Alternatively, you can enter all of your data into a qualitative data analysis program and have it run the analysis.

- There is no simple set of rules or formula for reporting the results of a qualitative analysis. You might use quotes to illustrate the deeper meanings of how people experience the phenomena in question. You might present longer case vignettes. You might even blend in quantitative aspects, such as noting how many people expressed a particular concept.

10.6 Exercises

1. Go to the website https://bigcrunch.io/v/qdLz6FVFAhDU3pAcqLDmrt and create a pie graph and a bar chart for the following frequency distribution:

Age	Frequency	Percentage
70 and older	20	10
60 to 69	30	15
50 to 59	40	20
40 to 49	50	25
30 to 39	30	15
20 to 29	20	10
19 and younger	10	5

2. Using an online standard deviation calculator, calculate the mean and standard deviation for the following frequencies regarding the number of nights each of twenty homeless individuals slept in a shelter last month:
    0, 0, 0, 0, 0, 1, 1, 1, 1, 1, 1, 1, 2, 2, 2, 3, 3, 28, 30, 30

    Interpret the results.

10.7 Additional Reading

- Grbich, C. (2007). *Qualitative Data Analysis: An Introduction*. London: Sage.
- Miles, M. B., Huberman, A. M., & Saldana, J. (2020). *Qualitative Data Analysis* (4th ed.). London: Sage.

Chapter 11

Analyzing Data from Outcome Evaluations

WHAT YOU'LL LEARN IN THIS CHAPTER

You'll learn how to use various inferential data analysis techniques to analyze and present the results of the outcome evaluation designs discussed in Chapters 6 and 7 – evaluations that seek to make causal inferences about program effectiveness. You'll learn about the concept of statistical significance and the inferential statistics that are used to calculate it. You'll learn about mistakes that are commonly made when interpreting those statistics and the need to calculate the strength of program effects and their meaningfulness. You'll also learn about examining program effects in relation to program costs. Although analyzing program effectiveness typically is done using inferential statistics, the chapter will end with a brief look at how qualitative data analysis can also be used in outcome evaluations.

11.1   Introduction

Whereas the data analysis techniques discussed in Chapter 10 were for descriptive purposes, and the statistics described therefore are termed *descriptive* statistics, the techniques to be discussed in this chapter are for the purpose of inferring whether the outcome difference between groups, or between pretest data and posttest data, can be attributed to chance – that is, when the differences are not statistically significant. Therefore, the techniques to be discussed in this chapter are called *inferential* statistics. The chapter will begin with an explanation of the meaning of inferential data analysis, its utility, and its different types. Then it will discuss its limitations and why it is important to have a nuanced and balanced outlook regarding whether differences between groups are statistically significant. Then it will discuss the importance of going beyond statistical significance and considering the meaningfulness of differences that are *statistically* significant but perhaps not of a *magnitude* that is significant for *practical* purposes, which involves calculating and interpreting effect sizes and considering how meaningful the differences are in *practical* terms. It will also discuss the importance of assessing the costs of alternative interventions, programs, and policies in connection to their effects and benefits. The chapter will end with a brief look at how qualitative data analysis can be used in outcome evaluations.

11.2   Inferential Statistics

If you have ever played Scrabble or a card game, you know that just due to chance sometimes one player gets almost all the best Scrabble tiles or the best cards in the deck. Chance can also influence whether the best outcome scores are in one group versus another. Consequently, any time your outcome scores favor one group over another, or the posttest group of scores over the pretest group, savvy stakeholders will want to see an inferential statistic that indicates the probability that mere chance – and not the policy, program, or intervention being evaluated – could have caused the difference. When that probability is very low – usually at 0.05 or lower – chance is deemed implausible. When that happens the results are called *statistically significant*.

There are many types of inferential statistics that can be used to calculate the probability that the results can be attributed to chance. They are called *statistical significance tests*. Which test to use depends on the nature of the data. For example, a chi-square test is commonly used when the outcome data are in a yes/no format, such as when examining whether participants get re-arrested or referred for child maltreatment. A *t*-test is often used when comparing the mean scores of two groups or of pretests versus posttests. Analysis of variance (ANOVA) is used when comparing the means of more than two groups. Delving into all the different types of statistical tests and their calculations goes way beyond the scope of this book. You can take a course on statistics if you want to learn about that. If you do not take such a course – or even if you do and it leaves your head spinning – you'll need to find someone with statistical expertise to help you with the inferential analysis of your outcome data. To do the calculations, you'll need statistical software like SPSS or SAS and perhaps someone who knows how to use that software. Alternatively, you can go online and enter a search term like *t-test calculator*, *chi-square calculator*, or *ANOVA calculator*. Those online calculators let you enter your scores and then do the calculations for you. For example, a *t*-test calculator might show you a result like the following:

The *t* value is 3.34. The *p* value is 0.001. The result is significant at $p < 0.05$.

Different tests of significance are needed because outcome measures and study designs can be of diverse types, requiring statistical calculations of different kinds for their analysis. For example, comparing two means at the ratio level of measurement requires different calculations than when the outcome measure is at the ordinal level of measurement. An example of an ordinal level would be having treatment recipients provide a number from 1 (very rarely) to 5 (very often), perhaps with a midpoint of 3 (occasionally). The numbers are ordinal because they do not mean the actual number. For example, 5 (very often) does not mean five occurrences or five times more often than 1 (rarely). In contrast, at the ratio level of measurement the numbers really mean the number of something. For example, if one person binge drank five times last month and another did so one time, then five means five times, not very often, one means one time, not rarely, and five actually is five times more often than once.

Table 11.1 lists some of the more commonly used bivariate statistical significance tests and when they are used. The term *bivariate* means that only two variables are included, such as a group variable (i.e., treatment versus control) and an outcome variable (i.e., number or proportion of incidents, scale scores, etc.). There are additional tests that involve controlling for additional variables, which are called *multivariate* tests. Those more complex tests go beyond the scope of this book, and you can study statistics to learn more about them. For example, one multivariate test is called analysis of covariance (ANCOVA). It controls for pretest scores when comparing posttest scores. A bivariate alternative to ANCOVA in Table 11.1 is a *t*-test of change scores. Either of those two approaches would be preferable to a simple *t*-test when comparing the posttest scores of two groups that were quite different at pretest. For example, if Treatment A recipients improve from a pretest mean score of 40 to a posttest mean of 50, and Treatment B recipients improve from a pretest mean score of 20 to a posttest mean of 40, it would be misleading to just compare the mean of 50 with that of 40 because recipients of Treatment B started out with a lower score and actually improved more.

11.2.1 p Values and Significance Levels

Despite their different mathematical formulas and calculations, the different significance tests have essentially the same aim: to tell you the probability that the difference in outcome between the groups in your evaluation can be attributed to chance. They will all show that probability as a *p* value. For example,

Table 11.1 *Commonly used bivariate statistical significance tests when comparing the outcomes of two or more groups*

Name of significance test	When to use
t-test	When comparing the means of two groups when the outcome variable is at the ratio or interval level of measurement
Non-parametric *t*-test alternatives	When comparing the means of two groups when the outcome variable is at the ordinal level of measurement
Analysis of variance (ANOVA)	When comparing the means of three or more groups when the outcome variable is at the ratio level of measurement
t-test with change scores	When comparing the mean change from pretest to posttest of two groups
Chi-square	When comparing proportions in two or more groups with nominal data

if p equals 0.04, that means that your result can occur 4 times out of 100 just due to chance (i.e., the luck of the draw). The p value often gets confused with the significance level, but the difference between the two is important. The significance level is nothing more than some arbitrary cutoff point that social scientists have traditionally been willing to deem low enough to rule out the plausibility of chance as the explanation for the results. The traditional cutoff point is usually set at 0.05. Thus, if the significance test produces a p value of 0.04 ($p = 0.04$), the result would be deemed statistically significant and not due to chance.

11.2.2 Type II Errors

If the p value is above the significance level cutoff point (usually 0.05), the result is deemed not significant because chance cannot be ruled out. I mentioned above that the difference between the p value and the significance level is important. Here's why. Suppose your p value is somewhere around 0.06 or 0.07. It would be above a 0.05 significance level but still would show that your result can occur only 6 or 7 times out of 100 just due to chance. Although that is more than 5 times out of 100, chance would still seem pretty improbable. In fact, it would mean that there is a 93 or 94 percent probability that your results are *not* attributable to chance. So, if you get that result and conclude that the results did not support the effectiveness of the policy, program, or intervention being evaluated, you would be taking a pretty big risk of being in error when implying that the policy, program, or intervention is ineffective when it really might be effective. The error you would be risking is called a Type II error.

When evaluating outcomes in the social and human services, Type II errors can be very important and perhaps deserve a lot more emphasis than they get in many statistical texts or courses that focus so much on calculation of the p value and whether it meets the traditional cutoff point. For example, suppose you are evaluating a promising new program to prevent child maltreatment by parents with a substance-abuse disorder. Being effective with that target population would be quite a challenge, and at the time of writing I am unaware of any interventions for that population and outcome objective with strong research support regarding their effectiveness. If you make a Type II error when interpreting your inferential data analysis, you could be dismissing a program that might help a lot of children avoid maltreatment and a lot of parents the agony of being found guilty of child neglect or abuse. That's why you should not overrely on statistical significance when interpreting your outcome findings and why you should be sure to give ample emphasis to the remaining aspects of outcome data analysis to be discussed in this chapter.

11.3   Mistakes to Avoid When Interpreting Inferential Statistics

Table 11.2 lists four mistakes commonly made when interpreting the inferential statistics involved in outcome evaluations. These mistakes are often related to Type II errors and an overreliance on statistical significance. But, before elaborating on each of these mistakes, I want to make sure that I am not minimizing the importance of statistical significance. As I mentioned earlier, virtually any time that you have two or more groups of numbers the means or proportions of the two groups will differ at least to some degree. To illustrate this, every semester I divide the students in my program evaluation class into two groups. In one group are students who were the first-borns in their biological family, and in the other group are students who had older siblings. Then I ask them to count the number of letters in their last names. Almost every semester there is a difference in the mean number of letters between the two groups. To attribute that to anything but chance makes no sense to me because their birth order has nothing to do with their last names, and older and younger siblings in their original biological families will almost always have the same last names. (Even if there was a remarriage between the birth of the older and the birth of the younger, the chances are that the newest last name would be shared by the children.) The fact that differences in means for those two groups can be found consistently – differences that it would seem silly to attribute to anything other than chance – illustrates how easy it is to get *some* differences in outcomes between groups in an evaluation even when the program, policy, or intervention being evaluated is utterly worthless. Consequently, if we disregard statistical significance when attributing differences to treatment effectiveness, we are taking a big risk of another type of error – called a *Type I error* – in which we would be recommending the provision of ineffective programs, policies, or interventions to people who won't be helped by them and by providers who will be wasting their resources on something worthless instead of pursuing more effective alternatives to help people in need. Without forgetting the importance of Type I errors, let's now discuss the mistakes listed in Table 11.2.

11.3.1 Overreliance on Statistical Significance

This error can result in the remaining errors to be discussed and that appear in Table 11.2.

11.3.2 Disregarding Sample Size (Statistical Power)

Suppose I claim to be able to see the future, and to prove it I give you a coin and predict that if you flip it twice it will come up heads each time. Suppose you do so and it comes up heads each time. "Pure luck!," you'd say as you note that the

Table 11.2 *Mistakes commonly made when interpreting inferential statistics*

Type of mistake	Implication
Overreliance on statistical significance	Overlooking Type II errors, effect size, and substantive significance
Disregarding sample size (statistical power)	Sample size affects Type II error risk as well as the chance that a trivial result will be statistically significant
Disregarding effect size	Weak effects can be statistically significant with large samples; strong effects can fall short of significance with small samples
Overlooking substantive (practical) significance	Some strong effect sizes might not be meaningful; some weak effect sizes might be meaningful

odds of that result happening by chance are one in four (or one-half times one-half). "Okay," I respond, " if you are not impressed by the 100 percent accuracy of my prediction then flip it eight more times and it will come up heads again all eight times (making ten heads in a row)." Suppose you do so and it comes up heads every time. Then you might begin to wonder about my super powers, or, more likely, you'd look and notice that I gave you a two-headed coin. Why not say "Pure luck" after ten flips? Because the odds of ten successive heads are one-half to the tenth power, or less than one in a thousand (< 0.001).In other words, an outcome that is based on a large number of observations (i.e., a large sample) is less likely to be attributable to chance than the same outcome based on a small number of observations (i.e., a small sample). Using the same logic (that is, the same laws of probability), suppose I randomly assign four parents at risk of child maltreatment into two groups of two, and then have one group listen to an old Elvis Presley record to see if that will prevent child maltreatment, and then find that both listeners had no child maltreatment incident while the other two both did have such an incident. Would you say "Wow, a 100 percent effect-ive intervention!"? I hope not, because there would be a much greater than 0.05 probability that my results were due to chance. (The actual probability would be 0.17.) But what if instead of having my "treatment" group listen to Elvis singing "Hound Dog," I actually provided them with an effective intervention. Given the probabilities with a sample size that small, I would have had no chance of getting a statistically significant result even with a 100 percent effective interven-tion. These silly examples illustrate that as sample size increases, the probability of obtaining a statistically significant result (i.e., ruling out chance) increases, and that as sample size decreases the probability of obtaining a statistically sig-nificant result decreases.

The statistical term for that probability is *statistical power*. How to calculate statistical power goes way beyond the scope of this book and also beyond the scope of most introductory statistics texts and courses. Some books provide tables that show the statistical power for corresponding sample sizes (e.g., Rubin, 2013, p. 149), and there are some online calculators for it. Regardless of whether you find your statistical power in a table, online calculator, or via a statistical consultant, if your sample size is small you should take your power (or at least your small sample size) into account when interpreting any results that are not statistically significant. Pointing out your low statistical power or your small sample size when discussing your results will help dissuade readers from dismissing the possible value of your program and the need to test it out more, ideally with a larger sample. You should also consider statistical power when *planning* an outcome evaluation design because it will help you decide how big your sample needs to be to have a good chance of obtaining statistically significant results. Alternatively, it might not be feasible to get a sample large enough to provide ample statistical power. However, that might not discourage you from going ahead with the evaluation, especially if you expect to find a strong, meaningful effect size. Such an effect size, coupled with a high risk of a Type II error (low sample size), can be cited in making the case for supporting the potential value of your program and the need to test it further.

11.3.3 Disregarding Effect Sizes

As discussed in Chapter 7, effect sizes depict how much of a difference the intervention makes on the outcome goal. They do it in a way that can permit comparisons across evaluations that have different designs and different kinds of outcome measures. They are important to know so that the strength of the impact of one intervention approach can be compared with the strength of alternative approaches, as you will see soon when the calculation and interpretation of effect sizes are discussed. Another reason why it is important to consider effect sizes is that the *p* value does not tell you the *strength* of a program's impact. It is tempting to think that if Intervention A's *p* value is lower (more statistically significant) than Intervention B's, then Intervention A had stronger effects. However, suppose Intervention A is evaluated in a local agency with a sample size of 100 participants, including 50 who receive the tested intervention and 50 who do not receive it. The recipients have a re-arrest rate of 38 percent versus 62 percent for the non-recipients. A chi-square test will produce a *p* value of 0.02. Suppose Intervention B is tested statewide or regionally with 10,000 participants, 5000 who receive the intervention and 5000 who do not. The recipients have a re-arrest rate of 48 percent versus 52 percent for the non-recipients. A chi-square

Table 11.3 *Illustration of two chi-square results with different sample sizes*

Result A (sample size = 100)		
Outcome*	Intervention A	Control group
Re-arrested	19 (38%)	31 (62%)
Not re-arrested	31 (62%)	19 (38%)

*$p = 0.02$

Result B (sample size = 10,000)		
Outcome*	Intervention B	Control group
Re-arrested	2400 (48%)	2600 (52%)
Not re-arrested	2600 (52%)	2400 (48%)

*$p < 0.0001$

test will produce a *p* value that is less than 0.00001. That *p* value is much lower than Intervention A's *p* of 0.02 despite Intervention A having a much better (38 percent) re-arrest rate than did intervention B. Both *p* values are statistically significant at the 0.05 significance level, but due to the sample size difference the more impressive *p* value is for a less impressive effect. These (fictitious) results are displayed in Table 11.3. You might want to use an online chi-square calculator to plug the numbers in and see the results. You might also want to play around by changing the proportions and sample sizes to see what different chi-square results emerge.

11.4   Calculating and Interpreting Effect Sizes

As mentioned above, different types of effect size statistics are needed for different forms of outcome data. For example, when the data involve comparing groups in terms of the proportion of their participants who get re-arrested (as in Table 11.3), the appropriate effect size statistics are *odds ratios* and *risk ratios*. When the data involve comparing mean outcome scores between two groups, the applicable statistic is the *between*-group effect size, which is called Cohen's *d*, which equals the difference between the two group means divided by the pooled standard deviation of the outcome scores across both groups. In *one-group* pretest–posttest evaluations a *within-group* effect size statistic can be calculated, which equals the difference between the posttest mean score and the pretest mean score divided by the pooled standard deviation across sets of scores. The relatively simple formulas for the between-group and within-group

Table 11.4 *Formulas for between-group and within-group effect sizes*

Between-group formula (Cohen's d)[a]	Within-group formula
(treatment group mean *minus* control group mean) *divided by* pooled standard deviation	(posttest mean score *minus* pretest mean score) *divided by* pooled standard deviation

[a] The means are for outcome (or posttest) scores. The pooled standard deviation is across all outcome scores.

effect sizes are displayed in Table 11.4. Let's begin by examining within-group effect sizes because they can be used to add value to the simplest (and inferentially weakest) outcome evaluation design: the one-group pretest–posttest design.

11.4.1 Within-Group Effect Sizes

Chapter 7 discussed the value of within-group effect sizes in that they can be compared with published average (aggregated) within-group effect sizes of the treatment and control groups in the various RCTs that provided the research support for the intervention being evaluated in an agency's one-group pretest–posttest evaluation. You can reexamine Chapter 7 if you want to learn more about that process and how it enhances the value of one-group pretest–posttest outcome evaluations. Here we'll just look at a user-friendly way to calculate the within-group effect size, using online calculators. The first step is to use an online *standard deviation* calculator to compute the group's pretest mean and standard deviation and posttest mean and standard deviation. The next step is to enter those means and standard deviations into an online *effect size* calculator. Box 11.1 shows how to complete these steps using some fictitious data given in Table 11.5 and the online calculators. At the bottom of Box 11.1 you can see three effect sizes, Cohen's d, Gates' *delta,* and Hedges' g. The latter two (Gates' *delta* and Hedges' g) are *within-group* effect sizes. As you can see, the difference between them is rather trivial (0.06), and both indicate that the posttest mean is about three tenths to about one-third of a standard deviation better than the pretest mean. The published benchmarks against which you can compare your within-group effect size probably use Hedges' g, which adjusts for the different sample sizes of the various studies from which the benchmark effect sizes were aggregated. So, to be precise, you can use Hedges' g, which adjusts for your sample size, when comparing your within-group effect size against the benchmarks.

Box 11.1   Calculating a Within-Group Effect Size

Table 11.5 *Some fictitious data for calculating a within-group effect size*

Case number	Pretest score	Posttest
1	30	20
2	40	30
3	50	45
4	35	30
5	40	35
6	35	25
7	40	35
8	35	30
9	30	21
10	40	32
11	30	20
12	35	30
13	40	31
14	35	25
15	35	24
16	50	40
17	45	40
18	25	17
19	30	27
20	40	33
21	45	31
22	35	26
23	40	30
24	30	20
25	35	25
26	40	30
27	43	36
28	37	29
29	33	27
30	30	22

Step 1. Enter the pretest scores in the online calculator www.alcula .com/calculators/statistics/standard-deviation/. Enter the scores as com-ma-separated data (numbers only):

30,40,50,35,40,35,40,35,30,40,30,35,40,35,35,50,45,25,30,40,45,35,40,30,35, 40,43,37,33,30

Click on **Submit Data**

Result:

Mean = 36.93

Standard deviation = 5.94

Step 2. Replace the pretest scores in the box with the posttest scores to get the posttest mean and standard deviation:

20,30,45,30,35,25,35,30,21,32,20,30,31,25,24,40,40,17,27,33,31,26,30,20,25, 30,36,29,27,22

Click on **Submit Data**

Result:

Mean = 28.86

Standard deviation = 6.45

Step 3. Go to the online effect size calculator www.socscistatistics.com/ effectsize/default3.aspx.

Step 4. Scroll down to the **Enter Your Values** boxes and enter your pre-test mean, standard deviation, and sample size in the Group 1 boxes:

Mean: 36.93

Standard deviation: 5.94

Sample size: 30

Step 5. Enter your posttest mean, standard deviation, and sample size in the Group 2 boxes:

Mean: 28.36

Standard deviation: 6.45

Sample size: 30

Click on **Calculate**

Result:

Cohen's d = 1.30

Gates' *delta* = 1.36

Hedges' g = 1.30

11.4.2 Between-Group Effect Sizes

If your evaluation is comparing the mean posttest scores of two groups, you would follow the same steps as in Box 11.1 except that, instead of inserting pretest and posttest scores and calculating pretest and posttest means and standard deviations, you would insert each group's posttest scores and calculate each group's means and standard deviations. Then you would enter those means and standard deviations in the effect size calculator box just as in Box 11.1. Cohen's d would be your between-group effect size, which equals 1.30 in Box 11.1, meaning that the treatment group mean is about three tenths of a standard deviation better than the control group mean. As discussed in statistics books (such as Rubin, 2013), between-group effect sizes that are at least 0.80 are considered to be strong, meaning that the treatment is having a relatively strong impact on the target problem or goal. Between-group effect sizes that approximate 0.50 are considered to have a moderate impact, and between-group effect sizes that are near or below 0.20 mean that the treatment is considered to be having – at best – a weak impact. Meta-analyses of studies that have aggregated the between-group effect sizes of published RCTs have provided the basis for those considerations.

Cohen's d is like a z-score, which is a statistic that represents how many standard deviation intervals a particular value falls above a mean. Likewise, Cohen's d shows how many standard deviations the treatment group mean falls above the control group mean. A table of z-scores (Rubin, 2013, p. 88) shows that a strong Cohen's d of 1.3 indicates that the treatment group's mean is better than 90 percent of the control group scores. A strong Cohen's d of 0.80 indicates that the treatment group's mean is better than 79 percent of the control group scores. A moderate Cohen's d of 0.50 indicates that the treatment group's mean is better than 69 percent of the control group scores. These same proportions would apply to within-group effect sizes, but would represent the proportion of pretest scores exceeded by the posttest mean.

11.4.3 Why Divide by the Standard Deviation?

You might be wondering why we need to divide the difference in outcome scores by the standard deviation. Why isn't it enough to just say that one group's mean of 37 is better than another group's mean of 28? The answer is that dividing by the standard deviation enables us to compare the relative strengths of different interventions that are evaluated with different outcome measures. Suppose, for example, that the data in Table 11.5 are scores on a scale on which parents self-report their knowledge and attitudes about parenting. Suppose an evaluation of a different positive-parenting intervention uses as its outcome measure the number of times each parent is observed exhibiting an abusive behavior, and finds a mean of 4 for the treatment group versus 7 for the control group. Suppose that the pooled standard deviation is 1. Cohen's d would equal 7 minus 4 divided by 1, or $d = 3$, meaning that the treatment group's mean is three standard deviations better than the control group's mean, indicating a much stronger effect than in Table 11.5. By comparing the effect sizes, we can make the different results comparable despite their different outcome measures and the difference in the range of scores possible on the different measures. Thus, if your outcome evaluation results have a Cohen's d of 3 you would not only be able to mention your statistical significance and the raw number difference in outcome between groups; you could also legitimately conclude that the effectiveness of your program, policy, or intervention is very strong compared with most outcome evaluations.

11.4.4 A Caution

If your treatment and control group pretest scores are far apart to begin with, Cohen's d could be inapplicable and misleading. Suppose, for example, that you are evaluating the impact of a voluntary positive-parenting class in a family service agency. Parents (or prospective parents) who opt to participate in the program might be more motivated than the non-participants to learn to be good parents. Consequently, due to a selectivity bias the participants may already have read more and learned more about positive parenting than the non-participants before the class began and before the pretest was administered. Suppose the participants' pretest mean score is 60, and the non-participants' mean is 40. Let's further suppose that the class has a weak impact, such that the participants' mean increased to 64, while the non-participants' mean stayed at 40. Finally, suppose that the posttest standard deviation of both groups was 8. Dividing the 24-point difference at posttest by the standard deviation of 8 would result in an extremely strong Cohen's d of 3.0, meaning that the class had a very strong impact on positive-parenting scores, with the participants' mean exceeding more than 99 percent of the non-participants' scores. But the participants' mean was higher to begin with and increased only by 4 points (from 60 to 64 – a 7 percent increase). Thus, the misleading Cohen's d of 3.0 would seriously exaggerate the impact of the class.

As discussed in Chapter 7, whenever your comparison groups design is vulnerable to a selectivity bias, you can extend it to a switching replication design by providing the intervention to the non-participants after the posttest. Suppose you did so and their scores also increased by 4 points (a 10 percent increase from 40 to 44). Rather than using Cohen's d, it might make more sense to calculate a within-group effect size for each group to convey the approximate degree of impact the class was having. Another caution, however, is that you would need to test the statistical significance of the difference in change scores to assess the probability that it could be due to chance.

11.4.5 Odds Ratios and Risk Ratios

For outcome measures that are at the nominal (yes/no) level of measurement and that therefore cannot be calculated in terms of means and standard deviations, the applicable effect size statistics are *odds ratios* and *risk ratios*. To explain these two effect sizes, let's use the example of re-arrest rates in an evaluation of an in-prison pre-release program that aims to prevent re-arrest after release.

Odds Ratios. Suppose that 20 of the 100 recipients of the program get re-arrested as compared with 50 percent of the 100 non-recipients. With only 20 out of 100 re-arrests, 80 of the 100 (80 percent) of the program recipients had a successful outcome, as indicated by an 80 percent success rate, whereas 50 out of 100 (50 percent) of the non-recipients had a successful outcome, which is a 50 percent success rate. The 20 percent re-arrest rate of the recipients means that 80 percent (80 out of the 100) avoided re-arrest, and thus this group had an 80 percent success rate. Thus, there were 4 successful outcomes for every unsuccessful outcome, because 80 is 4 times 20. The ratio of successful outcomes to unsuccessful outcomes therefore is 4 (or 4 to 1). In contrast, the ratio of successful to unsuccessful outcomes for the non-recipients is 50/50, or 1 (1 to 1). The odds ratio for this evaluation therefore is 4 because the odds of a successful outcome for the recipients (4 to 1 or 4/1) are four times greater than the odds of a successful outcome for the non-recipients (1 to 1 or 1/1).

Risk Ratios. Risk ratios are akin to odds ratios except that instead of pertaining to desirable (successful) outcomes they pertain to undesirable (unsuccessful) ones. Using the results in the above re-arrest example, the program recipients had a 20 percent rate of undesirable outcomes (rearrests), whereas the non-recipients had a 50 percent rate of undesirable outcomes. The risk ratio is calculated by dividing the rate of undesirable outcomes of the recipients by the rate of undesirable outcomes of the non-recipients. In this example it would be 0.20 divided by 0.50, which equals 0.40. The 0.40 risk ratio means that the risk of re-arrest for the recipients was only 4/10 (four-tenths) the risk of the non-recipients. With odds ratios, the higher the number, the better, because odds ratios pertain to desirable outcomes. An odds ratio that does not exceed 1, therefore, is disappointing because it would mean that the ratio of successful outcomes for recipients is no better than the ratio for non-recipients. The reverse is the case with risk ratios, in which the desirable result is less than 1, meaning that the risk

Table 11.6 *Illustration of desirable and undesirable odds ratios and risk ratios regarding graduating versus dropping out*

Nature of outcome measure	Desirable outcome	Undesirable outcome
Graduation rate	Odds ratio > 1	Odds ratio < 1
Dropout rate	Risk ratio < 1	Risk ratio > 1

of an undesirable outcome is lower for the recipients than for the non-recipients. And a risk ratio of more than 1, heaven forbid, would mean that recipients fared worse than non-recipients. Table 11.6 illustrates desirable and undesirable odds ratios and risk ratios.

11.5 Overlooking Substantive (Practical) Significance

The mistake listed in the bottom row of Table 11.2 which appeared earlier in this chapter pertains to the *substantive significance* of your outcome results. Other terms for substantive significance are *practical significance* and *clinical significance*. Each of these terms refers to the meaningfulness of the results. Some strong effect sizes might not be meaningful, and some weak effect sizes might be meaningful.

To illustrate what is meant by the substantive significance, or meaningfulness, of a finding, consider the example of a positive-parenting intervention. Suppose Intervention A has a statistically significant result with 40 percent of recipients being found to have committed a future incident of child abuse or neglect as compared with 50 percent of the non-recipients. Those proportions would yield an odds ratio of 1.2 and a risk ratio of 0.8 because the 60 percent successful outcomes among recipients is 1.2 times the 50 percent successful outcomes among non-recipients, and the 40 percent undesirable outcomes among recipients is 0.8 times the 50 percent undesirable outcomes among non-recipients. Those ratios might not knock your socks off, but remember that they refer to found incidents of child abuse or neglect.

Next, suppose that an evaluation of Intervention B uses scores on a self-report scale of knowledge and attitudes about parenting – one with a serious vulnerability to a social desirability bias – as the outcome measure and gets a statistically significant result with a very strong Cohen's *d* of 2.0, meaning that the recipients' mean score is 2 standard deviations better than the non-recipients' mean score (or better than 79 percent of the non-recipient scores).

It would be a mistake to conclude that the strong effect size for Intervention B automatically means that Intervention B's effects are more meaningful than

Intervention A's effects. Many child welfare practitioners might conclude the opposite, arguing that they'd prefer an intervention that will reduce the incidence of child abuse or neglect by 20 percent (from 50 percent to 40 percent) rather than an intervention that has a stronger effect on a self-report scale vulnerable to a social desirability bias – a scale that might have little bearing on what parents actually do with their children, especially when they experience stress. In fact, when I present this example to my program evaluation students, virtually every one of them responds by deeming the Intervention A outcome to have more substantive significance than the Intervention B outcome.

As you may have already surmised, interpreting the substantive significance of a finding involves making value judgments about the nature of the evaluation, the magnitude of the effect size, and the meaningfulness of the outcome measure. A strong effect size found for a practically unimportant outcome measure or in a shoddily designed evaluation can have less substantive significance than a weaker effect size found in a well-designed evaluation with a more meaningful outcome measure. Only when two evaluations are equivalent regarding strength of design and meaningfulness of the outcome measure will the larger effect size tend to have more substantive significance.

11.6   Cost-Effectiveness and Cost–Benefit Analyses: Evaluating Efficiency

In light of budgetary constraints, administrators and other stakeholders are likely to wonder about the cost and efficiency of programs and interventions. However, in light of those budgetary limits, costs should also be of concern to everyone who cares about helping people. Suppose, for example, that a child welfare intervention has practitioners making home visits to each family four days per week and has an odds ratio of 1.5, meaning that for every successful outcome (no future incident of child maltreatment) among the non-recipients, there are 1.5 successful outcomes among the recipients. Let's call it Intervention A and assume that its cost limits its caseload size to a maximum of 100 recipients, who in an evaluation would be compared with 100 non-recipients. The 1.5 odds ratio would mean that 75 of its 100 recipients had a successful outcome if 50 of the 100 non-recipients had a successful outcome. Suppose another child welfare intervention – we'll call it Intervention B – is somewhat less intensive, involves two (half as many) visits per week, and can therefore afford to serve twice as many clients as Intervention A. Suppose its odds ratio is 1.2, in which there were 120 successes for its 200 recipients and 100 successes for its 200 non-recipients. Because Intervention B could serve twice as many clients as Intervention A, it was able to achieve 45 more successes than Intervention A despite its less impressive odds ratio. Therefore, if you are a service provider who doesn't care one whit about administrative costs, and who cares only about preventing child maltreatment, you would prefer that your agency's finite budget be spent on Intervention B – the less effective but more efficient option – so that twice as many families could receive services and consequently a lot more incidents of child maltreatment could be prevented.

The two main ways to evaluate efficiency are *cost-effectiveness analysis* and *cost–benefit analysis*. Both approaches examine the costs of providing a program. They differ in that cost–benefit analysis also tries to estimate the monetary value of the outcome – that is, the monetary value of the *benefits*. Monetizing benefits, however, is much more complex and requires a lot more assumptions than does monetizing costs. Moreover, it's hard to attach a dollar figure to intangible humanistic benefits like reducing family conflict, alleviating a retired combat veteran's PTSD symptoms, providing respite to a caregiver of a loved one suffering from dementia, helping nursing home residents feel less depressed and better about their lives, or comforting terminally ill hospice patients in their final days.

Because cost-effectiveness analysis is less complex, avoids dubious assumptions about the monetary value of social welfare outcomes, and does not try to attach a dollar figure to the value of the psychosocial well-being of program recipients, you are much less likely to become involved in a cost–benefit evaluation in your career than in a cost-effectiveness evaluation that only involves assessing the costs of a program, not the monetary value of its benefits.

But trying to assess the costs of a program is itself complex and requires technical expertise in cost accounting. For example, Newcomer *et al.* (2015) identified some (not all) of the costs of an after-school dropout prevention program that aimed to reduce the incidence of dropping out of high school by high-risk students. The costs are listed in Box 11.2.

Box 11.2   Costs of an After-School Dropout Prevention Program

- Costs to students
  - Loss of wages from after school part-time jobs
- Costs to school and others
  - Loss of classroom use after school
  - Costs to parents regarding taking time off from work and transporting students
  - Consultant wages related to training teachers and setting up the program
  - Cost of computer software created for after-school dropout programs

- Cost of texts
- Salaries and benefits of full-time and part-time teachers for after-school work
- Extra building maintenance costs after normal hours (i.e., janitor, etc.)
- Materials and supplies (workbooks, paper, pencils, marker pens, etc.)
- Travel costs for field trips
- Costs of additional insurance

Attaching a dollar figure to the costs in Box 11.2 is not as straightforward as you might imagine. It involves accounting concepts such as "variable versus fixed costs, incremental versus sunk costs, recurring versus nonrecurring costs, hidden versus obvious costs, future costs, opportunity costs, and so forth" (Rubin & Babbie, 2017, p. 330). Consequently, if you ever do conduct a cost-effectiveness evaluation, you are probably going to need to consult an accountant. Although they acknowledged the difficulty in monetizing the benefits of program outcomes, Newcomer *et al.* attempted to identify some of the key benefits of the dropout prevention program. Those benefits are listed in Box 11.3.

After completing the inferential data analysis in a cost-effectiveness analysis, the next step is to calculate the *cost-effectiveness ratio* by dividing the sum of program costs by the number of outcome successes attributable to the program. For example, if the total cost of the dropout prevention program is $200,000, and only 10 of its 100 participants wind up dropping out of high school – compared with 60 of the 100 non-participants – then the program prevented 50 dropouts (10 versus 60). Dividing the $200,000 cost by the 50 successes means that the program cost per dropout prevented was $4,000. If a *cost–benefit ratio* were completed with those results, it would compare the monetized benefits of those 50 successes with the total cost of the program. Thus, if each prevented dropout saved society $50,000, it might not be too difficult to convince legislators to allocate more funding to the dropout prevention approach because 50 times $50,000 equals $250,000, which exceeds the cost of the $200,000 program by $50,000. Thus, the case could be made that society will profit $50,000 for every $200,000 it spends on funding programs like it. Not a bad investment! Moreover, the cost of renewed funding of the existing program would be less than $200,000 because sunken start-up costs would not be required for some equipment and some consultants to train teachers and set up the program.

However, cost-effectiveness analyses and cost–benefit analyses require one more step, which involves performing a *sensitivity analysis*. A sensitivity analysis

---

Box 11.3   Some Key Benefits of a Dropout Prevention Program

- Monetized benefits (and losses) to participants
  - Increased participant earnings
  - (Participant loss of welfare payments)
  - (Increased participant taxes)
- Monetized benefits to others
  - Increased tax revenue
  - Decreased welfare payments
  - Reduced incarceration and judicial costs (assuming that more dropouts means more crime)
- Non-monetized benefits to participants
  - Self-confidence associated with graduating from high school
  - Being a better educated citizen
- Non-monetized benefits to others
  - Crime victims' pain and suffering of crime victims (assuming that more dropouts means more crime

---

is completed using computer software and adjusts the costs and benefit dollar amounts according to alternate assumptions regarding things like renting versus buying, tapering off of program effectiveness over time, changes in tax rates, increases in wages, inflation, and so on.

11.7   Qualitative Data Analysis

Qualitative data are most commonly used to generate new insights and deeper understandings, such as identifying some needs of homeless people that had not been considered in advance or deepening an understanding of why some home-less people prefer street living over shelters. However, some have suggested that qualitative data analysis methods can be used to generate and test ideas about whether a program was effective and why. Suppose, for example, a one-group pretest–posttest evaluation finds improvement from pretest to posttest. Even if the quantitative data regarding the difference between pretest and posttest are not statistically significant, in-depth qualitative case studies can be conducted with cases that did and did not exhibit improvement to try to ferret out what program or client factors distinguish the improvers from their counterparts who did not improve. Maybe the program really is effective, but only when certain program elements are experienced as helpful by certain clients. And when the pre-to-post improvement is significant, a qualitative analysis can foster a deeper understanding of the elements of the program that clients perceived as most helpful and why, and the ways in which clients changed as a result of those elements. Newcomer *et al.* (2015) discuss conducting a qualitative comparative analysis (QCA) for the purpose of yielding causal inferences. They recommend using software that can "compare the constellations and interactions among conditions and the outcome" (Newcomer *et al.* 2015, p. 582). The analysis can be rather complicated. For example, Newcomer *et al.* (2015, p. 582) mention a "minimization algorithm, using Boolean logic (or $+$, $/$, and $\times$) that identifies the specific combination of variables that are sufficient for occurrence or non-occurrence of the outcome."

11.8   Chapter Main Points

- Statistical significance tests assess the probability that mere chance – and not the policy, program, or intervention being evaluated – could have caused the difference in outcomes between treatment conditions. When that probability is very low – usually at 0.05 or lower – chance is deemed implausible. When that happens the results are called statistically significant.
- Different tests of significance are needed because outcome measures and study designs can be of diverse types, requiring statistical calculations of different kinds for their analysis. Four common tests are *t*-tests, analysis of variance, and chi-square.
- Despite their different mathematical formulas and calculations, the different significance tests have essentially the same aim: to tell you the probability that the difference in outcome between the groups in your evaluation can be attributed to chance. They will all show that probability as a *p* value.
- The significance level is nothing more than some arbitrary cutoff point that social scientists have traditionally been willing to deem low enough to rule out the plausibility of chance as the explanation for the results. The traditional cutoff point is usually set at 0.05. If the *p* value is below the cutoff point, the result is deemed statistically significant. If it is above the cutoff point, the result is deemed not significant because chance cannot be ruled out.
- Failing to rule out chance risks a Type II error, which can be an important error, especially when the *p* value is close to being significant, the sample size is small, and the difference between groups might be meaningful.
- As sample size increases, the probability of obtaining a statistically significant result (i.e., ruling out chance) increases, and as sample size decreases the probability of obtaining a statistically significant result decreases.

- The term *statistical power* refers to the probability of obtaining a statistically significant result.
- Effect sizes depict how much of a difference the intervention makes on the outcome goal. They do it in a way that can permit comparisons across evaluations that have different designs and different kinds of outcome measures.
- Four mistakes commonly made when interpreting inferential statistics are as follows: (1) overreliance on statistical significance; (2) disregarding sample size (statistical power); (3) disregarding effect-size; and (4) overlooking substantive (practical) significance.
- Cohen's *d*, a between-group effect size, equals the difference between two group means divided by the pooled standard deviation of the outcome scores across both groups.
- In *one-group* pretest–posttest evaluations a *within-group* effect size statistic can be calculated, which equals the difference between the posttest mean score and the pretest mean score divided by the pooled standard deviation across sets of scores.
- Between-group effect sizes and within-group effect sizes both show how many standard deviation intervals the mean of one group of outcome scores falls above the mean for the other group of outcome scores.
- If the treatment and control group pretest scores are far apart to begin with, Cohen's *d* could be inapplicable and misleading due to a selectivity bias.
- For outcome measures that are at the nominal (yes/no) level of measurement and that therefore cannot be calculated in terms of means and standard deviations, the applicable effect size statistics are *odds ratios* and *risk ratios*.
- Odds ratios depict the ratio of the fraction of successful outcomes for recipients divided by the fraction of successful outcomes for non-recipients. A desirable odds ratio should exceed 1.0.
- Risk ratios depict the ratio of the fraction of unsuccessful outcomes for recipients divided by the fraction of unsuccessful outcomes for non-recipients. A desirable risk ratio should be less than 1.0.
- The two main ways to evaluate efficiency are *cost-effectiveness analysis* and *cost–benefit analysis*. Both approaches examine the costs of providing a program. They differ in that cost–benefit analysis also tries to estimate the monetary value of the outcome – that is, the monetary value of the *benefits*.
- Monetizing benefits is much more complex and requires a lot more assumptions than does monetizing costs. Moreover, it's hard to attach a dollar figure to intangible humanistic benefits.

11.9   Exercises

1. Using your school's online literature database, try to find one outcome evaluation of a program, policy, or intervention for each of a through d, below.
   Discuss what you find with your classmates and instructor.
   a. The results supported effectiveness, and the authors addressed the effect
      size or substantive significance of the findings.
   b. The results supported effectiveness, but the authors did not address the
      effect size or substantive significance of the findings.
   c. The results did not support effectiveness, and the authors mentioned
      statistical power or the possibility of a Type II error.
   d. The results did not support effectiveness, but the authors did not men-
      tion statistical power or the possibility of a Type II error

2. Suppose your one-group pretest–posttest evaluation found the following
   scores:
   Pretest scores: 10, 11, 12, 13, 14, 15, 16, 17, 18, 19
   Posttest scores: 14, 15, 16, 17, 18, 19, 20, 21, 22, 23
   a. Go to the online calculators mentioned in this chapter for calculating
      standard deviations and means (www.alcula.com/calculators/statistics/
      standard-deviation/) and effect size (www.socscistatistics.com/effectsize/
      default3.aspx).
   b. Find your within-group effect size for the above scores.
   c. Interpret the implications of your effect size regarding how well your
      agency's practitioners are implementing TFCBT in light of the bench-
      marks reported in the article by Rubin *et al.* (2017) in the References and
      discuss your interpretation with your classmates and instructor.

3. Go to the online statistical power calculator website at www.danielsoper.
   com/statcalc/calculator.aspx?id = 47. When you get to that site, calculate
   power for a *t*-test at three different levels of Cohen's *d*: weak (0.20), moderate (0.50), and strong (0.80). Note the minimal sample size you would need
   for each level.

4. Suppose the dropout rate in a high school is 50 percent among very-high-risk
   entering ninth graders. Suppose an evaluation of a new dropout prevention
   program finds that 80 of the 100 entering ninth graders graduate in four
   years.
   a. What are the odds ratio and risk ratio for the results of the dropout pre-
      vention program (compared with the pre-existing dropout rate)?
   b. Suppose the total monetized cost of the dropout prevention program was
      $90,000. What would its cost-effectiveness ratio be?

c.   In light of the likely estimated monetized benefits to students and society, do you think the cost–benefit ratio of the program would strongly support advocating its future funding? Why or why not? (You need not estimate actual dollar values to answer this; very rough guesses will suffice.)

11.10 Additional Reading

- Enter the search term "within-group effect-size benchmarks" and read at least two of the benchmarking articles you find.
- Cohen, J. (1988). *Statistical Power Analysis for the Behavioral Sciences* (2nd ed.). New York, NY: Lawrence Erlbaum Associates.
- Johnson-Motoyama, M., Brook, J., Yan, Y., & McDonald, T. P. (2013). Cost analysis of the strengthening families program in reducing time to family reunification among substance-affected families. *Children and Youth Services Review*, 35(2), 244–252.
- Ragin, C. (1987). *The Comparative Method: Moving beyond Qualitative and Quantitative Strategies*. Berkeley, CA: University of California Press.

Chapter 12

Writing and Disseminating Evaluation Reports

> **WHAT YOU'LL LEARN IN THIS CHAPTER**
>
> You'll learn how to write and disseminate an evaluation report in a manner that will appeal to, and improve the chances for utilization by, stakeholders. You'll see the importance of tailoring the writing style and format of the report to your target audience, and how that might require you to write differently than when you write for an academic audience, like your professors. You'll learn about the components of an evaluation report and tips regarding the contents and style of each component. You'll also get some tips for improving your writing in general.

12.1   Introduction

Now that you've learned the ins and outs of designing and conducting an evaluation, here comes what might be for you the hard part: communicating your work in such a way as to have an impact on your target audience. Just how hard will depend on how well you have comprehended the previous chapters of this book and whether you have successfully completed courses in which you had to write and then receive critical appraisals of your writing. If you did complete such courses, you probably learned that good writing does not come easy. Often the thing you write seems perfectly clear to you, because you know what you are thinking and trying to say, and you understand your topic. But your readers might not share your expertise, and they can't read your mind. Consequently, if you are receiving feedback on your drafts, you might have to go through several revisions before the feedback reassures you that your writing is clear, understandable, and interesting to read. I've found that to be the case with some of my best doctoral students – those who consistently exhibit mastery of research concepts in their exams and in their class participation, but who have difficulty writing about their own dissertation ideas in a way that is terse, clear, and understandable. So, if the prospect of writing an evaluation report daunts you, you are not alone. In the case of writing evaluation reports, the challenge is greater because you are no longer writing to please professors and instead writing for an audience that probably will get alienated by a report that contains academic jargon. Let's begin this chapter, then, by considering how to tailor your report to your audience.

12.2   Tailor to Your Audience

Being a successful writer is like being a successful standup comedian. You need to tailor what you say and how you say it to your audience. You would not tell dark humor jokes about death in a eulogy at a funeral, but you might do so in a standup routine with an audience of young adults at a local comedy club. By the same token, you should not write for an audience of non-academic administrators or other stakeholders like you would write for a doctoral dissertation committee comprised of persnickety pedants. If you want your report to have an impact on decision-makers, you should begin by determining who are the key decision-makers you want to make sure will read your report and what writing style and format are most likely to influence them.

Likewise, you should write your report in a politically sensitive manner. Doing so is vital if you want stakeholders to utilize your report and seriously consider implementing its recommendations. You should imagine how you would react to your report draft if you were one of the stakeholders. Imagine how you would feel upon seeing your report if you had their responsibilities and had to worry about how your conclusions might reflect upon how well they were carrying out those responsibilities and their chances to achieve certain aspirations (securing more funding, for example). Having imagined yourself in their shoes, you should try to anticipate the kinds of objections they might have to your conclusions and the reasoning for those objections.

12.3   Writing Style and Format

Key decision-makers, like most administrators and stakeholders, have neither the time nor the inclination to carefully read lengthy, academic-style reports filled with the kinds of details that might thrill some of your professors. For them, the report needs to be short (perhaps no more than ten pages) and snappy, with mostly short sentences in active voice and language that most high-school sophomores would understand easily. As suggested by Grob (2015), the report should have an uncluttered layout, use bright colors, and put the main points in large, bold font and perhaps set aside from the narrative. But, as with many good things in life, you should not overdo it. You are not writing a comic book. Your audience should not feel like they are being talked down to. Striking the right balance is a lot easier for me to recommend than for you to do. Like learning to walk a tightrope, you'll need some practice. Also, you should show drafts incrementally to colleagues and request their blunt critical feedback to each iteration as you try to get the report right.

12.4   Involve Key Stakeholders

If you want to improve the chances that your evaluation will have an impact, you should include key stakeholders like program administrators and other staff members in developing the report. Their inclusion is especially important regarding the conclusions and claims you develop in the report. In fact, before you develop conclusions and claims, you should ask them to suggest the conclusions and claims that they would make in light of your findings. Patton (2008) suggests asking them to identify which of their conclusions and claims are the most important and which – in their view – have the strongest support in your data analysis. For example, outcome evaluation findings that support program effectiveness, but lack statistical significance, might lead to a claim that the program appears to be effective. That claim might fit in the category of very important, but not in the category of having strong support. Patton further recommends that, after engaging stakeholders in the process of suggesting conclusions and claims, you should engage in a dialogue with them regarding the conclusions and claims that will appear in the final report. Those that appear should follow from and be supported by your data, and you should distinguish between those conclusions or recommendations that are strongly supported by the data and those with less support. Ultimately, your report's conclusions and recommendations should not be yours alone. Instead, they should result from a collaboration with key stakeholders.

12.5   Ethical Issues

Although you should be sensitive to stakeholder concerns and collaborate with them in developing conclusions and recommendations, you should resist the temptation to go overboard in trying to please them. Resisting that temptation might be difficult, especially if you are an in-house evaluator whose job performance will be rated by one or more stakeholders. And if you are an external evaluator whose income depends at least in part on securing future evaluation contracts, it will be tempting to stay in the good graces of stakeholders by slanting your conclusions to their liking. Writing a misleading report out of self-interest concerns, however, is unethical. Although you should not arrogantly and insensitively ignore the input and views of stakeholders, you should not abandon your scientific integrity in an effort to please them. It might be hard to decide where to draw the line in being responsive to stakeholders in your conclusions and recommendations, but your own self-interest should not influence that decision. You should be honest in presenting your findings and conclusions, but, as Posavac and Carey (1985, p. 295) admonish, you should not be "honest to the point of being tactless."

    With these caveats in mind, let's now look at each section of the report with an eye to how to tailor each section to an audience of key decision makers, administrators, and other busy stakeholders.

12.6   Report Components

The report should be preceded by an executive summary. The first section of the report should be the introduction, which might include (or precede) a brief literature review, followed by your methodology, findings, discussion and recommendations, references, and appendices – in that order. Let's now take a closer look at each of those sections, beginning with the executive summary.

12.6.1 Executive Summary

For busy executives and other key decision-makers, the executive summary might be the only part of your report that they read carefully. Grob (2015) calls it the most important part of your report and suggests that it not exceed two pages (although there is not universal agreement about that maximum, it should not be much more than a page or two longer). Grob further recommends that the executive summary should concentrate on findings and recommendations, putting findings a little more than halfway through the first page, and putting recommendations around the middle of the second page. The coverage of the methodology in the executive summary should be brief and in plain language, perhaps no more than a short paragraph. The summary should be easy on the eyes, with fonts and margins that are of an ample size (but don't overdo the typographical enhancements). Avoid footnotes; they come later, if at all. Use headlines and paragraphs that begin with sentences that contain the paragraph's main points. The report that follows the executive summary can flesh out the details of the summary (Grob, 2015). An example of a narrative of a fictitious executive summary without the bells and whistles of colors, special spacing, etc. appears in Box 12.1.

Box 12.1   An Example of an Executive Summary Narrative

Executive Summary

This evaluation asked whether caregivers of older individuals can be trained to effectively provide evidence-based life review therapy to alleviate depression among older adults with mild cognitive impairment. Using a one-group pretest–posttest design with no control group, we relied on two indicators to answer that question:

- Ratings of the fidelity of recorded life-review sessions between caregivers and care recipients; and
- A mean within-group effect size statistic and its comparison with published benchmarks that depict the average degree of improvement among life review recipients in the published research supporting the effectiveness of life review when provided by mental health professionals.

We also assessed whether having caregivers provide the intervention would improve the quality of the relationship between the caregiver and care recipient.

Findings

- **Caregivers can be successfully trained to provide evidence-based life review therapy with treatment fidelity.**
  A national trainer and expert in life review therapy gave high ratings to the fidelity of videotaped sessions of caregivers providing life review therapy.
- **Caregivers can provide life review therapy effectively to alleviate depression among older adults with mild cognitive impairment.**
  Care recipients improved on average about as well as did recipients of life review in the published studies supporting its effectiveness and far above the average degree of improvement by control group participants.
- **Having caregivers provide the life review intervention *might* improve the quality of the relationship between the caregiver and care recipient.**
  The scores on the scale measuring the quality of the relationship between the caregiver and recipient improved substantially, with a strong effect size.
  However, with no control group and no published benchmarks on the impact of life review on quality of relationship, this finding is only tentative.

Recommendations

Our findings strongly support the plausibility of the notion that caregivers can be successfully trained to provide life review effectively and with fidelity to alleviate depression among older adults with mild cognitive impairment. The findings also tentatively suggest that providing the intervention might improve the quality of the relationship between the caregiver and care recipient. Therefore, our evaluation supports the following recommendations:

- Unless and until stronger, more controlled outcome evaluations yield findings that contradict ours, agency efforts to recruit and train caregivers to provide life review therapy to their care recipients should continue to be funded;
- Unless and until stronger, more controlled outcome evaluations yield findings that contradict ours, funding should be provided to train caregivers in more agencies nationwide in light of the baby boomer generation's reaching old age and the consequent likely shortage of resources to help reduce depression among older adults;
- Provide funding for randomized clinical trials to see if findings like ours are replicated in control group designs.

12.6.2 Introduction and Literature Review

The first part of the main narrative of your report should succinctly introduce readers to the problem that your evaluation has addressed. Summarizing the existing literature and research on the problem as briefly as possible (while not omitting important parts in a biased fashion), it should tersely convey the extent and importance of the problem, what has been done before by others to address the problem, and how all of that provided the rationale for your evaluation and its aims. In short, readers should be able to understand why your evaluation was needed, its importance, and its objectives. Although accomplishing all this probably will require briefly reviewing some literature, this section could be simply labeled *Introduction*. Some (Royse *et al.*, 2016) have suggested having a separate *Literature Review* section, but in the interests of brevity and appealing to a non-academic audience, you might want to briefly summarize the relevant literature within the Introduction section. Or not – remember your *audience* and write your report in a manner that you think will maximize its impact on them.

Regardless of where you cover prior literature, be sure to avoid tediously reporting the details of related works separately. For example, if four separate sources have documented the needs of an aging baby boom generation – let's call the four authors Burns, Dylan, Ginsberg, and Rubin – you might say, in one sentence, "Four recent studies have shown that the aging of the baby boom generation has resulted in a shortage of mental health professionals to meet the increasing prevalence of depression among older adults (Burns, 2015; Dylan, 2016; Ginsberg, 2018; Rubin, 2019).

The priority of the Introduction section is that the reader should immediately see the need and importance of your evaluation. The sequence of the Introduction's elements can be remembered with the mnemonic *PRO*, as follows:

- **Problem**: Scope, importance, prior efforts
- **Rationale**: Why your evaluation was timely, needed, and important
- **Objective**: The aims of your evaluation

You might want to use bold subheadings for each of the above elements if you think that will work best for your audience.

12.6.3 Methodology

The next section of your report describes the details of how your evaluation was conducted; that is, its evaluation *methods*. To make this section more user-friendly, you might want to use bold subheads for each main component of the methodology, as follows:

- **Design** (if not already reported in your evaluation aims)
  - Quantitative? Qualitative?

- ○ Logical arrangements
- **Participants**
  - ○ How many people participated?
  - ○ How were they selected or recruited?
  - ○ What were their characteristics?
- **Measurement**
  - ○ Measurement instruments used (scales, etc.)
    - ○ Cite source(s) regarding their reliability/validity
  - ○ Data collection methods

12.6.4 Results (Findings)

This section reports the results of your data analysis. If you think your audience would prefer some brief interpretation or discussion of each result at the time it is presented, you might want to label this section *Findings* instead of *Results*. Otherwise, you can wait for the next section (Discussion) for all the interpretations and discussion. Keeping your audience in mind, you should not overwhelm readers with all of your results or the statistical minutiae of the results. You should limit this section to the most important findings, only – those that have the greatest bearing on the main implications and recommendations of your report. You might find this difficult to do; it is only normal for investigators – scientific researchers and evaluators alike – to think that all of their findings are important. This is another area in which it is advisable to show a draft of your report to some colleagues and request their blunt critical feedback. You should keep in mind the astute admonition by Chronbach *et al.* (1980) regarding the impulse to document everything as "self-defeating thoroughness" (cited by Royse *et al.*, 2016, p. 388).

Infographics. Your audience will probably want to see your main statistical findings portrayed pictorially using infographics, such as graphs or charts. You can create visually appealing graphs and charts using word processing programs or statistical software like Excel or SPSS. There also are many online sites that can help you create infographics. Some offer to do so for free, but be forewarned, they might require payment to allow you to download your creation. Just like statistical findings, however, you should not overwhelm your readers with too many infographics. Present them sparingly, just to highlight your key findings. Some tips suggested by Newcomer *et al.* (2015) for using infographics in evaluation reports are as follows.

- Limit the number of graphs or charts to about one or two that pertain to your most important findings.

- Keep them simple, with just a few slices in a pie chart, just a few bars in a bar graph, and just a few rows and columns in a table.
- Make the text and numbers large enough to read.

Two commonly used types of infographic are pie charts and bar graphs, as displayed in Figures 12.1 and 12.2. Notice the different titles for the two pie charts

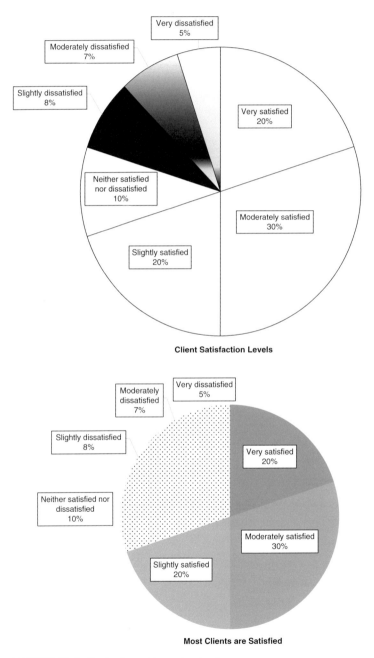

FIGURE 12.1 Illustration of two pie charts.

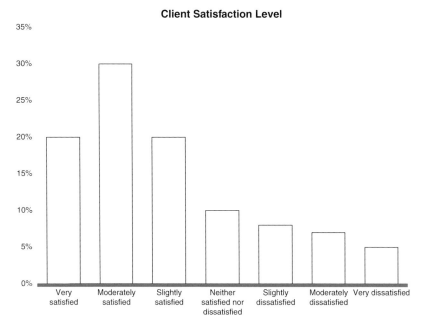

FIGURE 12.2 Illustration of a bar graph.

in Figure 12.1. The first is accurately titled "Client Satisfaction Levels." The second goes a step further. To convey the main point of the chart, it is titled "Most Clients are Satisfied." Either title would be acceptable, but you might opt for the second title if you think your audience would prefer a title that goes beyond blandly labeling the data in the infographic and interprets the story conveyed by the picture. You might notice in these figures that perhaps the pie chart – especially the top one – has too many slices. It might be easier on the eyes of stakeholders if it were reduced from seven to five levels of satisfaction (i.e., from seven to five slices).

12.6.5 Discussion

In this section you can discuss alternative ways to interpret your results and explain the interpretation that you think is the most appropriate. Then you should develop recommendations for action based on your conclusions, followed by an acknowledgment of the most relevant limitations of your methodology. For example, suppose an outcome evaluation uses a switching replication design to assess the effectiveness of a program that aims to improve positive parenting and prevent child maltreatment among parents with substance-use disorders thought to be at high risk for child maltreatment. Suppose the sample size is small, with low statistical power and with results that fall a tad short of statistical significance but with a meaningful effect size. Box 12.2 illustrates part of a possible Discussion section for that scenario.

> **Box 12.2   Illustration of Part of a Discussion Section for an Outcome Evaluation**
>
> The lack of statistical significance in our outcome findings means that we cannot with certainty rule out chance as the reason that our treatment group results were better than the control group results. However, several considerations imply that it would be a serious mistake to conclude that our program was ineffective. One is that our small sample size limited our chances of getting statistically significant results, due to low statistical power. That, combined with our strong and clinically meaningful effect size and the fact that our results were close to being statistically significant, implies a serious risk of a Type II error (deeming an effective program to be ineffective). The main methodological limitation of our evaluation was the lack of random assignment of participants to treatment versus control conditions. However, research design textbooks agree that our use of a switching replication made our design one of the strongest quasi-experimental designs in that it controlled for a selectivity bias almost as well as a randomized clinical trial. Therefore, our findings imply the following recommendations.
>
> **Recommendations**
>
> - Provide funding that will enable our program to continue unless or until another treatment approach for the target population is found to be more effective.
> - Provide enough funding to enable our program to treat a larger number of clients and thus be amenable to a further evaluation, this time with adequate statistical power.

You should avoid the temptation to omit mentioning the limitations of your evaluation. No evaluation in our field is flawless. Don't fear looking incompetent by acknowledging your evaluation's flaws. If you acknowledge your limitations, you'll look more competent than if you don't acknowledge them. However, don't go overboard when acknowledging your limitations. You don't want your readers to think that your evaluation (and their reading it) was a waste of time. In fact, it's probably a good idea to couple each limitation with a brief explanation of why your evaluation has value despite that limitation. For example, if you were unable to use randomization when forming your treatment and control groups, you might mention that you compensated for that by using a switching replication design or by noting the fact that each group's characteristics and pretest scores were very similar. Likewise, if 50 percent of your agency's clients did not respond to your client satisfaction survey, and if most of those who did respond reported being dissatisfied, you could support the value of your survey despite the non-response flaw by noting that, even in the unlikely case that all of the non-respondents were satisfied, your survey has found that at a minimum a sizeable subgroup of clients were not satisfied.

Discussing Negative Findings. Many outcome evaluations produce results that imply that a program is ineffective. Stakeholders with a vested interest in results that depict the program as successful probably will be disappointed with such findings. To increase the chances that they will incorporate your recommendations – perhaps by modifying the program's services – rather than become defensive and attack your methodology, you should discuss the negative findings tactfully, perhaps commenting on how skillful the providers were in implementing the program's interventions or the commendable extra efforts they exerted in being responsive to client needs. Rather than portray the program as a failure, emphasize feasible, practical recommendations for improving it. Ideally, you would have alerted stakeholders in the planning stage of your evaluation of the possibility of disappointing results and your obligation to report such results.

Although you should be tactful in discussing negative findings, you should expect – and resist – efforts by stakeholders to pressure you to hide such findings or spin them in a biased way to make the outcome look more successful than it really was. As discussed in Chapter 9, resisting such pressures will be more difficult if you are an in-house evaluator whose performance ratings or job security can be jeopardized by unhappy stakeholders. It might also be difficult if you are an external evaluator who has close collegial relationships with the disappointed stakeholders or who hopes to secure future contracts for evaluations involving the agency. But resist them you must; as an ethical evaluator you are obligated to report negative or positive findings and to do so in an unbiased fashion. Moreover, if stakeholders fear that your findings will endanger their program's funding, all the tact in the world might not prevent them from being displeased with you.

What If Parts of the Evaluation Could Not Be Completed? It is not uncommon for a well-designed evaluation to contain elements that could not be completed. Sometimes this happens due to unforeseen external events. Sometimes it is because certain evaluation participants fail to follow through as planned. For example, you might be conducting an outcome evaluation of a treatment intervention in a residential treatment center for youths with behavioral problems. Suppose that the treatment manual calls for ten weekly therapy sessions. Suppose further that your evaluation plan calls for a switching replication design in which the control group will receive the intervention after both groups are posttested and then receive another posttest ten weeks later. The plan might even include qualitative interviews with each youth after the quantitative portion of the evaluation has been completed. Suppose that, while you are in the midst of your evaluation, the state agency overseeing residential treatment centers for youths enacts a new policy requiring that no youth remain in a residential facility for longer than three months (about twelve weeks). If so, you would not have enough time to complete the switching replication part of your design, which requires twenty weeks. Likewise, you would not have time to complete the after-treatment qualitative interviews.

Your findings would be limited to the first posttest. Your design has been weakened because, without its switching replication element, it is much more vulnerable to a selectivity bias (given the very real possibility that without random assignment the two groups might not be equivalent). The design has been further weakened by the loss of its qualitative component.

How do you handle this unanticipated snag in the design when writing your report? To begin, you should not feel that this unfortunate development reflects negatively on your competence as an evaluator, because there was no way for you to anticipate it. Things like this commonly happen even with the best evaluators and their best-laid plans. You simply must do the best you can with the limitations in your design (for example, reporting the first posttest results, only) and then making sure that in your Discussion section you mention the elements of the design that could not be completed, explain why you were forced to jettison them, and point out how their loss weakened your design.

Nobody is perfect, not even the best evaluators, and sometimes – being human – design elements get lost due to imperfections in their design or in the way they implemented it. Even then, the Discussion should be thorough about what happened and the consequent limitations in the evaluation. To omit that coverage in your Discussion – or even to downplay it – would be dishonest and unethical. Don't be shy about laying it all out there for the readers. Stuff happens even to the best of us.

12.6.6 References

Immediately after you have concluded your discussion section and made your recommendations, you should provide a References section that lists – in alphabetical order of the first author's last name – all of the literature that you have cited in your report. You could use the format like the one used in the narrative and References of this book. For example, when citing a previous book that I wrote, in the narrative you might say, "Rubin (2013) suggested that …." Or, "statisticians have recommended … (Rubin, 2013)". Then, in your reference section you could list that citation as follows:

Rubin, A. (2013). *Statistics for Evidence-Based Practice and Evaluation* (3rd ed.). Belmont, CA: Brooks/Cole/Cengage Learning.

The American Psychological Association (APA) provides a helpful guide for citations and references at https://apastyle.org. However, remember your audience; the reference format you choose should be one that your audience prefers. If you are in any doubt, it's probably best to use the APA style.

12.6.7 Appendices

Depending on the length and complexity of your report and the various tables and infographics that you'd like to include, you might want to attach an appendix to the end of it. The appendix could include tables and infographics that you feel are too important to omit but that were too tangential to your main findings and conclusions to insert in the main body of your report. Other possible inserts for an appendix might include copies of measurement instruments or materials provided to participants, such as informed consent forms, and so on.

12.7   Summary of Mistakes to Avoid

Box 12.3 summarizes the main mistakes to avoid in writing your report. The last item in the list is one that was mentioned just briefly in this chapter, but important nonetheless. Your report will be much more readable if the sentences are written in *active voice*, which means that the subject of the sentence is the doer of the action in the sentence. If the sentence is structured in such a way that the subject is the recipient of the action, then the sentence is written in *passive voice*. An example of active voice would be "The participants completed the pretests

---

Box 12.3   Summary of Some Common Mistakes to Avoid When Writing Evaluation Reports

- Crowding too much narrative on the same page
- Insufficient or excessive use of infographics and typographical enhancements (bold or large font, italics, etc.)
- Overly complex tables, graphs, and charts
- Using technical jargon geared to an academic audience
- Lengthy, complex, awkward sentences or paragraphs that use needless words
- Using passive voice

after they provided their informed consent." An example of passive voice would be "The pretests were completed by the participants after the informed consent was provided by them." Notice that, in addition to being in active voice, the first sentence is shorter and snappier. You should try to keep your sentences short and snappy throughout your report. In conclusion, try to follow this "golden rule" suggested by Newcomer *et al.* (2015, p. 764):

- Make the message jump off the page.
- Make sure nothing else does.

12.8   Dissemination

If you want to maximize the likelihood that your findings and conclusions will be read and utilized, you should remember that reports are not the only means of disseminating those findings and conclusions. You can also present them at conferences, at community meetings, in press releases, through an E-newsletter or listserve, in a blog post, or in a social media post. The various dissemination options are not mutually exclusive; you can use multiple ones. Each has its advantages and disadvantages. Press releases, for example, can reach a broad audience, but require a newsworthy topic. The E-newsletter and listserve options reach people quickly, but rely on having a thorough list of intended recipients and having those recipients opening your email message, which conceivably could get filtered into their junk mailboxes.

Table 12.1 *Online resources with tips on disseminating evaluation reports*

Site	Web address
Adolescent Prevention Program Tip Sheet	https://teenpregnancy.acf.hhs.gov/sites/default/files/ resource-files/Dissemination%20of%20Evaluation%20 ResultsTipSheet_508-Compliant_FINAL_8-1-14_0.pdf
Informal Science	www.informalscience.org/evaluation/ reporting-dissemination
Centers for Disease Control and Prevention	www.cdc.gov/healthyyouth/evaluation/pdf/brief9.pdf
Health Bucks Evaluation Toolkit	www.centertrt.org/content/docs/Intervention_ Documents/Intervention_Evaluation_Materials/Health_ Bucks/Health_Bucks_Evaluation_Toolkit.pdf
Charity Channel.com	https://charitychannel.com/six-steps-to-effective- program-evaluation-step-6-communicate-your-results/

The choice of dissemination methods should depend on your target audience, and how they are most likely to receive and read what you have to say. The current widespread use of social media, for example, makes that a good choice for quickly reaching a broad audience that can read your post for free. Youthful audiences, especially, might be appropriate for the social media option. The downside of social media posts (as well as blog posts), however, is that they might have less credibility than alternative dissemination options, they require an ongoing effort to maintain followers, and content control can be impeded through comments by followers. Some online resources with tips on disseminating evaluation reports are listed in Table 12.1.

12.9   Chapter Main Points

- Tailor your report to your audience. If you want your report to have an impact on decision-makers, you should begin by determining who are the key decision-makers you want to make sure will read your report and what writing style and format are most likely to influence them.
- The report needs to be short (perhaps no more than ten pages) and snappy, with mostly short sentences in active voice and language that most high-school sophomores would understand easily. The report should have an uncluttered layout, with the main points in large, bold font and perhaps set aside from the narrative.
- Show drafts of your report incrementally to colleagues and request their blunt critical feedback to each iteration.
- The executive summary should concentrate on findings and recommendations. The coverage of the methodology in the executive summary should be brief and in plain language, perhaps no more than a short paragraph. The report that follows the executive summary can flesh out the details of the summary.
- The introduction section should tersely convey the extent and importance of the problem, what has been done before by others to address the problem, and how all of that provided the rationale for your evaluation and its aims. In short, readers should be able to understand why your evaluation was needed, its importance, and its objectives.
- The methodology section should describe your design, participants (number, characteristics, how selected or recruited), measurements, and data collection methods.
- Your results section should not overwhelm readers with all of your results or the statistical minutiae of the results. You should limit this section to the

most important findings only – those that have the greatest bearing on the main implications and recommendations of your report.

- Portray your main statistical findings using infographics, but present them sparingly, just to highlight your key findings.
- Your discussion section should discuss alternative ways to interpret your results and explain the interpretation that you think is the most appropriate. It should develop recommendations for action based on your conclusions, followed by an acknowledgment of the most relevant limitations of your methodology.
- To promote utilization of your recommendations by program personnel, you should write your report in a politically sensitive manner. Discuss negative findings tactfully.
- Involve key stakeholders in developing your report. Collaborate with them in developing conclusions and recommendations.
- Resist efforts to pressure you to spin negative findings in a biased way to make an outcome look more successful than it really was. Although you should be sensitive to stakeholder concerns and collaborate with them in developing conclusions and recommendations, you should resist the temptation to go overboard in trying to please them.
- It is unethical to write a misleading report out of self-interest concerns.
- If some elements of your design could not be completed, explain why you were forced to jettison them, and point out how their loss weakened your design.
- Reports are not the only means of disseminating your findings and conclusions. You can also present them at conferences, at community meetings, in press releases, through an E-newsletter or listserve, in a blog post, or in a social media post.

12.10 Exercises

1. Quickly write a one-page double-spaced summary of something you did recently. Explain why you did it that way. After you finish, read what you wrote. What sentences or paragraphs were written in an overly lengthy, complex, or awkward way, using passive instead of active voice? Rewrite the page to improve those parts. Show your two versions to a friend and ask them to tell you which version they liked better and why.
2. Look at a paper you have previously written for one of your classes. Scrutinize it in the same way you did in exercise 1, above.

3. Make up a fictitious evaluation of a program, policy, or intervention. Draft an evaluation report of its fictitious elements. Ask your classmate to do the same. Read and critically appraise each other's reports in light of this chapter's main points.

12.11 Additional Reading

- Birchfield, R. W. (1988). *The New Fowler's Modern English Usage* (3rd ed.) New York, NY: Oxford University Press.
- Strunk, W., Jr., & White, E. B. (1999). *The Elements of Style* (4th ed.). New York, NY: Longman.

More Tips for Becoming a Successful Evaluator

You've come a long way since Chapter 1. You've learned about the different purposes and types of evaluation, how to assess needs, how to survey clients and program staff, how to measure program outcomes, the logic and utility of feasible outcome designs, how to strengthen the causal logic of feasible outcome designs, how to conduct and interpret single-case outcome designs, practical and political pitfalls in outcome evaluations, how to analyze and present data from formative and process evaluations and from outcome evaluations, and how to write an evaluation report in a manner that will improve its chances of being read and utilized. This epilogue will examine things that you can do throughout the evaluation process to increase the chances that your report and evaluation will be successful. Some of the tips were mentioned in previous chapters, but warrant repeating because of their importance. Other tips will be new.

Planning the Evaluation

If you want your evaluation report to be useful, don't wait until you get to the report stage to start promoting its utility. Start from the moment you start planning the evaluation. Find out what the intended users of the evaluation think about the evaluation and what information they hope to get from it. Design the evaluation to address those information needs. Doing so requires that you learn all you can about the evaluation's stakeholders. You should not just focus solely on stakeholders who are at the top of the decision-making hierarchy, despite their importance. You should learn about stakeholders at all levels of the hierarchy. For example, front-line, service-providing staff, too, will be affected by your evaluation. Your results and recommendations might influence their future work, and they might experience your evaluation procedures as a burden on their current work. If service-providing staff members were not involved in planning the evaluation protocol, and if they do not understand it, they might be more likely to forget about or resist complying with the protocol, not to mention their likely disregard for the evaluation report.

When you involve service providers in the evaluation planning, do not just explain things to them. Listen and be responsive to their concerns. If they feel burdened by the evaluation protocol – perhaps regarding extra data collection or paperwork requirements – brainstorm with them regarding ways to alleviate the burden.

Key stakeholders who can influence how successfully your evaluation is carried out and whether its report and recommendations will be utilized should participate at the outset in determining the aims and methods of the evaluation. Involving them in that process and fostering their cooperation throughout the evaluation requires that you are skilled in developing and maintaining relationships. (Some of those skills will be examined later in this epilogue.)

Levels of Stakeholder Participation. Not everyone agrees on the extent of influence stakeholders should have regarding the technical aspects of evaluations. At one extreme is the argument that the limited technical expertise or competing vested interests of stakeholders could compromise the quality of the evaluation. Some stakeholders, for example, might want a methodologically biased evaluation that seems more likely to produce an outcome that portrays the agency in a good light. At the other extreme are empowerment-oriented evaluators who believe in giving stakeholders final decision-making authority over all aspects of the evaluation. The disagreement pertains mainly to whether stakeholders should influence the technical aspects of the evaluation regarding such things as the outcome design, measures, and data collection. In between those extremes is the strategy of selectively engaging different stakeholders in different ways regarding different steps of the evaluation or different aspects of evaluation planning.

Obtain Feedback to a Written Draft of the Evaluation Protocol. Regardless of the extent of stakeholder influence over the evaluation protocol, you should show the stakeholders a written draft of the protocol at the end of the planning phase and obtain their feedback to it. Doing so has two purposes. First, seeing everything in writing might help them realize logistical problems that hadn't occurred to them during the planning discussions. Feedback regarding those problems can help you improve the protocol. Second, if they tell you that they see no problems in the protocol, they are implicitly giving it their blessing, which can enhance the prospects for their ultimate utilization of the final evaluation report.

During Implementation of the Evaluation

Agency and stakeholder conditions that prevailed while planning the evaluation can change in important ways during the course of the evaluation. For example, economic downturns and changes in governmental political administrations can imperil agency funding, which in turn can intensify the political context of an outcome evaluation. Funding cuts can reduce the resources allotted to service provision, increase staff turnover, and thus imperil the agency's ability to continue implementing the program or intervention being evaluated in the way it was designed to be implemented. Maintaining good relationships and regular, ongoing regular streams of communication with stakeholders is vital to learning about these fluctuations and being able to adapt the evaluation to them in a manner that will be acceptable to stakeholders while trying to protect the quality of the evaluation. Changing the evaluation protocol without the involvement of, and buy-in by, stakeholders can imperil their propensity to be influenced by your report. Imagine, for example, how they might react upon learning of the changes for the first time when they begin reading your report. If they continue reading it at all, it might be with a foul mood.

Even if conditions do not change during the evaluation, having regular, ongoing communication with stakeholders will help maintain their support and ultimate utilization of the evaluation. For example, they are likely to appreciate briefings that provide incremental feedback with preliminary findings about what aspects of the program appear to be working better than others, whether short-term objectives are being reached, or other information that might help them make incremental improvements. After each meeting you should prepare a brief memorandum that lists the key decisions made in the meeting. Otherwise, it might be too easy for administrators or other busy stakeholders to forget about those decisions.

At the Conclusion of the Evaluation

Chapter 12 offered extensive tips regarding writing the evaluation report in a manner that will appeal to stakeholders. It emphasized tailoring the writing style and format of the report to the target audience. One tip that was not mentioned involves the importance of showing a preliminary draft of your report to stakeholders and encouraging their feedback. This process serves two purposes. First, there might be some glitches in your report. Stakeholder feedback can identify those glitches and help you improve the report. Second, engaging stakeholders in this process might enhance their sense that the report (and the evaluation) is responsive to their concerns and therefore might improve the chances that they will utilize it.

For the most part, the evaluation methods addressed throughout this book have been mainly technical. Despite the necessity of technical expertise, it alone won't make you a successful evaluator. You'll also need skills in building relationships – what many call *people skills*. You might have noticed the need for people skills while reading the above tips, such as tips regarding maintaining good relationships and good communication with stakeholders and being receptive to their feedback.

People Skills

The importance of people skills is evident at all levels of work in social and human service agencies. An important attribute of being a good manager or administrator, for example, is the ability to make staff members feel like their ideas have an impact and their work is valued. If you have taken courses in management or administration, you have probably already learned about the importance of managerial people skills. And if you have taken courses in service provision, you probably had to work on improving your people skills in the context of building a strong practitioner–client alliance. Examples of the importance of people skills are virtually boundless and can be applied to all walks of life, not just your work life. They apply to having good friends, a good marriage, and so on.

If you lack good people skills, this epilogue will not suffice to remedy the problem. All it can do is enlighten you about the problem and perhaps point you in the right direction toward alleviating it. People skills can best be improved by practice. If you have the chance, you can take courses that provide opportunities for role playing and getting feedback on those skills. Let's look now at some important people skills relevant to being a successful evaluator.

Show Genuine Interest in Others. Try to remember important aspects of other people's lives. Not forgetting their names, obviously, will help, but also remember things like their hobbies, important events in their lives and in the lives of their families, and so on. When you casually encounter them don't just say "Hi, how's it going?" and move on. Ask them things like "How did your kid's soccer game go?," "Did that repair shop do a good job fixing your car?," "Is your wife recovering well from her surgery?," and so on. When they answer, don't just say "Good," and then go away or change the subject. Show that you are genuinely interested by asking some follow-up questions. Most people can tell the difference between faking interest to try to be popular and genuine interest.

Try to Be Humorous. I can't tell you how to do this. It does not mean trying to be the office comedian, frequently annoying people with jokes. I'll just give you an example that involved me recently. An acquaintance at my tennis club recently commented about not seeing me for a while. I responded that I had been busy writing a book. "What's it about?," he asked. I replied, "Program evaluation." "How boring!," he moaned. "Maybe," I said, "but I got a contract for it to be a movie." He laughed pretty hard. Had I become defensive about him depicting my "masterpiece" as boring, his interaction with me would have been a lot less pleasant than it turned out to be thanks to my self-effacing humor.

Be Self-Assured. In the foregoing humor example, if I lacked self-confidence, I might have felt diminished by the *boring* comment, perhaps feeling a need to argue about my book's importance. But being self-confident does not require being cocky. You do not want others to think you are conceited, with an inflated image of yourself (which, by the way, can paradoxically convey the impression that deep down you are really insecure). You just need to be adequately self-assured so that when others criticize you or say something less than flattering – perhaps unintentionally, but even if it is intentional – you do not become defensive or lose your cool. Self-assurance will help you to remain open to criticism and to respond to it in a way that not only avoids unpleasantness, but also avoids appearing insecure to others.

Show Genuine Empathy. If you are learning clinical skills, you probably are already familiar with the concept of empathy. Being empathic means being able to understand what it's like to walk in someone else's shoes. That is, putting yourself in their place and imagining how they must be feeling – not only according to what they say, but also according to their body language. Showing genuine empathy is akin to showing genuine interest in others. It does not mean memorizing stilted responses like "I hear you saying that your boss really hurt your feelings." It has to be natural, like "Doggone! I'll bet that ticked you off!" The point here, however, is not to say the "Doggone …" comment or any other particular comment. The point is to just genuinely try to focus on what the other person is saying and feeling, and then react in a natural way to let them know you understand.

Active Listening. Being empathic requires active listening skills. Being a good listener requires patiently putting your own concerns out of your mind and focusing entirely on what the other person is saying. Being able to do that is aided by self-assurance. If your mind is bogged down by worries or self-doubts, it will be harder to concentrate entirely on what another person is saying. Try to recall times when you were telling a friend about something important to you and they changed the subject, such as by responding with something like "That reminds me of the time that I …." If you respond like that it will not endear you to the other person. Instead, it will make them think that the whole time they were talking your mind was preoccupied with your own interests. Just like becoming empathic, becoming a good listener takes practice, perhaps in role plays followed by feedback. As you become a better listener, you are likely to experience why it is often said that people are more likeable if they talk less and listen more.

As you can see, many of these skills are interrelated. Being skillful in one of them can make it easier to be skillful in others. The above skills will also help you develop additional people skills, such as leadership skills, motivational skills, communication skills, and conflict resolution skills. I encourage you to develop these skills. They will not only help you to become a successful evaluator; they will help you become more successful in your personal life and in any career path that awaits you.

I hope the tips in this epilogue will help your efforts to have your evaluations utilized. Investing a lot of work in an evaluation that gets ignored can be a real bummer. But seeing your evaluation get utilized can be a thrill.

References

Aikin, M. C., & Vo, A. T. (2018). *Evaluation Essentials* (2nd ed.). New York, NY: Guilford Press.

Alexander, L. B., & Solomon, P. (2006). *The Research Process in the Human Services: Behind the Scenes*. Belmont, CA: Brooks/Cole.

Alvidrez, J., Azocar, F., & Miranda, J. (1996). Demystifying the concept of ethnicity for psychotherapy researchers. *Journal of Consulting and Clinical Psychology*, 64(5), 903–908.

Armijo-Olivo, S., Warren, S., & Magee, D. (2009). Intention to treat analysis, compliance, drop-outs and how to deal with missing data in clinical research: A review. *Physical Therapy Reviews*, 14(1), 36–49.

Birchfield, R. W. (1988). *The New Fowler's Modern English Usage* (3rd ed.) New York, NY: Oxford University Press.

Bisson, J. L., Jenkins, P. L., Alexander, J., & Bannister, C. (1993). Randomized control trial of psychological debriefing for victims of acute burn trauma. *British Journal of Psychiatry*, 171(1), 78–81.

Blake, D. D., Weathers, F. W., Nagy, L. M., *et al.* (1995). The development of a Clinician-Administered PTSD Scale. *Journal of Traumatic Stress*, 8(1), 75–90.

Bloom, M., Fischer, J., & Orme, J. G. (2009). *Evaluating Practice: Guidelines for the Accountable Professional* (6th ed.). Boston, MA: Allyn & Bacon.

Bond, G. R., Drake, R. E., Mueser, K. T., & Latimer, E. (2001). Assertive community treatment for people with severe mental illness: Critical ingredients and impact on patients. *Disease Management & Health Outcomes*, 9(3), 141–159.

Carlier, I. V. E., Lamberts, R. D., van Uchelen, A. J., & Gersons, B. P. R. (1998). Disaster-related post-traumatic stress in police officers: A field study of the impact of debriefing. *Stress Medicine*, 14(3), 143–148.

Chronbach, L. J., Ambron, S. R., Dornbusch, S. M. *et al.* (1980). *Toward Reform of Program Evaluation*. San Francisco, CA: Jossey-Bass.

Cohen, J. (1988). *Statistical Power Analysis for the Behavioral Sciences* (2nd ed.). New York, NY: Lawrence Erlbaum Associates.

Cohen, J. A., Mannarino, A. P., & Deblinger, E. (2006). *Treating Trauma and Traumatic Grief in Children and Adolescents*. New York, NY: Guilford Press.

CSWE. (2015). Educational Policy and Accreditation Standards, www.cswe.org/getattachment/Accreditation/Accreditation-Process/2015-EPAS/2015EPAS_Web_FINAL.pdf.aspx.

Dimidjian, S. (Ed.). (2019). *Evidence-Based Practice in Action: Bridging Clinical Science and Intervention*. New York, NY: Guilford Press.

Embry, D. D., & Biglan, A. (2008). Evidence-based kernels: Fundamental units of behavioral influence. *Clinical Child and Family Psychology Review*, 11(3), 75–113.

Ferguson-Colvin, K. M., & Maccio, E. M. (2012). *Toolkit for Practitioners/Researchers Working with Lesbian, Gay, Bisexual, Transgender, and Queer/Questioning (LGBTQ) Runaway and Homeless Youth (RHY)*. New York, NY: National Research Center for Permanency and Family Connections, Silberman School of Social Work.

Finckenauer, J. (1979). *Evaluation of Juvenile Awareness Project: Reports 1 and 2*. Newark, NJ: Rutgers School of Criminal Justice.

Fischer, J., & Corcoran, K. (2013). *Measures for Clinical Practice and Research*. New York, NY: Oxford University Press.

Fong, R., & Furuto, S. (Eds.). (2001). *Culturally Competent Practice: Skills, Interventions, and Evaluations*. Boston, MA: Allyn & Bacon.

Formative Evaluation Toolkit, Children's Bureau, www.jbassoc.com/wp-content/uploads/2019/01/Formative-Evaluation-Toolkit.pdf.

Gambrill, E. (1999). Evidence-based practice: An alternative to authority-based practice. *Families in Society*, 80(4), 341–350.

Gibbs, L., & Gambrill, E. (2002). Evidence-based practice: Counterarguments to objections. *Research on Social Work Practice*, 12(3), 452–476.

Grbich, C. (2007). *Qualitative Data Analysis: An Introduction*. London: Sage.

Grob, G. F. (2015). Writing for impact. In Newcomer, K. E., Hatry, H. P., & Wholey, J. S. (Eds.). *Handbook of Practical Program Evaluation* (4th ed.). Hoboken, NJ: John Wiley & Sons, Inc., 725–764.

Guillory, J., Wiant, K. F., Farrelly, M. *et al.* (2018). Recruiting hard-to-reach populations for survey research: Using Facebook and Instagram advertisements and in-person intercept in LGBT bars and nightclubs to recruit LGBT young adults. *Journal of Medical Internet Research*, 18(6), 20–26.

Hamilton, M. (1960). A rating scale for depression. *Journal of Neurology, Neurosurgery, and Psychiatry*, 23(1), 56–62.

Heckathorn, D. D. (1997). Respondent driven sampling. *Social Problems*, 44(2), 174–199

Hernandez, M., & Isaacs, M. R. (Eds). (1998). *Promoting Cultural Competence in Children's Mental Health Services*. Baltimore, MD: Paul H. Brookes.

Hough, R. L., Tarke, H., Renker, V., Shields, P., & Gladstein, J. (1996). Recruitment and retention of homeless mentally ill participants in research. *Journal of Consulting and Clinical Psychology*, 64(5), 881–891.

Housley, J., & Beutler, L. (2007). *Treating Victims of Mass Disaster and Terrorism*. Oxford: Hogrefe.

Johnson, B. R. (2004). Religious programs and recidivism among former inmates in Prison Fellowship programs: A long-term follow-up study. *Justice Quarterly*, 21(2), 329–354.

Johnson, C., Shala, M., Sejdijaj, X., Odell, R., & Dabishevci, K. (2001). Thought Field Therapy – Soothing the bad moments of Kosovo. *Journal of Clinical Psychology*. 57(10), 1237–1240.

Johnson-Motoyama, M., Brook, J., Yan, Y., & McDonald, T. P. (2013). Cost analysis of the strengthening families program in reducing time to family reunification among substance-affected families. *Children and Youth Services Review*, 35(2), 244–252.

Jones, J. H. (1981). *Bad Blood: The Tuskegee Syphilis Experiment*. New York, NY: Free Press.

Kirchherr, J., & Charles, K. (2018). Enhancing the sample diversity of snowball samples: Recommendations from a research project on anti-dam movements in Southeast Asia. *PLoS One* 13(8), e0201710, www.ncbi.nlm .nih.gov/pmc/articles/PMC6104950.

Kristof, N. (2007). Attack of the worms. *New York Times*, July 2, 2007, p. A19.

Krueger, R. A., & Casey, M. A. (2015). *Focus Groups: A Practical Guide for Applied Research* (5th ed.). Thousand Oaks, CA: Sage Publications, Inc.

Magnabosco, J. L.., & Manderscheid, R. W. (Eds.). (2011). *Outcomes Measurement in the Human Services: Cross-Cutting Issues and Methods in the Era of Health Reform* (2nd ed). Washington, DC: NASW Press.

Mayou, R. A., Ehlers, A., & Hobbs, M. (2000). Psychological debriefing for road traffic accident victims. *British Journal of Psychiatry*, 176(6), 589–593.

Merton, R. K. (1957). *Social Theory and Social Structure*. Glencoe, IL: The Free Press.

Miles, M. B., Huberman, A. M., & Saldana, J. (2020). *Qualitative Data Analysis* (4th ed.). London: Sage.

Miller, W. R., & Rose, G. S. (2009). Toward a theory of motivational interviewing. *American Psychologist*, 64(6), 527–537.

Miranda, J. (1996). Introduction to the special section on recruiting and retaining minorities in psychotherapy research. *Journal of Consulting and Clinical Psychology*, 64(5), 848–850.

Morrissey, J., & Goldman, H. (1984). Cycles of reform in the care of the chronically mentally ill. *Hospital and Community Psychiatry*, 35(8), 785–793.

Nandi, P. K. (1982). Surveying Asian minorities in the middle-sized city. In W. T. Liu (Ed.). *Methodological Problems in Minority Research*. Chicago, IL: Pacific/ Asian American Mental Health Research, 81–92.

Newcomer, K. E., Hatry, H. P., & Wholey, J. S. (2015). *Handbook of Practical Program Evaluation* (4th ed.). Hoboken, NJ: John Wiley & Sons, Inc.

Norton, L. M., & Manson, S. M. (1996). Research in American Indian and Alaska Native communities: Navigating the cultural universe of values and process. *Journal of Consulting and Clinical Psychology*, 64(5), 856–860.

Nunnally, J. C., & Bernstein, I. H. P. (1994). *Psychometric Theory*. New York, NY: McGraw-Hill.

Obernauer, C. (2013). 'Obamacare' vs. 'Affordable Care Act': Why Words Matter. Huffington Post online, October 4, 2013, www.huffpost.com/entry/obamacare-vs-affordable-care-act_b_4044579.

Patton, M. Q. (2008). *Utilization-Focused Evaluation* (4th ed.). Thousand Oaks, CA: Sage Publications, Inc.

Patton, M. Q. (2015). *Qualitative Research and Evaluation Methods* (4th ed.). Newbury Park, CA: Sage.

Posavac, E. J., & Carey, R. G. (1985). *Program Evaluation: Methods and Case Studies* (2nd ed.). Englewood Cliffs, NJ: Prentice-Hall, Inc.

Potocky, M., & Rodgers-Farmer, A. Y. (Eds.). (1998). *Social Work Research with Minority and Oppressed Populations*. New York, NY: Haworth Press.

Quoss, B., Cooney, M., & Longhurst, T. (2000). Academics and advocates: Using participatory action research to influence welfare policy. *Journal of Consumer Affairs*, 34(1), 47–61.

Ragin, C. (1987). *The Comparative Method: Moving beyond Qualitative and Quantitative Strategies*. Berkeley, CA: University of California Press.

Rose, S., Bisson, J., Churchill, R., & Wessely, S. (2002). Psychological briefing for preventing post traumatic stress disorder (PTSD). *Cochrane Database of Systematic Reviews*, 2002(2), CD000560.

Royse, D., Thyer, B. A., & Padgett, D. K. (2016). *Program Evaluation: An Introduction to an Evidence-Based Approach* (6th ed.). Boston, MA: Cengage Learning.

Rubin, A. (2009). Introduction: Evidence-based practice and empirically supported interventions for trauma. In Rubin, A., & Springer, D. W. (Eds.). *Treatment of Traumatized Adults and Children*. Hoboken, NJ: John Wiley & Sons, Inc., 3–27.

Rubin, A. (2013). *Statistics for Evidence-Based Practice and Evaluation* (3rd ed.). Belmont, CA: Brooks/Cole/Cengage Learning.

Rubin, A., & Babbie, E. R. (2016). *Essential Research Methods for Social Work* (4th ed.). Boston, MA: Cengage Learning.

Rubin, A., & Babbie, E. R. (2017). *Research Methods for Social Work* (9th ed.). Boston, MA: Cengage Learning.

Rubin, A., & Bellamy, J. (2012). *Practitioner's Guide to Using Research for Evidence-Based Practice* (2nd ed.). Hoboken, NJ: John Wiley & Sons, Inc.

Rubin, A., & Bowker, J. (Eds.) (1986). *Studies on Chronic Mental Illness: A New Horizon for Social Work Researchers*. New York, NY: Council on Social Work Education.

Rubin, A., & von Sternberg, K. (2017). A practitioner-friendly empirical way to evaluate practice. *Social Work*, 62(4), 297–302.

Rubin, A., Washburn, M., & Schieszler, C. (2017). Within-group effect-size benchmarks for trauma-focused cognitive behavioral therapy with children and adolescents. *Research on Social Work Practice*, 27(7), 789–801.

Sackett, D. L., Richardson, W. S., Rosenberg, W., & Haynes, R. B. (1997). *Evidence-Based Medicine: How to Practice and Teach EBM*. New York, NY: Churchill Livingstone.

Shadish, W. R., Cook, T. D., & Campbell, D. T. (2001). *Experimental and Quasi-experimental Designs for Generalized Causal Inference*. Boston, MA: Houghton Mifflin.

Shapiro, F. (1989). Efficacy of the eye movement desensitization procedure in the treatment of traumatic memories. *Journal of Traumatic Stress*, 2(2), 199–223.

Stein, G. L., Beckerman, N. L., & Sherman, P. A. (2010). Lesbian and gay elders and long-term care: Identifying the unique psychosocial perspectives and challenges. *Journal of Gerontological Social Work*, 53(5), 421–435.

Strunk, W., Jr., & White, E. B. (1999). *The Elements of Style* (4th ed.). New York, NY: Longman.

Surgeon General Report (2014). *The Health Consequences of Smoking – 50 Years of Progress*. Atlanta, GA: Centers for Disease Control and Prevention.

Thompson, E. E., Neighbors, H. W., Munday, C., & Jackson, J. S. (1996). Recruitment and retention of African American patients for clinical research: An exploration of response rates in an urban psychiatric hospital. *Journal of Consulting and Clinical Psychology*, 64(5), 861–867.

Thyer, B. A., & Pignotti, M. G. (2015). *Science and Pseudoscience in Social Work Practice*. New York, NY: Springer Publishing Co.

Wampold, B. (2015). How important are the common factors in psychotherapy? An update. *World Psychiatry*, 14(3), 270–277.

Weiss, E. L., Rubin, A., & Graeser, N. (2019). Transitioning to Civilian Life Scale (TCLS): Development, reliability, and validity. *Military Behavioral Health*, 7(1), 57–63.

Weisz, J. R., Ugueto, A. M., Herren, J., Afienko, S. R., & Rutt. (2011). Kernels vs. ears and other questions for a science of treatment dissemination. *Clinical Psychology: Science and Practice*, 18(1), 41–46.

Index

Locators in *italic* refer to figures; those in **bold** to tables.

Made in United States
Troutdale, OR
08/16/2023

12116212R10162